Popular Politics and Popular Culture
in the Age of the Masses

BRITISH IDENTITIES SINCE 1707
Vol. 6

Series Editors:

Professor Paul Ward
School of Music, Humanities and Media,
University of Huddersfield

Professor Richard Finlay
Department of History, University of Strathclyde

PETER LANG

Oxford · Bern · Berlin · Bruxelles · Frankfurt am Main · New York · Wien

Jeffrey Hill

Popular Politics and Popular Culture in the Age of the Masses

Studies in Lancashire and the North West of England,
1880s to 1930s

PETER LANG

Oxford · Bern · Berlin · Bruxelles · Frankfurt am Main · New York · Wien

Bibliographic information published by Die Deutsche Nationalbibliothek
Die Deutsche Nationalbibliothek lists this publication in the Deutsche Nationalbibliografie;
detailed bibliographic data is available on the Internet at http://dnb.d-nb.de.

A catalogue record for this book is available from the British Library.

Library of Congress Control Number: 2014930915

ISSN 1664-0284
ISBN 978-3-0343-0936-3

© Peter Lang AG, International Academic Publishers, Bern 2014
Hochfeldstrasse 32, CH-3012 Bern, Switzerland
info@peterlang.com, www.peterlang.com, www.peterlang.net

This publication has been peer reviewed.

Printed in Germany

Contents

Acknowledgments

I gratefully acknowledge the permission given by editors and publishers to reproduce, in whole or in part, textual material that originally appeared in the following books and journals.

The Editor, *Transactions of the Historic Society of Lancashire and Cheshire* for 'The Lancashire Miners, Thomas Greenall and the Labour Party, 1900–1906', *Transactions of the Historic Society of Lancashire and Cheshire*, vol. 130, (Nov) 1981, 115–30.

The Committee, North West Labour History Society for 'Social Democracy and the Labour Movement: The Social Democratic Federation in Lancashire', North West Labour History Society, *Bulletin* 8, 1982–1983, 44–55.

The Executive Editor, *International Review of Social History* for 'Manchester and Salford Politics and the Early Development of the Independent Labour Party, *International Review of Social History*, 26 (1981), 171–201.

The Editors, *Northern History* for 'Lib-Labism, Socialism and Labour in Burnley, c. 1890–1918', *Northern History* xxxv, 1999, 185–204.

The Editor, *Sport in History* for '"Connie" – Local Hero, National Icon: Cricket, Race and Politics in the Life of Learie Constantine', *Sports Historian*, 22 (1), 2002, 79–99.

Taylor and Francis Publishers for 'Cricket and the Imperial Connection: Overseas Cricketers in Lancashire in the Inter-war Period', in J. Bale and J. Maguire eds, *Worlds Apart: Sports Labour Migration in the Global Arena* (London: Frank Cass, 1994), 49–62.

Edinburgh University Press for 'Rite of Spring: Cup Finals and Community in the North of England' in Jeff Hill and Jack Williams eds, *Sport and Identity in the North of England* (Keele: Keele University Press, 1996), 85–111.

Peter Lang Publishers for '"You Don't Upset the Shaygets": Howard Jacobson's *The Mighty Walzer*' in Jeffrey Hill, *Sport and the Literary Imagination: Essays in History, Literature and Sport* (Oxford/Bern: Peter Lang, 2006), 171–90.

CHAPTER ONE

Lancashire and the North West

I

Writing of the town of Bochum in the late nineteenth and early twentieth century the American historian of Germany, David F. Crew, made an
important point about the relationship between the local and the national
in historical perspective: 'it is a question of asking how and in what ways
and to what extent local areas participated in, contributed to, were affected
by and reacted to the larger-scale social, economic and political transfor-
mations that changed much of Europe during this period.'[1] A similar point
was made equally plainly by one of the foremost historians of North West
England, John Marshall. Marshall, who had done as much as anyone to
champion local and regional approaches, felt strongly that such histories
must be related to the wider discourse of national and international developments, lest they descend into mere antiquarianism.[2]

These prescriptions have long been honoured in relation to the North
West of England, Lancashire in particular.[3] The region has been a continuing

1   David F. Crew, *Town in the Ruhr: A Social History of Bochum 1860–1914* (New York:
     Columbia University Press, 1979, 7–10).
2   John D. Marshall, *The Tyranny of the Discrete: Discussion of Problems of Local History
     in England* (Aldershot: Scolar Press, 1997).
3   The North West as a region has usually been regarded as the old counties of
     Lancashire, Cumberland and Westmoreland; sometimes Cheshire and parts of
     Staffordshire have been included, as in Fawcett's 'Lancastria' (C.B. Fawcett, *Provinces
     of England: a study of some geographical aspects of devolution*, London: Williams and
     Norgate, 1919). I incline here to the former definition, but add the industrialised
     areas of Cheshire around Manchester. Each of the constituent counties of these

focus of interest for historians and social commentators interested in the big picture. Most have given prominence to the material and intellectual features of the North West.[4] Size has much to do with this. During the period to which this book refers the region possessed an economy and a population greater than that of many European countries. There were almost five million people living in the North West on the eve of the First World War, many of them employed in the various branches of cotton production. It was the region's dominant industry – and a leading one for the country itself – accounting for perhaps a quarter of Great Britain's export trade earlier in the twentieth century. 'Britain's bread', as a later government slogan had it, 'hangs by Lancashire thread.' It therefore appeared to many, at least until global trading relations underwent a profound change in the interwar years, that this was an area of considerable importance: a 'world region', so to speak, to be seen in much the same light as were later centres of international dynamism such as the West European 'golden triangle' or California's Silicon Valley.

As the site of the world's first industrial revolution the North West of England was assured a historic significance: not simply one region among many, but a *primus inter pares*. In this sense it has been a barometer by which to gauge the economic, social and political climate of Britain as a whole. It was the first of Britain's highly urbanised and industrialised areas, with almost two thirds of its population living in towns by the mid-nineteenth century. By the end of the century a significant proportion was immigrant, some half a million Irish in origin and mostly Catholic: a source of social

---

regional constructions was altered in the local government reorganisations of 1974. Lancashire lost much of its old territory, and became a new county, roughly a third of its former size, based on Preston. For this book, however, I follow another leading historian of the county, J.J. Bagley, in seeing Lancashire as being 'what it has meant since the Middle Ages, when Roger of Poitou first brought the area under his rule and when Edward III first created the county palatine.' (J.J. Bagley, *A History of Lancashire*, London: Phillimore, 1976 edn., p. 11.): ie, the Lancashire of pre-1974, which included Liverpool and Manchester, Warrington and Widnes, and the areas 'beyond the sands' of Cartmell and Furness.

4   The historian A.J.P. Taylor (a Lancastrian himself) was exceptional in acknowledging the region's other charms: '... the best country in the world ... and the nicest people' (A.J.P. Taylor, 'Manchester', *Encounter*, March 1957, 5).

and cultural discord that spilled over into politics. Thus many of the features of 'modern' society were evident here for the first time. It was this that in the 1840s had drawn Friedrich Engels, a futurologist if ever there was one, to write about Manchester, the city at the region's heart, the 'shock city of an age'[5], and the one to which many analysts of modern society were to follow him at one time or another.

In its politics the region was, in the nineteenth and early-twentieth centuries, at the forefront of progressive movements that carried national and international weight. 'Peterloo' had early been a symbol of resistance to power unjustly wielded. The Chartists flourished here, with their mass meetings on Blackstone Edge outside Rochdale. The Anti-Corn Law League drew much of its momentum from Lancashire; among its leaders John Bright was a local man, Richard Cobden MP for Stockport. The Pankhursts of Manchester inspired the Suffragette movement. Free Trade was created here, celebrated intellectually in the ideas of the Manchester School, and at much the same time in bricks and mortar in the form of the Free Trade Hall, for many years the home of the Hallé Orchestra. It was in Lancashire that the Labour Party made its first sizeable electoral impact in the General Election of 1906, fought in this part of the world very largely to defend Free Trade.[6] Since the Reform Act of 1832 the constituencies of the region have been a 'pendulum' whose swings, together with London, determined the outcome of national elections.[7] It is little wonder that inhabitants of this part of England felt themselves to be distinctive, in the vanguard of modernity: 'what Lancashire thinks today ... the rest of the world thinks tomorrow' according to an old saw. Stuart Rawnsley's claim for the North of England – 'No other region has such an intensified sense of place' – aptly applies to the mentality of the north-western corner of it during this period.[8]

5   Asa Briggs, *Victorian Cities* (Harmondsworth: Penguin Books, 1968 edn), 96.
6   See Jeffrey Hill, 'Working-Class Politics in Lancashire, 1885–1906: A Study in the Origins of the Labour Party', unpublished PhD thesis, Keele University, 1971, ch. 12.
7   A.J.P. Taylor. 'What Lancashire Thinks Today ...', *New Statesman*, 14 May 1971.
8   Stuart Rawnsley, 'Constructing the North' in N. Kirk ed., *Northern Identities: Historical Interpretations of 'The North' and 'Northernness'* (Aldershot: Ashgate,

Much of the self confidence evident in the decade before the First World War arose from an unshakeable belief in the region's industrial strength, founded on cotton and supported by coalmining, chemicals and engineering.[9] But any expectations this might have aroused in the future longevity of the region's economic strength would have been profoundly misplaced. Faith in continued prosperity was quickly dashed, 'fatally undermined' (in Trevor Griffiths's stark phrase) within ten years of the Great War's end.[10] In 1934 the writer J.B. Priestley, after visiting the weaving town of Blackburn while compiling his *English Journey*, noted that the cotton trade 'is almost finished … Few of them there now believe that it will ever return.'[11] It was a gloomy though prescient vision, shared by many others in the industry. Even before Priestley wrote, the local newspaper in Nelson, a town less badly affected by the depression than Blackburn, cannily summed up the historic dimensions of the situation when it pointed out that 'we are passing through an epoch in our industrial life, not one of those periods of bad trade that we have been accustomed to in past years. We see no genuine reason for optimism.'[12] The downturn in the region's economy was sudden, and

2000), 3. I have resisted the temptation to enter into a discussion of 'the spirit of the North', a theme recently explored in very readable form by Stuart Maconie, *Pies and Prejudice: In Search of the North* (London: Ebury Press, 2007) and Paul Morley, *The North (and Almost Everything In It)* (London: Bloomsbury, 2013). Against them, however, must be set the more judicious study by Dave Russell, *Looking North: Northern England and the National Imagination* (Manchester: Manchester University Press, 2004).

9   There is a strong hint of hubris in Ben Bowker's comment on pre-1914 Lancashire: 'if the Lancashire of 1880 had been quietly proud and the Lancashire of 1900 aloofly proud, the new Lancashire was arrogant.' B. Bowker, *Lancashire Under the Hammer* (London: Hogarth Press, 1928), 19.

10   Trevor Griffiths, *The Lancashire Working Classes c. 1880–1930* (Oxford: Clarendon Press, 2001), 5. Compare John Walton's equally stark reference to the region's 'sharp and irreversible decline' from the 1920s (J.K. Walton, 'The North West' in F.M.L. Thompson ed, *The Cambridge Social History of Britain 1750–1950: volume 1, Regions and Communities* (Cambridge: Cambridge University Press, 1990), 408.

11   J.B. Priestley, *English Journey* (Harmondsworth: Penguin 1977 edn.), 262.

12   *Nelson Leader*, 23 May 1930. On the overall economic situation in Lancashire at this time see Lars G. Sandberg, *Lancashire in Decline: A Study in Entrepreneurship,*

largely unrelieved. Writing some thirty years after Priestley, and in defiance of the 'affluence' that was often attributed to Britain in the 1950s and 1960s, the geographers Freeman, Rogers and Kinvig were able to pronounce of the North West that 'coal and cotton are no longer inexhaustible employers of labour, and the need for regeneration is all too clear.'[13] At the beginning of the twenty-first century it is by no means clear that the hoped-for regeneration has occurred. And industrial decline can provoke moral collapse. Places once intimately associated with those old radical and progressive causes have been, in the recent past, susceptible to the enticements of the far Right.[14] The whirligig of time does indeed bring in its revenges.

Such economic misfortunes were happening in a different social setting. Between the last quarter of the nineteenth century and the beginning of the Second World War there came into being in the North West a civil society that exhibited new forms of behaviour. It was a society not only bigger and more populous but one which displayed qualitative differences from the initial industrial society of Lancashire that had attracted so much attention a generation or two earlier. We might refer to this newer manifestation as 'modern', in the sense that features of social life were emerging that were to become commonplace almost everywhere in twentieth-century Britain: for example, the consolidation of class identities and relationships as a principal form of social identity and dynamism; the acceptance of urban life as the 'normal' context of civilised living; a slow decline in the attachment to religious belief and behaviour; the rise of new institutions in associational life, from trade unions to the Women's Institute; the increasing

---

Technology and International Trade Columbus, OH: Ohio State University Press, 1974), a study which seeks to defend cotton bosses against charges of inertia in their business management. See also John K. Walton, *Lancashire: A Social History, 1558–1939* (Manchester: Manchester University Press, 1987), ch. 14.

13 T.W. Freeman, H.B. Rogers and R.H. Kinvig, *Lancashire, Cheshire and the Isle of Man* (London: Thomas Nelson and Sons, 1966), 1.

14 The far-right British National Party experienced some success in local elections in the early years of the twenty-first century, becoming for example the second largest party on the town council in Burnley. By 2012, however, it had lost all its seats in the town (<http://www.guardian.co.uk/politics/2012/May/04/local-elections>).

dependence upon the provision of goods and services in the market place, with the consequent commercialisation of popular culture; and, a process evident especially during the First World War, a marked expansion of the role played by various agencies of the state in day-to-day life. One effect of the combined force of these changes was a greater presence of people in public life; what had once been the preserve of the few was now invaded by the many, a process that sociologists might refer to as 'massification'. The problem it raised was not only one of numbers and space. As Raymond Williams has pointed out the words 'mass' and 'masses' connote many things, some positive, others negative; they bring into consideration all manner of issues covering taste, education, knowledge, politics, and religion that presaged a new kind of society in Europe.[15]

Two outstanding characteristics of the social arrangements of mass society provoked doubt and debate. One was the involvement in politics of new groups of the population, often considered by old elites to be unready either to form intelligent opinions or make sensible choices. There was an indication of such thinking in the rush to 'educate' new voters following the reforms that brought women and many men into parliamentary elections for the first time in the decade after the First World War. Such 'masses', it was thought, could be seduced by the blandishments of demagogues. The other concern was aroused by the increase in the amount of leisure time among those who previously had known little. The question of how this time might be used occasioned doubts, especially when leisure became the target of intensified commercial activity. People's attainment of a level of 'enjoyment' in life came to be determined by what they could afford to pay rather than what they created for themselves. This purchased leisure became a passive activity lacking the vitality that had defined the Victorian concept of 'recreation'.[16] Such concerns were notably evident on the political Left, where it was felt that mass culture might too readily

---

15   Raymond Williams, *Keywords* (London: Fontana/Croom Helm, 1976), 158–63.
16   See, for example, J.B. Priestley, 'When Work Is Over', *Picture Post*, 4 January 1941, 39.
      See also Jeffrey Hill, '"What Shall We Do With Them When They're Not Working?":
      Leisure and Historians in Britain', in Brett Bebber ed, *Leisure and Cultural Conflict
      in Twentieth-Century Britain* (Manchester: Manchester University Press, 2012), ch. 1.

acclimatise people to the ways of capitalism. It accounted in part for the formation of an oppositional cultural life within socialist movements. The big European workers' parties were active in this, with the Germans well in the lead, but Britain was not without smaller-scale versions, pockets of which were to be found in Lancashire.[17]

II

The essays in the present volume have been prompted in various ways by this general discourse on 'the age of the masses'. They deal with popular politics and popular culture, two subjects that have customarily been treated in isolation from each other. Yet, as historians of political behaviour have now come to recognise, the political and the cultural are but complementary aspects of a single social process. Those seeking political changes in the late-nineteenth and early-twentieth centuries did so in the presence of some powerful new forces in popular culture, which as Eric Hobsbawm noted many years ago, introduced significant qualitative improvements in people's lives.[18] The influence of popular culture consequently set constraints on what was possible in politics. Moreover – a point noted forcibly by recent historians of political allegiance – politics cannot be understood simply by relating belief to a prior and pre-determining economic and social 'experience'.[19] Instead,

17   See Dick Geary ed., *Labour and Socialist Movements in Europe Before 1914* (Oxford: Berg Publishers, 1989); Denis Pye, *Fellowship Is Life: The National Clarion Cycling Club 1895–1995* (Bolton: Clarion Publishing, 1995); Jeffrey Hill, *Nelson: Politics, Economy, Community* (Edinburgh: Keele University Press, 1997), chs 4, 6. J.B. Priestley's peppery contribution to the famous 'Plan for Britain' issue of *Picture Post* captures some of this very well. (Priestley, 'When Work Is Over', *Picture Post*, 39–40.)

18   Eric J. Hobsbawm, *Labour's Turning Point 1880–1900: extracts from contemporary sources* (Hassocks: Harvester Press, 1974).

19   Pre-eminent among them: Jon Lawrence and Miles Taylor 'Introduction: electoral sociology and the historians' in Lawrence and Taylor eds, *Party, State and Society:*

people's ability to 'think' politically depends on the existence of a language through which their beliefs can be articulated. To understand this language we need, as the Italian philosopher Antonio Gramsci argued, to understand the texts and practices of the popular culture that frames it.[20]

A further characteristic of the collection is its methodology; or, more precisely, the influences from which the methodologies at work here have been shaped. Changing paradigms of historical analysis are present. Whilst the essays are all based upon sources that historians would recognise as 'primary', and are therefore 'empirical' in terms of their evidence, there is nonetheless a movement towards ideas, concepts and theories developed from the inter-disciplinary project of cultural studies; and a concern therefore to bring historical enquiry into contact with ideas developed in cognate disciplines. In the later work this brings forth a 'postmodern' inflection, though one employed not in the abstract form to which this paradigm sometimes gives rise, but in the service of empirical historical enquiry.

In Part I the essays cluster around the subject of politics, and have as their focus the theme of change, innovation and adaptation in a formative period of political transformation. The early ones (Chapters Two to Four) were written as a contribution to the debate over the rise of the Labour Party and the decline of the Liberals, an issue that has now perhaps lost some of the momentum it once possessed. They deal with the problems of establishing the new political strategy of independent labour representation (Chapter Two) and of attempting to implant socialism of different kinds in often unpromising terrain (Chapters Three and Four). The more recent political essays (Chapters Five and Six) reveal a shift of emphasis; less concerned with a 'forward march of labour', and more attuned to the survival of 'old' political cultures such as Lib-Labism (Chapter Five), and

---

Electoral Behaviour in Britain Since 1820 (Aldershot: Scolar Press, 1990), 1–26. Also Mike Savage and Andrew Miles, *The Remaking of the British Working Class 1840–1940* (London: Routledge, 1994).

20   G. Nowell Smith and Q. Hoare, *Selections From the Prison Notebooks* (London: Lawrence and Wishart, 1971). See also Gareth Stedman Jones, *Languages of Class: Studies in English Working Class History 1832–1982* (Cambridge: Cambridge University Press, 1983).

with the continuing popularity of Toryism as a political creed into the first truly democratic age of British politics (Chapter Six). This latter discussion also brings to the fore a gender dimension sometimes overlooked by political historians, especially those concerned with labour history. In all of the essays (and the same is true in those of Part II) particular attention is give to *local* histories, and their relationship to national and even global developments.

Part II leads us into popular culture. If a displacement of status and religious loyalties by those of social class is one of the chief themes of political change in Britain at this time, it is paralleled in cultural life by the rise of a commercial mass culture alongside older voluntary and mutualist associations. If politics during this period was increasingly bowing to the interests of 'the people', this was certainly the case in cultural life. The aspects of this process that are most closely scrutinised in Part II relate to something with which the North West has, since the late-nineteenth century, become firmly associated in the popular mind: sport.

The sport of this region had important influences on the development of sport more generally, both in Britain as a whole and internationally. Northern influences continue into the present day, as the success of association football teams such as Manchester United and Liverpool has shown. Historians of sport have recognised this, and accorded to the region its due place in the creation of what is sometimes referred to as 'modern sport'.[21] What have more often been overlooked, however, are the global dimensions to be found in sport, and their particular relationship to the local. Some aspects of sport in the North West resulted from and contributed to the region's international role. In cricket, the sport most responsive to this, international, imperial and local interests interacted to produce a set of powerful influences shaping people's views about themselves and their communities (Chapters Seven and Eight). Among such communities was the 'imagined' one of the North itself. This particular notion of place contributed greatly to the distinctiveness

21   A recent example is Dave Russell ed., *Sport in Manchester* (Manchester: Manchester Centre for Regional History, 2009). See also Richard Holt, *Sport and the British: A Modern History* (Oxford: Oxford University Press, 1989).

of the region. 'Northern-ness' and its associated forms of local patriotism, and their relationship with 'nation', are the subject of Chapter Nine, which examines the rituals attached to association football's Cup Final and the 'meanings' inscribed in its attendant rituals. During the period in question the medium though which many of these meanings were communicated, and which was absolutely fundamental to the emergence of modern sport, was the provincial newspaper press. Historians of sport have recognised the rich vein of information provided in newspapers, and mined it accordingly. What has been less recognised is the way the newspaper text worked on its readers. In Chapter Nine we see it creating the sense of local identity that so sustained the development of sport in this period. It does so by utilising in particular a sense of 'other', in this case the capital city London.[22]

III

In these ways, therefore, this is also a book about a personal intellectual journey. It charts the interests of an individual historian over a period of some forty years. The milestones and landmarks that have provided direction along the route are therefore important. They are provided by the work of numerous historians whose influences shape the content of the book. The earliest essays arose from doctoral research carried out in the late 1960s. One of the major scholars from this period for a historian interested in the Labour Party was Henry Pelling, in particular his *Origins of the Labour Party 1880–1900*, which had first appeared in 1954.[23] Pelling

---

22   I have further explored this point in 'Anecdotal Evidence: Sport, the Newspaper Press, and History', in Murray G. Phillips, ed., *Deconstructing Sport History: A Postmodern Analysis* (Albany, NY: State University of New York Press, 2006), 117–29.

23   Henry Pelling, *The Origins of the Labour Party, 1880–1900* (Oxford: Oxford University Press, 1965 edn).

disentangled in this work the many threads of political and social thought
and action that combined to produce a new form of politics at the end
of the nineteenth century. The book developed a theme of 'independent
labour representation', a notion that appealed (often for different reasons)
to both trade unions and socialist bodies. Together they constructed a
new political instrument – the Labour Representation Committee – to
create a parliamentary presence for the labour interest. A local example of
its early work is illustrated in Chapter Two. There was however a certain
'whiggish' tone in Pelling's work. It took its bearings from what was later
to happen – notably the decline of the Liberal Party after the Great War
and its replacement by the Labour Party as the main alternative to the
Conservatives. Pelling, it could be argued, accorded this pre-1914 political initiative greater significance than its impact at the time might have
warranted. After all, the new Labour Party, a name adopted in 1906, had
fewer MPs throughout the pre-war years than the Irish Nationalists, a
party and its leader (John Redmond) now largely forgotten. What Pelling
probably also over-emphasised was the importance of socialist bodies in
this process. The two main ones – the Independent Labour Party (ILP)
and the Social-Democratic Federation (SDF) – were both always small
parties, though they contained quite influential individuals. The Labour
Party was never formally socialist before 1914, though in 1918 and largely as
a result of wartime collectivism it adopted a new constitution that included
a statement (Clause IV) calling for the public ownership of the means of
production, distribution and exchange. Quite what this implied is uncer-
tain. When faced, for instance, with the financial crisis of 1931 two of the
Party's earliest socialist activists, James Ramsay MacDonald and Philip
Snowden – who both assumed high ministerial office in the 1920s – chose
to save capitalism by joining a coalition (the National Government) with
the Conservatives. Socialism, it seemed, was something that could only
result from a stable capitalist base. This, however, is not to suggest that
Pelling was completely wide of the mark in his emphasis on socialism.
There were areas, in Lancashire and elsewhere, where it was important
in the creation of a local labour movement and significantly shaped its
political ideology. Manchester was one such area (Chapter Four), Nelson

another.[24] Any analysis of the changes in politics in these places in the two decades before 1914 that does not take into account the work of the ILP, and to a lesser extent the SDF, would be a misleading one.

Socialism is the subject of Chapters Three and Four. What we might call a 'centre-periphery' approach emerges (especially in relation to the SDF), pointing up a number of local variations from what had been understood to be the national 'model' of behaviour. Interpretations of the SDF's failure to establish a firm socialist base, as advanced for example by Henry Collins,[25] are reviewed in the light of local conditions and tactics in the North West. This approach was later taken up in far more comprehensive form in a fine book by Martin Crick,[26] and reveals a different picture from that of London. What, however, was severely lacking in most work done at this time was the question of gender, a subject not squarely tackled until the appearance of Karen Hunt's study of women and the 'woman question' in the SDF.[27] Hunt, quite properly criticising much labour history for its male centred-ness, directed her attention not only to women within the SDF (scrutinising women's circles in, for example, Rochdale and Northampton) but gave most prominence to the perennial and still important issue of the relationship between socialism and feminism. The SDF never fully resolved this problem – female social democrats were always on the margins of the party when they tried to challenge the priority given to class and economics with questions about the place of women – just as, according to Hunt, it continued to bedevil the Labour Party into the late-twentieth century.

Hunt's work is therefore a necessary corrective to the emphasis given here, which is on questions of strategy, in particular the notion of the 'labour alliance', a theme prominent in Pelling's work. The ILP's success in

---

24   Hill, *Nelson*, chs 4, 6.
25   Henry Collins, 'The Marxism of the Social-Democratic Federation', in A. Briggs and J. Saville ed., *Essays in Labour History*, vol. 2 1886–1923 (London: Macmillan, 1971), 47–69.
26   Martin Crick, *The History of the Social-Democratic Federation* (Ryburn/Keele University Press, 1994).
27   Karen Hunt, *Equivocal Feminists: The Social Democratic Federation and the Woman Question, 1884–1911* (Cambridge: Cambridge University Press, 1996).

Manchester is one of the achievements of this strategy in the years before 1914. But this too should be contextualised by more recent studies. Mark Bevir's *The Making of British Socialism* is noteworthy in that it scarcely touches upon this issue, though it does have quite a lot to say about the SDF.[28] Bevir also eschews electoral tactics in the localities. For him the forging, or not, of alliances to secure the aim of labour representation is not what socialism is about. Indeed his study is far more a broad history of ideas. The Labour Party is not neglected, but unlike many previous scholars Bevir does not see socialism as synonymous with working-class organisations. To an extent his work is motivated by the desire to 're-revive' socialism, so to speak, in the light of critiques from neo-conservatives of the late-twentieth century ignorant of the richness of socialist thought and its relevance to the contemporary world. The work of both Hunt and Bevir thus extend and augment the discussion of socialism to be found in Chapters Three and Four.

The tendency noted by Bevir, of compressing research on political change into a limited Labour Party mould, had already seemed to be an unduly circumscribed approach after four important earlier interventions on this subject. The first, in the early 1970s, was Peter Clarke's outstanding *Lancashire and the New Liberalism*.[29] His organising concept for analysing political behaviour was, just as with Pelling, social class. But instead of making the Labour Party the beneficiary of class identities in politics Clarke set out to show that the Liberals were equally capable of making a pitch on this ground. What is more – and this was ground-breaking in the context of the historiography that had gone before – he argued that change could result from conscious political initiatives: that it was not only a question of responding to the slow unfolding of social and economic circumstances. The New Liberalism, or Progressivism, hatched by C.P. Scott, Lloyd George and Winston Churchill during the middle phase

28   Mark Bevir, *The Making of British Socialism* (Princeton NJ: Princeton University Press, 2011).

29   P.F. Clarke, *Lancashire and the New Liberalism* (Cambridge: Cambridge University Press, 1971).

of the Liberal administration that took office at the end of 1905, promised
to be the template on which to build a new coalition of forces in which
Labour might settle as a junior partner to the Liberals. In other words, a
British version of what the Democratic Party in the USA became under
F.D. Roosevelt.

The second important work came in the mid-1980s, with Martin
Pugh's excavating of the records of the Primrose League.[30] In terms of
popular politics Pugh demonstrated beyond question that Toryism easily
outnumbered rival left-leaning movements. The Primrose League had,
in Bolton alone, probably more members than the whole of the socialist
movement in the North West put together. It was not formally joined to
the Conservative/Unionist Party, but the League's essentially *social* purpose,
with emphasis on family, church and empire, unequivocally buttressed
the ideologies promoted by the party. Moreover, the League was a most
accomplished recruiter of women and young people.

Thirdly, there is the work of Mike Savage, who is his analysis of
working-class politics in the town of Preston offers a layered model of the
potential strategies available to labour groups, depending on the nature of
the local labour market as well as the historic traditions of popular action
in particular places.[31] Savage, more theoretically orientated than the other
writers, greatly expands our conceptual understanding of working-class
politics, proposing three 'capacities', as he terms them, for action: they are
economism, mutualism, and statism – each likely to exist simultaneously
in industrial communities but to produce different outcomes. The fourth
intervention of importance in this respect is that of Duncan Tanner in
1990.[32] It was Tanner, with a combination of breadth and depth of analysis, who most effectively contested the Pelling school by demonstrating a
continuing vitality in Liberalism in the years before the First World War.

30   Martin Pugh, *The Tories and the People, 1880–1935* (Oxford: Blackwell, 1985).
31   Michael Savage, *The Dynamics of Working Class Politics: the Labour Movement in
      Preston 1880–1940* (Cambridge: Cambridge University Press, 1987).
32   Duncan Tanner, *Political Change and the Labour Party, 1900–18* (Cambridge:
      Cambridge University Press, 1990).

Chapters Five and Six bear the imprint of these studies. Chapter Five, on political change in the cotton and mining town of Burnley, is influenced by both Savage and Tanner in seeking to bring back into the centre of discussion two traditions that were marginalised in Pelling's conclusions: social democracy, and Lib-Labism – both seen as anachronistic in the context of independent labour representation.

Chapter Six takes up themes from Clarke and Pugh, arguing that the 'new' liberalism perceived by Clarke in the Edwardian years was supplanted by a 'new' Toryism that developed after the War. It further cultivated some of the features of the Primrose League illuminated in Pugh's work. For much of the nineteenth and twentieth centuries Lancashire had a strong association with the Conservative Party. Before 1945, and in comparison with similarly industrialised regions, the North West was never particularly fertile ground for parties of the left, and as the franchise was extended in 1918 and 1928 the Conservatives, far from declining in Lancashire, successfully adapted their political style to new circumstances. In the interwar years Toryism sloughed off some of the religious sectarianism that had characterised its pre-1914 persona and assumed a political stance of a stridently anti-socialist nature that reached out to the newly enfranchised female voter.

Closing the politics section of the book with an affirmation of the Tory Party's continuing popular appeal dispels some of the whiggish perspectives on the Labour Party nourished in the twenty years following the General Election of 1945. What credibility Labour retained rested on one thing: the demonstrable strength and importance of the trade union movement. As independent working-class institutions the trade unions were absolutely indispensable as a core element for any party aspiring to challenge the political status quo of Edwardian and post-war Britain. But even with the organised labour movement as its foundation, greatly expanded as this was during the War, the Labour Party's reach remained limited. Rural workers, those in the newer industries of the South and Midlands, women, and white collar workers all proved difficult to recruit into a reliable body of support until the breakthrough of 1945. The 'masses' extended far beyond the Labour Party's interwar following. It is an inescapable fact of twentieth-century British electoral politics that the Labour Party has had no automatic claim to more than a section of working-class votes. For twenty-five years after the Second World War it might have been more likely than any of its rivals to mobilise them. But for much of the rest of the century it was no more (and sometimes much less) than the party of the *organised* working class, a very different thing. It was in this form that it eventually challenged the Liberals by the inter-war years. But this was a time, it should be remembered, of extraordinarily poor electoral performances by Labour. Its parliamentary results, only in 1929 impressive enough to make it seem a major national party, were nonetheless good by comparison with Labour's generally feeble municipal returns outside a few strongholds.[33] We are aptly reminded by Duncan Tanner that 'a very large percentage of the working class evidently did not vote Labour' during these years.[34]

IV

A point of much debate, and some discord, in historians' practice over recent years has been the 'cultural (or linguistic) turn'. Contrary to what some have felt I have long regarded the ideas and concepts associated with it as potentially very enriching for our understanding of history – and certainly not to be dismissed out of hand. Part II contains some of my own explorations of cultural and linguistic significations in society, based upon case studies of sport.[35] As with many others, an important source of

33   Sam Davies and Bob Morley, *County Borough Elections in England and Wales, 1919–1938: A Comparative Analysis* (Aldershot: Ashgate Publishing, 3 vols 1999–2006).

34   Duncan Tanner, 'Class Voting and Radical Politics: the Liberal and Labour Parties, 1910–1931' in Lawrence and Taylor, *Party, State and Society*, 123. McHugh's study of Manchester bears out some of these points; Declan McHugh, *Labour in the City: The Development of the Labour Party in Manchester, 1918–1931* (Manchester: Manchester University Press, 2006), esp. ch. 4.

35   See for example Jeffrey Hill, *Sport, Leisure and Culture in Twentieth-Century Britain* (Basingstoke: Palgrave Macmillan, 2002); *Sport and the Literary Imagination: Essays*

inspiration in my taking up this subject came from the publication in 1980 of Tony Mason's *Association Football and English Society*.[36] It was the first British work to offer a historical understanding of sport from a fully fledged academic scholar. It is true that James Walvin, just a few years earlier, had brought out *The People's Game*, itself a fine study of football, though with a less intensive penetration of primary sources than Mason's work.[37] Both were pioneering initiatives in British terms, showing that sport, which had been almost entirely overlooked in the academy, could be treated in the same scholarly manner as the other topics historians had traditionally fixed on. Both were a legacy of the important shift in emphasis that in the 1960s brought about a new kind of social history. Mason, in fact, had worked for many years in the Centre for Social History at Warwick University, one of the chief sources for that current of creative thinking.

It was the subject matter of Mason's book that inspired me, rather than its methodology.[38] In many ways it was a traditional history, showing none of the theoretical influences that in the later 1970s were beginning to introduce 'structuralism' and other aspects of continental European philosophy to British academics. But it did make a bold breakthrough into new territory, and opened up new ways of thinking about 'working-class history'.

in *History, Literature, and Sport* (Oxford: Peter Lang, 2006); Jeff Hill and Jack Williams ed., *Sport and Identity in the North of England* (Keele: Keele University Press, 1996).

36   Tony Mason, *Association Football and English Society, 1863–1915* (Brighton: Harvester Press, 1980).

37   James Walvin, *The People's Game: The Social History of British Football* (London: Allen Lane, 1975).

38   The historiography of sport has developed rapidly and extensively in the time since Mason's book appeared. Most of what has been published has applied a Masonian 'empiricist' methodology – research in the primary sources coupled with strong analysis in the write up. Few historians have taken up alternative approaches inspired by 'postmodern' ideas. For an interesting and important excursion into this other world, see Douglas Booth, *The Field: Truth and Fiction in Sport History* (London: Routledge, 2005). Booth's signposts deserve to be followed. An attempt at a route map is to be found in my own *Sport in History: An Introduction* (Basingstoke: Palgrave Macmillan, 2011).

It showed above all that, whilst working men and women were interested in trades unionism and labour politics, what increasingly consumed much of the attention of men (and possibly some women) was sport: and from September to April in particular, football.

At around the same time inspiration was found in the Open University's course on *Popular Culture* (U203), which signposted a theoretical route in 'culture'. This wide-ranging programme (which, interestingly, contained nothing on sport) was important for the ways in which it defined popular culture as contested terrain, and matched theory to empirical case studies. Whilst its Gramscian emphases might to some now appear rather old hat, the course nonetheless remains a landmark in how to 'do' cultural studies. Pre-eminent among its attributes is an insistence on the political. As one of the course's champions, the sociologist Stuart Hall, once noted:

> Popular culture is one of the sites where [the] struggle for and against a culture of the powerful is engaged: it is also the stake to be won or lost in that struggle. It is the arena of consent and resistance. It is partly where hegemony arises, and where it is secured. It is not a sphere where socialism, a socialist culture – already fully formed – might be simply 'expressed'. But it is one of the places where socialism might be constituted. That is why 'popular culture' matters. Otherwise, to tell you the truth, I don't give a damn about it.[39]

Popular Culture brought to the fore a powerful idea drawn from structural linguistics. It had to do with language, and argued for its determining function – that language constitutes thought rather than being an expression of it. In this simple formulation lies much of the force of an intellectual movement that has caused a fluttering in traditional historical dovecotes, by challenging an empiricist methodology that had become installed as the orthodoxy practically ever since history first became an established discipline in the academy.

The particular virtue of the cultural/linguistic turn in relation to sport is in its placing emphasis on the ideological influences of sporting practices and texts. Many sport historians had come to see sport and

---

39   Stuart Hall, 'Notes on Deconstructing "the Popular"', in Raphael Samuel ed., *People's History and Socialist Theory* (London: Routledge and Kegan Paul, 1981), 239.

leisure as processes 'shaped', or even 'determined', by economic, political, demographic, intellectual and other forces. Sport and leisure emerge in this way as social activities that have their existence only as by-products of other, *prior* developments. A clear example of this is the study of the influences that account for the emergence during the second half of the nineteenth century of association football as the 'people's game'. Several studies of this process have established that it was a combination of changes in work patterns, transport, business organization and the communications media that enabled association football to take the form it did. Such an approach is helpful, enabling us to understand how the process of modernization affected sport, but it stops short of according any autonomous agency to sport itself. The history of sport becomes a 'window', so to speak, through which to study developments in other areas of society.

To counteract this approach the essays in Section II seek to bring out the ways in which sport and leisure are processes which themselves have a determining influence over people's lives. The practices and texts of sport and leisure exist not simply as something shaped by other forces, but as cultural agencies with a power to work on their participants and consumers ideologically. In other words, they are processes from which we derive *meaning*. In their manifold activities are inscribed and structured habits of thought and behaviour that contribute to our ways of seeing ourselves and others, to a making sense of our social relationships, and to the piecing together of some notion of what we call 'society' or 'community'. Features as diverse as gender, nationalism, hero-worship, bodily exercise, and commercialism are all produced and re-produced through, among many other things, sport and leisure activities.

Sport and leisure, then, are not in themselves fixed categories. What they *seem* to us to be is to an extent dependent upon how they are *represented* to us. This process of mediation is a central theme of the essays. The language is in all these cases a written one (though it might equally be visual, or oral): representing visions of themselves to readers, whether through ideas of community or the sporting hero, who himself might be a symbolic figure of community (Chapters Seven, Eight and Nine). In these cases the medium is the newspaper press, the chief source of representation

in sport for the first half of the twentieth century.[40] It is generally taken to
be a source of factual information, although the 'objectivity' of the facts
is filtered through the linguistic and narrative conventions that frame the
press reporters' copy.[41] This might introduce an element of imagination.
When the source of mediation is avowedly imaginative fiction – a novel, for
example (Chapter Ten) – it poses a further problem for the historian. Can
creative literature be a historical 'source', and if so how should it be interro-
gated? This question reminds us of a remark by the American anthropolo-
gist Clifford Geertz: 'Believing, with Max Weber, that man is an animal
suspended in webs of significance he himself has spun, I take culture to
be those webs, and the analysis of it therefore not to be an experimental
science in search of law, but an interpretive one in search of meaning.'[42]

V

Chapter Seven examines an early example in sport of what, at a later date,
would almost certainly be described as 'globalisation'. The fourteen cricket
clubs of the Lancashire League, an association formed in the early 1890s
and based on weaving towns in the north east of the county ('East Lancs'
in popular speech), had been in the forefront of change in the cricket
world before the Great War. It saw the promotion of a commercial ethos
at the level of club cricket. It revealed a different mentality about cricket

40   Compared with later years, when television and corporate advertising assumed the
      major role, and 'heroes' had more often than not become 'celebrities'. See David
      L. Andrews and Steven J. Jackson ed, *Sport Stars: The Cultural Politics of Sporting
      Celebrity* (London: Routledge, 2001).
41   I have explored this theme further in Jeffrey Hill, 'History and Text: a case of linguistic
      determinism?' *Japan Journal of Physical Education and Sport*, 27 (2010), 95–112.
42   Clifford Geertz, *The Interpretation of Cultures: Selected Essays* (New York: Basic
      Books, 1973), 5.

from that which flourished in the South of England. This was one of the reasons why it was overlooked in the mainstream literature on the game.[43]

Much emphasis in the Lancashire League was placed upon the employment of professional players ('pros' – limited by the early-twentieth century to one for each club). They came to have a dominant effect on the development of the League. Their presence drew spectators and bolstered club finances. In the early years of the League these players were for the most part men who had played domestic county cricket, though occasionally a player from overseas was introduced. After 1918 however there was a rapid expansion in the employment of the overseas 'pro'. Nelson cricket club played an important part in this development. Beginning with the employment in 1921 of a famous Australian player, E.A. 'Ted' McDonald, Nelson pursued cricket success, crowd appeal and financial returns throughout the 1920s. The club's quest culminated in the engagement in 1929 of a relatively unknown Trinidadian, Learie Constantine, who was an immediate success and who stayed with Nelson until 1937, becoming the most renowned player the club and the League had ever known. Constantine's crowd appeal was immense and his presence in Lancashire was strongly supported by all the clubs in the League, which began a pursuit of their own to find similarly attractive stars. The result was a League that, by the mid-1930s, drew upon cricket resources from an international sphere, with players from various parts of the then Empire converging upon the northeast corner of Lancashire to earn their living. The process continued into the post-war years, fading only by the 1970s when professional cricket internationally began to provide greater opportunities for players. The Lancashire League's phase of the international 'pro' was important not only for cricket. It brought the small weaving communities, whose economies had long been linked to global trade, into new cultural contacts. Overseas

---

43 See Jeffrey Hill, '"First Class" Cricket and the Leagues: Some Notes on the Development of English Cricket, 1900–1940', *International Journal of the History of Sport*, 1 (May 1987), 68–81. Also Peter Davies with Robert Light, *Cricket and Community in England, from 1800 to the Present Day* (Manchester: Manchester University Press, 2012); Jack Williams, *Cricket and England: A Cultural and Social History of the Inter-War Years* (London: Frank Cass, 1999), ch. 8.

players represented a new kind of 'modernity'. Alongside other cultural innovations such as the cinema it introduced a shift in the social bearings of the communities in which these sportsmen performed their art.

This theme is taken up in Chapter Eight, where the approach is informed by the ideas of Frantz Fanon and C.L.R. James on colonial and postcolonial relationships.[44] The subject is the career of the cricketer Learie Constantine, encountered in the previous chapter as the talisman of internationalisation of league cricket in Lancashire, from the late 1920s to his death in 1971. Constantine's position as one of the first West Indian cricket 'superstars' gave him a prominence in the Caribbean and England that enabled him to enjoy a celebrated career after he retired from full-time cricket in the late 1930s. In England he was admired as a writer and broadcaster, and a man who had achieved status as a barrister in spite of having had little formal education when younger. After living in Nelson until 1949 he returned in 1954 to his native Trinidad, to work with the local nationalist movement led by Eric Williams. In the early 1960s he came back to London as the High Commissioner of Trinidad and Tobago. For all his adult life, therefore, Constantine was to a greater or lesser extent in the public eye. Rather than recount his sporting achievements emphasis falls on the ways in which ideas of Constantine were channelled through various media, principally the press and radio. His life is approached as a series of narratives about localism, gender, race and Englishness. The time spent by Constantine in Nelson is seen as a particularly important phase of his life – significant both for Constantine himself and the town of Nelson. It emphasises the function of the written text in the construction of heroism and identity, revealing an intriguing story of how a black Roman Catholic could become the greatest local hero the then thoroughly white, Protestant town of Nelson had produced.

44   On James see: C.L.R. James, *Beyond a Boundary* (London: Hutchinson, 1963); Kenneth Surin, 'C.L.R. James and Cricket' in A. Bateman and J. Hill ed., *The Cambridge Companion to Cricket* (Cambridge: Cambridge University Press, 2011), ch. 9. On Fanon: Frantz Fanon, *Black Skin, White Masks* (London: Pluto Press, 1967 edn); Nigel C. Gibson, *Living Fanon: Global Perspectives* (Basingstoke: Palgrave Macmillan, 2011).

The importance of the *text* in communicating ideas of sport and place is a central concern in Chapter Nine, which takes as its theme the celebrations, from the 1880s to the 1960s, witnessed in northern towns whose football clubs (association and rugby) had appeared in national cup finals. During this time, a formative one in the establishment of both association football and rugby league, many clubs from the North of England, and particularly Lancashire, enjoyed success, winning League titles and appearing in the final of the FA Cup, England's leading association football competition. The emphasis in this discussion is not on the game itself but on the ways in which football clubs were represented as symbols of the towns whose names they bore. A club's appearance in the cup final – played in London, initially at the Crystal Palace, then from 1923 onwards at the new stadium at Wembley (known as the Empire Stadium) – represented for the town something out of the ordinary, an opportunity not only to celebrate sporting achievement but to enjoy a degree of national recognition otherwise not normally conferred on northern industrial towns. A striking feature of the cup final was the mass movement of spectators to London, often reported by the press as a 'northern invasion'. This event was construed as a symbolic 'taking' of the capital, an assertion of the northern presence in the metropolis and the country at large. The crowd rituals associated with it were a significant part of the 'invasion', and conformed in many ways to the idea of liminality noted by anthropologists in the study of practices such as pilgrimage and holiday-making.[45] They were extensively and lovingly reported in the provincial press as expressions of local identity. Press reports, it is argued, should not simply be treated as 'reportage' (though there is factual information in abundance) but equally as examples of a linguistic construction of attitudes and identities; of the press talking to its readers in a language that produced signifiers of a complex set of territorial identities ranging from town, to region, to nation. There are, in the humble local newspaper, important pointers to some of the processes

---

45   See, for example, V. and E. Turner, *Image and Pilgrimage in Christian Culture: Anthropological Perspectives* (Oxford: Basil Blackwell, 1978).

through which identity is created and understood, as well as about the nature of historical sources and enquiry.[46]

This leads us on to a final question about 'texts'. Can the literature of fiction usefully be employed as a source in reconstructing the past? Many historians have given this question short shrift, arguing that the imaginative text has no place alongside proper 'evidence'. Chapter Ten seeks to challenge that position through a detailed reading of Howard Jacobson's novel *The Mighty Walzer* (1999). It is a partly autobiographical work, with a keen ethnographic sense of Jewish communities in North Manchester in the 1950s. It could perfectly well take its place in that long-established sequence of writing about the city by political and social observers. Ethnicity and sport – both a major part of Manchester cultural life – are Jacobson's principal subjects. Among other things he is concerned to show how sport helps sustain ethnic identity. The table tennis leagues of the city provide one means through which the principal character, Oliver Walzer, comes of age. He is a dextrous though unorthodox player whose view of sport is equally unconventional. Oliver's narrative, given from the perspective of his deracinated present as an itinerant lecturer, is in one sense a nostalgic remembrance of a lost Manchester – a 'roots' novel. It provides a fertile text for the examination of the problematical notion of identity. In other respects, though, it gives us subversion on a grand scale: about Jewishness, assimilation, family life, and above all sport. Would the Victorian public school framers of sport as a code of morality and manliness recognise their creation after its envelopment in the table tennis leagues of 1950s Manchester? Literary fictions are more than simply a 'reflection' of social and cultural life. They are an active ideological force that helps to construct for us a vision of the cultural environment and its people. At the same time they can provide the element of *critique* that is notably lacking in many texts on sport.[47]

---

46   See Hill, 'Anecdotal Evidence' in Phillips ed, *Deconstructing Sport History*, ch. 5.
47   See G.K. Peatling, 'Rethinking the History of Criticism of Organised Sport', *Cultural and Social History*, 2, 3 (2005), 353–71; John Bale, *Anti-Sport Sentiments in Literature: Batting for the Opposition* (London: Routledge, 2008).

VI

Jacobson's novel brings us firmly into the post-1945 years. It stands as something of an ethnic postscript to the main period under review, which began with a limited franchise in Britain and ended with the vote for everyone over the age of 21. What had been the world's first industrial society had only by the late 1920s become a democracy. The essays trace some of the effects of this transition on social, cultural and political identity.

Whilst to some extent it has been possible to generalise about the transition from a regional perspective, the local environment has always been foregrounded: here are found what John Walton has called 'sub-regional experiences' with striking contrasts.[48] There is, therefore, no typical case, but if we were to seek a particular place where many of these changes come together, the town of Nelson would provide a good example.

Nelson was a 'new town' that had developed from a scattering of small settlements in the north-east corner of Lancashire in the 1870s. Many among its labour force were migrants, some from far afield but most from handloom weaving communities in the nearby Yorkshire dales. The town's politics were distinctive. An alliance of ILP socialists and the cotton weavers' trade union made up a powerful force that dominated Nelson local government. With the exception of 1931 it returned Labour candidates, first in the Clitheroe seat and then in the new constituency of Nelson and Colne, well into the years after the Second World War. Nelson (more so than Colne) provided the constituency's radicalism, and it was Nelson that acquired from the press the title 'Little Moscow'. It made for good copy, though was politically inaccurate. Nelson had a strong radical tradition stretching back to its beginnings, imported by its Nonconformist immigrants. It was nurtured in a host of voluntary associations, most of them chapel related, that fashioned cultural life. In the same tradition of mutualist self help the Co-op, building societies, socialist groups and trade unions followed. The Weavers' Institute exemplified the physical and intellectual

48   Walton, 'The North West', 357.

energy of this activity, the Co-operative retail nexus its business ethos. In its localism and earnestness Nelson was the antithesis of mass society, even while located within the international political economy of cotton. There was a strong attachment to place and social class, with undertones of religious and, in a labour market open to female work opportunities, gender identities.[49] In this spectrum of allegiances Nelson represented an incongruous mixture, a combination that produced what might best be described as parochial cosmopolitanism.

By the 1930s, however, this particular form of community was being challenged by new, American-inspired cultural forms: the cinema, the dance hall, popular music, radio and, for some, private motorised transport. The opening in Nelson in 1930 of Woolworth's department store – a direct American competitor to the mutualist Co-op with its 'divi' system[50] – symbolised many of these changes.[51] So too did the intrusion into its very localised sport of a money consciousness, exemplified in the presence of the overseas 'pros' in cricket.

After a brief resurgence in the fortunes of the cotton trade after the Second World War Nelson's economy slumped rapidly. It followed the rest of Lancashire in this respect. One response to the problem of economic regeneration was attempted in the recruitment of a new wave of immigrant labour, this time from South Asia. It offered little long-term salvation to business, while bringing in its train a variety of social and political concerns.[52] They were not dissimilar to those experienced following the Irish migrations into Liverpool and its surrounding towns a century earlier.

49   Gender questions in Nelson are dealt with in Jill Liddington and Jill Norris, *One Hand Tied Behind Us: The Rise of the Women's Suffrage Movement* (London: Virago, 1978), esp. chs viii and ix. Jill Liddington, *The Life and Times of a Respectable Radical: Selina Cooper (1864–1946)* (London: Virago, 1984) is yet more firmly focused on Nelson.

50   Members of the Co-operative Society were paid a regular dividend according to the amount of the goods purchased on their membership number.

51   American influences often provoked disapproval at this time. Aneurin Bevan's put down of Neville Chamberlain – 'a mind like Woolworth's; everything in its place, and nothing above sixpence' – is a case in point.

52   See Hill, *Nelson*, 137–41.

Together with the continued slump in the cotton trade, and the bleak economic prospects faced by the late 1960s, immigration disturbed the equilibrium of class identity that had delivered Nelson dutifully to the Labour Party since the beginning of the century.

Yet social class was always a fickle allegiance. In his detailed analysis of class formation in Wigan and Bolton, Trevor Griffiths has argued strongly that class feeling was only one part of a broader confection of multiple identities that made up Lancashire's social life.[53] Whilst class solidarity was generally present, especially in areas of strong trades unionism, it competed with a variety of other identities. Within them, sometimes obscured from the historian's gaze, were the persisting layers of localism – of the neighbourhood, the village, the town and, at times, the county – which this book seeks to uncover.

---

53   Trevor Griffiths, *Lancashire Working Classes*. John Walton has similarly dampened the emphasis on class (Walton, 'The North West', 413) and downplayed the idea of a *regional* identity (Luis Castells and John K. Walton, 'Contrasting Identities: North-West England and the Basque Country, 1840–1936' in Edward Royle ed., *Issues of Regional Identity: In Honour of John Marshall* (Manchester: Manchester University Press, 1998), 44–81.

PART I

CHAPTER TWO

The Lancashire Miners, Thomas Greenall and the Labour Party, 1900–1906

The Lancashire and Cheshire Miners' Federation (LCMF) was the first of the big county miners' unions to become affiliated to the Labour Party. It did so in 1903, a full six years before the general passage of the Miners' Federation of Great Britain (MFGB) from Liberal to Labour. This early alignment of the Lancashire Miners with the new party, though an event of some significance in Labour politics, has not elicited very much detailed comment from historians,[1] for whom the explanation for Lancashire's affiliation has been sought in the unique convergence of pressures affecting the miners of this region. It is generally recognised that the Lancashire Miners shared with their fellow workers in other coalfields a desire for parliamentary representation as a means of securing remedial legislation for the industry. Thus the LCMF had been a prominent campaigner for the Eight Hour Day ever since the issue had first been raised in the early 1890s and had later come to embrace a number of other legislative objectives, including the controversial demand for the nationalisation of the mining industry.[2] Consequently, the Lancashire Federation was no stranger to electoral activity and in 1892 and again in 1895 had mounted campaigns

---

1   The subject is dealt with in some depth in the following: Roy Gregory, *The Miners and British Politics, 1906–1914* (Oxford: Oxford University Press, 1968), 57, 63–4, 82–7; Raymond Challinor, *The Lancashire and Cheshire Miners* (Newcastle: Frank Graham, 1972), ch. 14. P.F. Clarke, *Lancashire and the New Liberalism* (Cambridge: Cambridge University Press, 1971) also discusses the electoral activities of the LCMF: pp. 320–2.

2   Lancashire and Cheshire Miners' Federation, *Reports, Minutes and Proceedings* (hereafter LCMF) (National Union of Mineworkers' Offices, Leigh), 14 November 1896.

in the Wigan coalfield to elect miners' leaders to Parliament. Indeed, the Federation President Sam Woods had represented Ince[3] as a Lib-Lab for three years from 1892. But historians have been quick to point out that a feature peculiar to the working class of this region held back the Miners in electoral matters; this was the notorious division of political loyalty in Lancashire between Liberal and Tory which, in contrast with other regions, gave rise to a large body of Tory working men and made it difficult, if not impossible, for a union like the LCMF to participate in elections with one or other of the established political parties.[4] There is, in fact, plenty of evidence to show that Tory colliers were always suspicious when LCMF officials of known Liberal sympathies campaigned for the labour interest, as happened when Sam Woods and Thomas Aspinwall contested Ince and Wigan in the 1890s. Because of this it was not possible for Lancashire to become an exponent of the Lib-Lab politics favoured by other mining districts and, consequently, the LCMF's record of labour representation compared with areas such as Yorkshire or the North East was generally poor. Therefore, it has been suggested, the Lancashire Miners turned at the earliest opportunity to a new party, offering a completely independent line, as the way out of their dilemma, and sank their old party differences in support for the cause of Labour.[5]

There seems little reason to disagree with the overall gist of this argument. Undoubtedly the LCMF was more willing than the miners' unions in other regions to consider the merits of a new party like the Labour Representation Committee (LRC). But one of the more problematical details of the case concerns the fact that the Lancashire Miners did not immediately join the LRC at its inception in February 1900 but instead waited over three years before eventually committing themselves in May 1903. In view of the alleged attractions of an independent stance this hiatus appears strange and, at the very least, requires some explanation.

3   Not Wigan, as stated by Gregory, *Miners*, 82.
4   See H.M. Pelling, *Social Geography of British Elections, 1885–1910* (London: Macmillan, 1967), ch. 12.
5   See Gregory, *Miners*, 57, 63–4, 82–7; Challinor, *Lancashire and Cheshire Miners*, ch. 14.

Furthermore, when the LCMF's electoral policy of the early 1900s is taken into account it becomes apparent that the decision to join the Labour Party was not the straightforward matter that previous accounts have tended to make it. It is, therefore, worth paying closer attention to the political developments of these years and in particular looking at two issues: the circumstances surrounding the Federation's decision to join the forces of independent labour in 1903 and, secondly, the subsequent attempt by Thomas Greenall to capitalise on this decision by contesting the constituency of Accrington as a Labour candidate. An investigation of these two aspects of LCMF activity will tell us quite a lot about the nature of early Labour politics, not only in the North West but in the country at large.

II

It is important to remember that much of the impetus for an independent political stance by the Lancashire Miners came from a relatively small cadre of officials within the Federation. The most prominent among them was Thomas Greenall. Greenall was one of the younger generation of miners' officials who, by the late 1890s, had marked themselves out as being the natural successors to the 'old guard' of leaders – men like Sam Woods, Thomas Ashton, Thomas Aspinwall and Robert Isherwood – whose efforts in the 1880s had been instrumental in the very formation of the Lancashire and Cheshire Federation.[6] In some ways the younger leaders, among whom could be numbered, in addition to Greenall, Thomas Glover, J.E. Sutton, Stephen Walsh and Jesse Butler, carried on the same traditions as their mentors. Greenall, for example, owed his rise to prominence in the union to the patronage of Sam Woods. Having started his working life at the age of 11 in the Thatto Heath colliery near St Helens, Greenall continued

6   Challinor, *Lancashire and Cheshire Miners*, chs 10–12.

to work in the pits until his early thirties when he attracted the attention of Woods, who appointed him Miners' Agent at Pendlebury. This was in 1889 and thereafter Greenall remained in the Pendlebury area, lending his support to the leadership's endeavours to create a stronger, more centralised Federation that would overcome the traditional autonomy of the districts,[7] an objective that was eventually secured by 1897. But where Greenall departed from orthodoxy was in his politics. By the mid-nineties he had broken away from Woods's Lib-Lab influence and joined the Independent Labour Party. At Pendlebury he became deeply involved in the ILP's campaign for social reform and labour representation, helping to spearhead a crusading movement for social justice on such questions as housing and infant mortality[8] and contributing frequently to the local socialist newspaper *The Pioneer*. In 1899 Greenall was in the forefront of a triple labour alliance between the local miners' and engineers' unions and the ILP which sponsored two successful candidates in the Pendlebury District Council elections of that year.[9] In this way Greenall reflected a noticeable trend on the part of the younger leaders away from the old Liberal or Tory politics of their seniors and towards the cause of socialism and independent labour. Butler and Sutton, for example, were also members of the ILP in the Manchester area where, from the mid-nineties, Sutton became a key figure in the local socialist movement, representing the ILP on the City Council and cultivating considerable electoral support among the miners of Bradford and Clayton.[10] Glover and Walsh too, though probably advanced radicals rather than socialists, had a record of support for independent labour.[11] It was natural, therefore, that they should seek to extend their interests in labour representation from a local to a national level when the opportunity presented itself.

7   *Wigan Observer*, 18 May 1892.
8   *The Pioneer* (Pendlebury), May, August, November, December, 1899.
9   *Pioneer*, March, April 1899.
10   *Manchester Guardian*, 2 November 1894.
11   T.C. Barker and J.R. Harris, *A Merseyside Town in the Industrial Revolution: St Helens, 1750–1900* (London: Frank Cass, 1993 edn), 459–60.

The inaugural conference of the LRC in February 1900 provided Greenall with just such an occasion. He attended as an LCMF delegate alongside Thomas Aspinwall, the long-serving Miners' Agent for Wigan. Like other trade unions on this occasion the LCMF had sent a delegation to the LRC meeting with a watching brief, but Greenall sought a more positive role. When the position of LRC Vice-Chairman was being decided he offered himself as a candidate, no doubt thinking that if elected his union's affiliation would be secured. Greenall did indeed gain election to the post[12] but on returning to Lancashire to consolidate his coup he suffered a reversal: after a number of postponed meetings and much disagreement over voting methods the LCMF finally decided by a very substantial majority in June 1900 not to join the LRC.[13]

The reasons for this decision have never been satisfactorily explained by historians of the miners. Gregory, for example, though emphasising the importance of the LRC for Lancashire, makes no comment at all on the 1900 vote. Raymond Challinor, on the other hand, seeks to explain it as a tactical delay, part of the necessary mental adjustment made by the Miners as they switched from being 'anti-Liberal' to becoming 'pro-Labour'.[14] Challinor is undoubtedly correct in stressing the fact that pro-Labour sentiments were stronger among the Lancashire men in 1903 than they had been in 1900 and, as Gregory points out, the Taff Vale case was partly responsible for this changed outlook.[15] But the whole business of the Labour Representation Committee was dependent upon rather more complex matters than simply the tide of opinion. There are two crucial issues to consider. In the first place, why should the LRC appear to the Lancashire Miners as a more neutral body than either of the conventional parties? Though it averred a working man's point of view it nevertheless contained many socialists and erstwhile Liberals who were no less likely to arouse the resentments of Tory colliers than

---

12 Labour Representation Committee (LRC), *Conference Report*, 1900, 8, 21. (People's History Museum, Manchester.)

13 LCMF, 31 March, 28 April, 26 May, 16 June 1900. The voting was 168 for, 359 against.

14 Challinor, *Lancashire and Cheshire Miners*, 232–3.

15 Gregory, *Miners*, 82.

had the Lib-Labs of former days. Secondly, and equally important, the LCMF was part of a wider community of miners, the MFGB, and its policies were influenced by its relations with this national movement. It is in the context of these two factors that the LCMF's attitude to the Labour party should be assessed.

The fact was that the newly created Labour Representation Committee posed something of a threat to the powerful loyalties that had grown up among the miners of the central coalfields during the course of the joint wages agitation of the 1890s. The MFGB had of course originally been established in 1889 to pursue the objective of collective wage bargaining and Lancashire, it should be remembered, had from the very outset been in the forefront of this movement. Whatever prosperity the colliers of Lancashire had experienced by the turn of the century much of it was due to the combined efforts of the MFGB. Coalfield solidarity, therefore, was more than mere rhetoric for the Lancashire Miners. The problem was, however, that industrial and political attitudes in the MFGB did not coincide. Lancashire's politics were not shared by other MFGB regions where the prevailing sentiments were those of traditional Lib-Labism, best exemplified in the hard-bitten anti-socialism of the Yorkshire Miners' Association and its President Ben Pickard.[16] Pickard, who was also President of the MFGB, was a long-standing opponent of independent labour representation and had fiercely opposed its socialist advocates. He regarded the LRC as a parasitic body formed by weak trade unions with an eye on the funds of powerful groups like the Miners. 'I should like to ask,' he exclaimed in a famous speech at the 1900 MFGB Conference, 'why we, as a federation, should be called upon to join an association to find money, time or intellect to focus the weakness of other trade unionists to do what you are doing for yourselves and have done for the last fourteen years.'[17] True to

16   For a very thorough discussion of this attitude see David Rubinstein, 'The Independent Labour Party and the Yorkshire Miners: the Barnsley By-Election of 1897', *International Review of Social History*, xxiii, 1978 (I) pp. 102–34.

17   17 MFGB, *Conference Report*, 1900 (MFGB records, NUM Yorkshire Area Offices, Barnsley – hereafter MFGB). See also R. Page Arnot, *The Miners* (London: George Allen and Unwin, 1949), 353ff.

his own staunch individualism Pickard had proposed as an alternative to the LRC a scheme which allowed the MFGB to retain complete control over its own parliamentary candidates and thereby perpetuate the Liberal sympathies of most of its membership. In 1901 the MFGB accepted its President's proposals and the Labour Fund Scheme, as it came to be known, was implemented.[18]

Viewed in this light the delicate nature of the LCMF's position becomes plain. The vote of June 1900 has to be seen as a recognition not only of the problem of divided loyalties among the Lancashire colliers themselves but also of the fact that a declaration in favour of the LRC might have seriously complicated relations with their fellow miners in other regions. These twin pressures were to have a recurring effect on LCMF attitudes during the next few years.

Any doubts there might have been about Lancashire's commitment to the *principle* of labour representation were dispelled, however, by the eagerness with which the Lancashire people exploited the Labour Fund Scheme once it came into operation.

Significantly much of the pressure came from below, that is to say from rank-and-file opinion, against the advice of the Federation leadership. The initial response of the LCMF leaders to Pickard's scheme had been a modest one, essentially confined to using it as an opportunity for placing Sam Woods in a local constituency.[19] Following his defeat at Ince in 1895 Woods had been MP for Walthamstow (Essex) but, as Thomas Greenall himself pointed out on one occasion, '... whilst on the whole the miners of Lancashire were pleased that Mr Woods was in the House of Commons [they] never relished the fact the same as when he represented a mining constituency in his own county.'[20] Shortly after the Labour Fund Scheme had been settled, therefore, it was proposed that Woods contest the Lancashire division of Newton-le-Willows as an MFGB candidate. But instead of this representing the sum

18   MFGB, Report of Executive meeting, 6 December 1901.
19   LCMF, 22 November, 28 December 1901.
20   Speech to the MFGB Conference, *Report*, 1901. Woods had lost the Walthamstow seat in 1900.

total of the LCMF's parliamentary candidates Woods's adoption served as the signal for a wave of further proposals from the more militant branches. By the end of 1902 a number of mining constituencies were under discussion in Federation meetings as likely places for future Labour campaigns; St Helens, Westhoughton, Radcliffe-cum-Farnworth, Eccles and Ince were all mentioned in addition to Newton. It seems more than likely that much of this discussion had been generated by the activities of Greenall and his fellow Agents and allies Thomas Glover and Stephen Walsh, the latter, though still a radical himself, now a spokesman for a socialist element within the Federation whose votes had helped him secure election as Agent in 1901.[21] In November 1902 the three men seized the initiative by recommending that, in addition to the candidature at Newton, the Miners should also sponsor their secretary, Thomas Ashton, at Ince and Greenall himself at Radcliffe-cum-Farnworth.[22] In some respects this proposal offered a neat solution for Lancashire: the three candidates would represent the complete spectrum of political opinion in the LCMF – Liberal (Woods) Tory (Ashton) and Socialist (Greenall) – and they would be contesting seats held by both political parties, thus illustrating the Federation's genuine independence; at the same time Lancashire would be obtaining its due reward from the Labour Fund Scheme since, on the basis of its membership, the LCMF was entitled to three candidates. But the idea was not without its critics. Some miners' representatives objected to the clandestine manner in which Greenall, Glover and Walsh had devised it whilst others disagreed with the particular constituencies chosen.[23] Above all, Thomas Ashton opposed it. No doubt as a lifelong Tory he was aware that much of the pressure arose from radical and socialist quarters and feared that conflict might be engendered with

21   LCMF, 27 April 1901. Walsh was elected Agent in 1901 following the death of Aspinwall. An analysis of the voting figures given in the LCMF reports suggests that in the final ballot he received votes transferred from the Social Democrat John Sparling, a Burnley miner who had polled quite soundly in previous ballots before dropping out. The Social Democratic Federation was strong in the Burnley area and a supporter of the Labour alliance principle through the LRC.

22   LCMF, 8 November 1902.

23   LCMF, 6 December 1902.

Tory miners which could undermine the Federation's industrial strength. In the past Ashton had always been careful to stress that, no matter what the personal party affiliations of its candidates might be, the LCMF '... [does] not recognise any politics except Labour.'[24] In 1894, for instance, at the time of Woods's and Aspinwall's campaign as Lib-Labs, he had reminded the membership that '... any candidate whose election expenses may be paid from the funds of the Federation must not lend his services to either political party unless an advantage is to be gained thereby affecting the workers generally.'[25] At the beginning of 1902, as pressure for more Labour candidates mounted, Ashton issued a strong appeal for caution: 'I think we ought not to be too forward in adopting candidates, there is plenty of time; let other districts in the (MFGB) have a little before we get ahead too far'.[26] Ashton clearly felt that a headlong rush into labour representation would once again raise the question of affiliation to the LRC and, in an endeavour to place a brake on proceedings, he refused to allow his own name to go forward as the candidate for Ince.

The interesting fact about Ashton's intervention, though, is the extent to which his counsel was disregarded by the Federation. As an official of long-standing his views usually commanded respect, especially among that body of Tory colliers for whom he had always been a leading spokesman; on many previous occasions a pronouncement by Ashton had been taken by the Federation at large to be a powerful indication of Tory feeling and the Lancashire Miners responded accordingly. This time, however, his caution had virtually no effect on the general desire to push ahead with a new electoral policy. Ashton's place at Ince was immediately taken over by Stephen Walsh and, as if to emphasise the drive for labour representation, the list of candidates was further extended in the following year when Thomas Glover was put up in his home town of St Helens.[27] Such manoeuvres suggested a new climate of opinion in which, by about 1903, the interests of

24   From a circular issued by Ashton to the Federation membership; LCMF, 12 April 1893.
25   LCMF, 10 February 1894.
26   LCMF, January 1902.
27   LCMF, 25 May 1903.

'the miners' as a whole were beginning to take precedence over traditional party loyalties; the experience of a decade and more of industrial solidarity seemed to have acted as a solvent on old sectional allegiances and produced almost a sense of class feeling among the Lancashire Miners.[28]

Certainly in the early years of the new century the issue of labour representation had assumed an urgency greater than probably at any time in the past. An intense crop of industrial problems were all demanding immediate attention – the evergreen issue of the Eight Hour Day, pressing concerns over safety regulations, old age pensions, compensation for injury and Nationalisation.[29] On top of these the Conservative government had introduced a tax of one shilling on every ton of exported coal and brought forth a flood of protest from the mining districts at the 'reckless interference with the principles of free trade to which we owe our commercial supremacy.'[30] Industrial action in itself seemed insufficient to tackle these matters and the general need for representation in the House of Commons was reflected in the frequency with which the subject was debated at LCMF conferences in the years after 1901. These conditions gave Greenall and his fellow Agents the opportunity to press the merits of the LRC, particularly since they were able to stress its independence from other parties. When, for example, Walsh was proposed for the constituency of Ince it was noted that he would stand '... on strictly independent lines irrespective of any political party.'[31] Glover set out his position even more bluntly the following year when he told an MFGB conference: '... if it was a question of coming out (at St Helens) as a Liberal or a Tory he personally might as well chuck up the position.'[32] Moreover, by 1903 the LRC itself had been able to display its credentials to the Lancashire Miners. In electoral terms there was the by-election success of David Shackleton to be taken into account at Clitheroe

28   For a discussion of the development of class attitudes in Lancashire at this time see Clarke, *Lancashire and the New Liberalism*, Parts V and VI.
29   LCMF, 14 November 1896; Thomas Ashton, *Three Big Strikes in the Coal Industry* (Manchester: MFGB, nd), vol 2, 81.
30   LCMF, 4 May 1901.
31   LCMF, 13 September 1902.
32   MFBG, *Conference Report*, 1904.

in 1902, whilst as far as ideology was concerned the LRC had shown itself, under the guidance of men like Ramsay MacDonald and Arthur Henderson, to be a moderate organisation whose left-wing was kept on a fairly tight rein. Equally significant was the LRC's flexibility in regard to affiliated members, making it possible for the LCMF to join without severing its ties with the MFGB. This important concession became apparent when pressure from the rank-and-file in Lancashire was building up to a point where it seemed that the LCMF would join with Labour, sooner rather than later. Informal contacts between Thomas Ashton and MacDonald had resulted in the discussion of the LCMF's existing links with the Labour Fund Scheme and Ashton raised the question of exemption from the LRC's Parliamentary Fund. MacDonald, doubtless anxious not to repel a valuable recruit, had made a non-committal reply which clearly found favour with Ashton for when the Federation eventually did become affiliated it did so on the cut-price basis of paying only the ordinary affiliation fee of ten shillings per thousand members and not subscribing to the Parliamentary Fund. The Lancashire Miners therefore joined the LRC whilst continuing to subscribe to the rival electoral fund of the MFGB, a situation which remained unchanged in 1904 when the payment to the LRC's Parliamentary Fund was made compulsory for all affiliates, the LCMF included.[33] This rather easy-going arrangement no doubt helped to appease some of the old guard Lancashire leaders who had feared that affiliation to the LRC would cause problems with other districts in the MFGB, though, as Challinor has pointed out, the LCMF deliberately underplayed its new alignment by sending relatively obscure delegates to LRC conferences.[34] Nevertheless, the general mood of the Lancashire Miners was such that when Harry

---

33   LCMF, 20 August 1904. The chief beneficiaries of the LCMF's contributing to both electoral funds were the two successful LCMF candidates of 1906, Walsh and Glover. They received salaries from both funds giving them a total annual income of £550. Though the Federation held back £100 of this from the LRC fund some branches nevertheless considered £450 to be exorbitant, but Conference voted in favour of their having it. (LCMF, 24 March 1906.)

34   Challinor, *Lancashire and Cheshire Miners*, 232. He states that the LCMF's delegation to the LRC conference of 1904 contained none of the senior officials – Woods,

Twist of Bamfurlong Miners, voicing the hopes of militant branches such
as Ashton's Green, Berry Field and Pendlebury as well as his own, raised
the question of formal LCMF affiliation to the LRC in April 1903 it went
through almost as a matter of course.[35]

III

Of the candidates put forward by the Lancashire Miners two, Glover and
Walsh, fought successful campaigns in the General Election of 1906. Woods,
however, suffered from constant ill health and was forced to withdraw
from active political work in 1904. His place at Newton-le-Willows was
taken by another LRC man, J.A. Seddon of the Shop Assistants, who
also secured a victory in 1906 with help from the Miners.[36] In many ways,
though, the most interesting case was that of Thomas Greenall himself. As
one of the prime-movers of independent labour representation it might
have been expected that he would gain most in electoral terms, yet it was
Greenall who came off worst. Ironically, his aspirations were blocked, not
by the old party loyalties he had been striving to overcome, but by the very
organisation he had helped bring into being. Greenall's experiences as a
Labour candidate amply repay close investigation for they illustrate very
clearly the intrusion of national politics into the activities of the LCMF,
Greenall's chosen constituency, Accrington, being involved in the secret
electoral pact negotiated between the Liberal and Labour Parties.
      He had originally been put forward as the LCMF candidate for
Radcliffe-cum-Farnworth but on his own initiative Greenall secured the

---

Ashton, or Aspinwall. The point is essentially valid, though since Aspinwall had died
in 1901 he could not have attended anyway.

35   LCMF, 25 April, 25 May 1903.
36   LCMF, 7 November 1903, 24 February 1906; LRC Minute Book, 30 June 1904
      (People's History Museum, Manchester).

Federation's approval to switch his campaign to the Accrington division in north-east Lancashire.[37] On the face of it this seemed a pointless manoeuvre since Accrington appeared less suited for a miners' candidate than did Radcliffe; though a fairly typical east Lancashire seat in that it was markedly working class in its social composition the Accrington division was dominated electorally by workers in the cotton weaving and textile engineering trades. The mining vote, confined to the pit villages of Altham, Hapton and Huncoat and the town of Clayton-le-Moors, was certainly less than 10 per cent of the electorate.[38] Moreover, Accrington was a strongly Nonconformist area and was reckoned traditionally Liberal. The seat was held by the prominent Wesleyan businessman Sir John Leese, who had won it by a comfortable margin in the 'Khaki' election of 1900, and had never previously attracted a strong labour interest.[39] Greenall, however, claimed that he had been promised good support from the local trade unionists and socialists and estimated that this would more than compensate for the lack of miners. At the start of his campaign in the autumn of 1903 he did indeed receive backing from both the local Trades Council and the influential United Textile Factory Workers' Association, two of whose Representatives – Wilkinson of the Weavers and Ashton of the Spinners – toured the constituency making speeches from the Labour platform.[40] On this basis Greenall's optimism for his new constituency seemed justified.

But there may have been other considerations for Greenall's change of plan. Though hard evidence on the point is lacking it seems more than likely that Greenall was aware of Liberal difficulties in Accrington which would make the seat an easy picking for Labour. During 1902 the incumbent

37   LCMF, 23 May 1903.
38   See Roy Gregory, 'The Miners and Politics in England and Wales, 1906–1914', unpublished DPhil thesis, Oxford Univ., 1963, p. 528; Pelling, *Social Geography*, 263.
39   The Manchester socialist John Hempsall had in fact contested Accrington in the 1900 General Election but obtained only 433 votes; his campaign was not supported by the major socialist parties. *Accrington Observer*, 22 September 1900.
40   *Northern Daily Telegraph*, 29 September, 16 October 1903; LRC, Minute Book, 5 September 1903.

M.P., Leese, ran into acute financial problems, causing him to make known his intention of resigning the seat at the next parliamentary election. This left the Accrington caucus with the task both of finding a suitable replacement and, at the same time, of keeping the matter secret. 'Secrecy', noted the Liberal Party Chief Whip, Herbert Gladstone, in his record of the affair, 'is all important, otherwise a Labour man would come out'.[41] But the local Liberals failed, probably on both counts; after protracted interviewing they selected an alternative candidate, Franklin Thomasson, in whom they seemed to have little faith, by which time Greenall had already made his move for the constituency.[42]

With two candidates in the field bidding for the 'progressive' vote Accrington represented a test case for the secret Gladstone – MacDonald pact. As far as dealings over Accrington were concerned, though, they revealed the pact to be a rather one-sided arrangement. It soon became clear that the Liberals regarded the constituency as their own preserve and would tolerate no Labour trespassing. Gladstone, for his part, was unable to exert much pressure for he had always pointed out that he possessed no real power to remove a Liberal candidate if the local caucus was determined to keep him.[43] At Accrington the Chief Whip made no serious attempt to displace the Liberal man but constantly urged MacDonald to remove Greenall with the offer of alternative constituencies. MacDonald's task was rendered difficult, however, since Greenall had come to regard his candidature as a matter of principle for the LCMF. He declared that Federation Labour candidates should be seen to be challenging a Liberal seat as well as Tory ones (as Walsh, Glover and, later, Seddon were). The point made sense in view of the difficulties surrounding the LCMF's affiliation and Ashton's warnings about the danger of party discord. Independence, in fact, had been the keynote of Greenall's opening campaign speeches and this made it hard for MacDonald to switch Greenall to a Tory seat where the local Liberals would have been more compliant. '[MacDonald] has

41   Viscount Gladstone Papers, British Library, BL Add MSS, Second Series, 46484, cxlv.
42   Gladstone Papers, 46484, cxlv.
43   Gladstone Papers, First Series 46106, cxxii.

seen Greenall and Greenall's friends', recorded Gladstone after an interview with MacDonald at the Leicester Isolation Hospital; 'he has done his best to persuade Greenall to take South Salford, but G. is obstinate and nothing will move him from Accrington.'[44] But in spite of the candidate's obstinacy MacDonald applied constant pressure to fulfil what he clearly saw as his part of the deal with Gladstone. His most effective weapon against Greenall was David Shackleton, the victor in the celebrated Clitheroe by-election of 1902 when the LRC scored its first parliamentary success in Lancashire. Understandably Shackleton enjoyed great popular esteem at this time, especially in the Accrington area: he was a native of the district, an official of the Haslingden Weavers and had strong personal connections with the local Liberals, having himself been until recently a member of their party. Shackleton emerged as a willing accomplice for MacDonald in the effort to remove Greenall and was probably aware of the existence of the secret arrangements. He appears to have had a number of meetings with Greenall in an attempt to persuade him that the Accrington candidature was hopeless and that Greenall should take up the offer of another seat. He blankly refused to support Greenall's platform, securing the approval of the LRC itself for this move,[45] and in this way did nothing but damage to Greenall's chances. It was Shackleton who suggested to Gladstone in the spring of 1904 that the surest way of removing Greenall would be to drop Thomasson and retain Leese as the Liberal candidate.[46]

This indeed proved to be the way out of the impasse as far as the architects of the electoral pact were concerned. Gladstone's success in securing for Leese the funds which allowed him to stay on in Accrington was the real factor, rather than the pressure exerted by MacDonald, that ultimately weakened Greenall.[47] He considered Leese to be a far tougher opponent than Thomasson (who retired from the contest through

44   Gladstone Papers, 46101, cxxii.
45   LRC, Minute Book, 30 October 1903.
46   Gladstone Papers, Second Series, 46485, cxlvi.
47   MacDonald also sent John Hodge and Arthur Henderson to persuade Greenall to move to Newton-le-Willows. (LRC, Minute Book, 27 Sept 1904.)

ill-health) and in fact estimated that it would cost upwards of another
£1,000 to mount a serious campaign against him, admitting that even
this amount might not guarantee success.[48] His decision to withdraw as
the LRC candidate for Accrington was therefore taken towards the end
of 1904, over a year after the campaign had opened. As an LCMF sponsored candidate, however, Greenall was obliged to explain his reasons
for withdrawing to the Federation and did so at two successive miners'
meetings in December of that year. The first meeting, held at Manchester,
provided an interesting sequel to the whole affair for it revealed both the
degree of secrecy that had shrouded the LRC's dealings and the depth of
feeling among some sections of the miners in favour of the Accrington
campaign, thus bearing out Greenall's assertions about the importance of
Accrington in the Lancashire Miners' electoral strategy. Unfortunately
for Greenall, however, it also involved a humiliating examination of
his personal qualities and resulted in an undue amount of blame being
apportioned to the candidate for the failure of the campaign. He was
bitterly attacked by some of the delegates, particularly those representing branches in the Accrington district, for neither attending the constituency frequently enough nor exhibiting sufficient will to win, the
implication being that he had lacked resolve and sought an excuse to
back out. Many miners seemed to sense a backstairs deal and refused to
accept Greenall's financial arguments for withdrawing,[49] thereby voicing
suspicions that had been in the air since the autumn of the previous year
when MacDonald had been forced to make a public denial of an allega-
tion that he was attempting to use Accrington as a quid pro quo with the
Liberals to cover a Labour free-run in nearby Clitheroe.[50] Accusations
of this kind were repeated at the second LCMF meeting held in Wigan
to listen to the LRC's explanation of the affair. The party's case was put
by Arthur Henderson and John Hodge who argued that the refusal to
support Greenall was based on the strategic consideration of preferring

48   LCMF, 5 November 1904.
49   LCMF, 5 November 1904.
50   *Northern Daily Telegraph*, 9 October 1903.

him to move to Newton-le-Willows, where the LRC candidate (now J.A. Seddon) was in difficulty because of poor health and shortage of money. Nothing was said about Liberal attitudes in Accrington itself, though many' delegates openly declared their suspicions of a political dodge and condemned Greenall for having too readily complied with it.[51] But without firm evidence it proved impossible to press these beliefs and the matter was referred to a committee of enquiry to be set up by the LCMF. It reported speedily and placed the full burden of guilt on Greenall's shoulders: '... he has not displayed that energy and courage in his candidature which he ought to have done ... he has been too apprehensive of defeat and has allowed himself to be too easily influenced by people's capricious opinions'.[52] The idea that the LRC had been involved in a secret political deal was categorically rejected. Such, then, was the verdict and on its basis the Lancashire Miners resolved to drop the Accrington candidature altogether. Greenall retired in ignominy.

It was an ironic outcome to his efforts. Though he may have contributed in part to his own downfall by switching too hastily from Radcliffe-cum-Farnworth the pressure applied by the LRC to keep him out of Accrington also figured largely; as Thomas Ashton later suggested the role of the LRC had been too leniently dismissed.[53] How far the Accrington business affected Greenall's future parliamentary prospects is difficult to judge. To be sure, he suffered many more setbacks as a candidate before eventually, at the age of 64, becoming Labour M.P. for Farnworth in 1922; this was a new constituency created after the First World War out of the division Greenall had originally been set to contest as one of the Lancashire Miners' very first group of Labour candidates.[54]

51   LCMF, 3 December 1904.
52   LCMF, 31 December 1904.
53   LCMF, 3 December 1904.
54   He was nominated for Leigh, a Liberal stronghold, as the LCMF candidate in the January Election of 1910 but came last in a three cornered contest. He was not adopted for December 1910, but put forward at Leigh again for 1915, the War of course intervening. In 1918 he fought Farnworth unsuccessfully.

IV

Four main points have emerged from the above discussion and all have
a wider relevance to the question of political change and the rise of the
Labour Party in this period. In the first place, we have seen that the transition of the Lancashire Miners to Labour was a more protracted business
than has been suggested in previous accounts. There seems little doubt
that fears of political discord in the miners' ranks, both in Lancashire and
in the national Miners' Federation, were responsible for the LCMF's decision not to affiliate to the LRC in 1900. Three years later conditions had
sufficiently changed to make it possible for the LCMF to take on its new
allegiance, though as the backlash to Greenall's withdrawal from Accrington
showed there was still a danger of alienating some sections of opinion if the
Federation was seen to be complying with pro-Liberal forces. Nevertheless
the subsequent successes of LCMF candidates served to vindicate the pressure for the Labour alignment and it might be suggested that this change
of direction betokened the rise of a new generation of miners to positions
of influence within the union: that, in fact, this was not just a change of
policy but one of those significant shifts of emphasis that periodically
affect all trade unions as new men with fresh experiences and ideas force
their way to the front. Secondly, the rather ambivalent relationship that
developed between the LCMF, MFGB and LRC may be seen as pointing up Lancashire's role as a bridge between rival organisations. Although
historians generally classify the LCMF M.P.s of 1906 with the Labour
group in the House of Commons we can see that the MFGB was equally
able to lay claim to their allegiance and perhaps by thus demonstrating that
the gulf between the two bodies could be spanned the Lancashire Miners
helped to precipitate the general adherence of the Miners' Federation to
the Labour Party in 1909. Thirdly, the electoral activities undertaken by the
Miners in Lancashire underline the point that the much discussed Liberal-
Labour pact actually involved few concessions for the Liberal Party. The
Accrington episode especially lends credence to the view expressed by one
recent writer on the subject that '... the pact with the Liberals was generous
to the LRC only insofar as it allowed its candidates to win Conservative

seats or hold on to ones already gained'.[55] Finally, the Accrington campaign further shows that by affiliating to the Labour Party the Lancashire Miners were submitting themselves to a degree of national control in the direction of their political affairs; Ramsay MacDonald's attempts to prevent Greenall's candidature represent in embryonic form the intrusion of a bureaucratic influence which, as the Labour Party evolved, served increasingly to bring about the subordination of local interests to the exigencies of national party strategies. In all these ways, then, the events leading up to Thomas Greenall's abortive campaign at Accrington illustrate some of the profound changes that were taking place in the British political system at the turn of the century.

55   David E. Martin, 'The Instruments of the People?: the Parliamentary Labour Party in 1906,' in David E. Martin and David Rubinstein, eds, *Ideology and the Labour Movement* (London: Croom Helm, 1979), 140.

CHAPTER THREE

Social Democracy and the Labour Movement: The Social-Democratic Federation in Lancashire

Lancashire is recognised as having been a key area in the development of the Social-Democratic Federation (SDF). Though accurate details of the movement's membership are hard to come by it seems reasonably certain that from about the early 1890s onwards a substantial proportion of the SDF's branches and members was located in the North West of England. Indeed, Lancashire was probably the Federation's most important provincial centre, often rivalling London in the extent and seriousness of its social-democratic activity.[1] However, few labour historians have seen fit to examine the SDP's development in this region. No doubt this is a reflection of the neglect from which the Federation has suffered nationally from historians, most of whom seem to feel that the organisation was a negligible force in working-class politics and contributed little or nothing to 'mainstream' developments.[2] This view has some massively influential support behind it, of course, starting with Engels and coming through to

---

1   The estimates of P.A. Watmough ('The Membership of the Social Democratic Federation, 1885–1902', *Society for the Study of Labour History Bulletin*, 34, (Spring 1977) 35–40) suggest that by the mid 1890s Lancashire had come to account for about a third of the SDF's national membership; by the early 1900s its paying membership was in excess of that of London, where membership figures were falling from the late 1890s onwards. Watmough shows that until 1902 London always possessed the largest number of branches, but whether this was true after 1902 may be doubted. In 1906 *Justice* claimed 44 branches in Lancashire which may have represented the largest figure for any one region (*Justice*, 22 November 1906).
2   Such tends to be the view of H.M. Pelling in his seminal work *The Origins of the Labour Party* (Oxford: Clarendon Press, 1965 edn).

Henry Collins.[3] It also contains a good deal of truth. The SDF was a small movement and though many political activists passed through its 'revolving doors' it was never at any one time a leading influence in working-class life nationally (though in some districts of London and Lancashire it may have been). The question is: why was the SDF unable to establish a more prominent place in the labour movement? The orthodox answer hinges on the fact that it failed to grasp the complexities of Marxism. Under the continuing influence of H.M. Hyndman, it is claimed, the SDF adhered to a rigid brand of socialism which produced stultifying tactics and ultimately consigned the Federation to the role of a sect.[4] A similar explanation has been offered to account for the failure of Marxism (in the form of Guesdism) in France.[5] The problem with these explanations is that they rest on certain features of party development that are more often assumed than demonstrated. It may well be the case with the SDF, for example, that its national leadership possessed theoretical shortcomings but there is no necessary connection between this fact and the failure of the movement to form strong links with the working class at grassroots level. In fact, there has been a tendency to regard the SDF as a unitary organisation (despite its name) and from this some important misconceptions have been perpetuated. The present essay seeks to shift the emphasis in discussing the SDF away from theoretical issues and towards the day-to-day activities of the local membership in order to suggest other explanations for the party's essential failure.

3   See Henry Collins, 'The Marxism of the Social Democratic Federation', in A. Briggs
     and J. Saville ed, *Essays in Labour History*, vol. 2, 1886–1923 (London: Macmillan,
     1971), 47–69.
4   Collins, 'Marxism of the SDF'.
5   Claude Willard, *Les Guesdistes: le mouvement socialiste en France, 1893–1905* (Paris :
     Editions Sociales, 1965).

I

In many ways it was appropriate that the North West should become a social-democratic stronghold; not only was it a region of long-standing radicalism, a former hub of Chartism (some of whose ideas the SDF was to take up), but it also loomed large in the minds of British Marxists as a society ripe for class struggle. From the earliest days of the SDF as an essentially London-based group of disillusioned ex-radicals gathered around the controversial figure of H.M. Hyndman, its leading figures had been anxious to lay down the movement's roots among the industrial workers of the North. The massed ranks of cotton workers and miners to be found in Lancashire attracted them as a potential advance guard of the proletarian army. Nobody represented this view better than Hyndman himself. He regarded the North as the perfect arena for social conflict and class confrontation, proclaiming in an important article written in 1881 that '... it has no middle class to break the force of collision between the capitalist and those whom he employs'.[6] In this way the northern industrial towns were invested with a special significance in the Marxist teleology; they were to signify – to use the title of the article just quoted from – 'The Dawn of a Revolutionary Epoch'. Hyndman's vision of a bi-polar society of bourgeoisie and proletarians no doubt owed something to the schematic representation of such in the *Communist Manifesto* though, in some ways, it was not an inaccurate picture of many Lancashire towns. What it significantly obscured, however, was the important cultural relationships not only within the working class itself but also between workers and bosses which contributed in part to Lancashire's celebrated working class Toryism and which, to the perceptive observer, might in turn raise doubts about the region's potential for sudden radicalization.[7] Nevertheless, on the basis

6 H.M. Hyndman, 'The Dawn of a Revolutionary Epoch', *Nineteenth Century*, IX (1881), 1–18.
7 On the working-class Toryism of the North West see P.F. Clarke, *Lancashire and the New Liberalism* (Cambridge: Cambridge University Press, 1971), chapters 2–4.

of Hyndman's somewhat flawed analysis, the SDF became committed at an early stage of its activities to converting the Lancashire working class to socialism, an aim the Federation was to pursue with enduring faith and some success over many years.

In the 1880s, when the SDF was in the process of establishing itself as a political movement, some of its attitudes and tactics in the North West do lend credence to the view that it was an intransigent body possessed of an alien creed. During this time local social democrats appeared to rely heavily on the guidance of London organisers when forming their branches, and there was thus imported into Lancashire a number of metropolitan attitudes which might not have been appropriate for the northern environment. Certainly they caused the early SDF to run counter to some of the established trends in Lancashire working-class politics.

By the mid-1880s social-democratic groups were active in Oldham, Rochdale, Blackburn, Darwen and, most notably, Salford. They concerned themselves for the most part with direct action on the question of unemployment, following the guidelines laid down in *The Manifesto of the Social Democratic Federation* which had been issued in February 1886 shortly after the Trafalgar Square riots in London.[8] This activity engaged Lancashire socialists in a year-round programme of street politics which included kerbside meetings, demonstrations and marches aimed not merely at publicising the plight of the unemployed, but at pressing for action by the municipal authorities. These techniques of unemployment agitation were in fact to become a signal feature of British left-wing politics for many years after, and an outstanding contribution by the SDF to working class action. They were exemplified (at this time) in the work of the SDF in Salford. Here, under the inspiration of the energetic Londoner John Hunter-Watts, a recruit to the SDF from the Secularist movement, the main thrust of social-democratic campaigning was seen in 1887 when the branch orchestrated a monster procession through the streets of the city culminating in the presentation to the Lord Mayor of a series of demands

8   *The Manifesto of the Social Democratic Federation*, 15th February 1886 (British Library of Political and Economic Science, London).

for the alleviation of the problems: '... that the local authorities organise the labour of the unemployed upon useful and productive work at fair rates of wages by carrying out necessary improvements', among which were numbered the demolition of slum dwellings, their replacement with sound workers' cottages, the construction of baths and gymnasia, and the provision of playing fields.[9] In the following year the campaign was pursued in the form of a mass rally on Blackstone Edge, near Rochdale, organised jointly by the Salford, Oldham and Bolton branches. According to an enthusiastic correspondent in *Justice*, the SDF newspaper, the occasion attracted a crowd of some 20,000 people and momentarily, at least, recalled the heroic days of Lancashire Chartism.[10]

Propaganda of this kind undoubtedly brought a new element into the politics of the working class and, at the same time, established a concern for municipal reform from which SDF groups in the region were rarely to depart in the future. But it was rather optimistically regarded as the only form of action required to make contact with the industrial proletariat. 'Neglect politics', advised Hyndman at this time, 'and use every available means to force temporary proposals upon the ruling class'.[11] This advice resulted in SDF branches moving away from conventional politics at a time when many local trades councils were beginning to get involved in modest municipal campaigns to achieve 'labour representation', expressing their labour consciousness for the first time at the ballot box.[12] 'Let us only recognise', urged Hyndman, 'that political action is after all quite secondary ... and more in the interests of the possessing classes – as likely to save them from attempts at violent revenge – than of the proletariat'.[13] On the question of trades unionism the SDF's position was even more rigid, its

9   *Justice*, 10 December 1887.
10 *Ibid.*, 5 December 1888.
11 *Ibid.*, 1 January 1887.
12 For these developments see J. Hill, 'Working Class Politics in Lancashire, 1885–1906; A Regional Study in the Origins of the Labour Party', (unpublished PhD thesis, Keele University, 1971), ch. 7.
13 *Justice*, 1 January 1887. The SDF in Bolton did in fact put forward six (unsuccessful) candidates in the municipal elections of 1887, though this was something of an

line neatly summed up in the circumstances surrounding the formation of the Federation's very first Lancashire branch at Blackburn in the early months of 1884. The occasion was a lengthy stoppage in the local weaving trade with the operatives trying to restore wage levels that had been cut during the Great Strike of 1878. It was quite plain from the reports sent back to *Justice* from the SDF's London representatives in Blackburn – J.L. Joynes, Jack Williams and James MacDonald – that they saw the strike as an opportunity to attack the trade unions involved, to denounce their sectional interests and to draw the attention of working people to the inadequacy of the industrial weapon in the proletarian struggle.[14] This objective was partly helped by the unsuccessful outcome of the dispute in the spring of 1884, following which *Justice* came out with a lengthy piece by one of the Federation's leaders, H.H. Champion, in which he counselled workers against attempting to emulate the unionism of the 'labour aristocrats'. The skilled men, he argued, should seek to join hands with the mass of the working population ('the men and women who suffer') to form one big union against poverty and exploitation.[15] Hostility on the part of the Federation's leadership (though Champion himself later retracted and left the SDF) remained a prominent feature of its policies, constantly reiterated in the columns of *Justice*. The upsurge of 'new unions' of the unskilled in 1889–1890 appeared to make little difference with *Justice* still expecting workers to channel their militancy into socialism through the SDF. This leader of 1891 captures the mood fairly well:

> the business of the social democrats as trade unionists is to permeate their trade unions with social democracy and on no account whatever to sacrifice to mere trade organisations that energy and enthusiasm which ought to be devoted to the spread of social democracy and social democracy alone. Look at it how we will, trade unionism, old or new, can never re-organise society ... every social democrat ought to belong to the trade union of his particular trade just as every sensible man in the middle class insures against death and disablement for the sake of his family. But trade

---

exception even for Bolton SDF. (*Bolton Weekly Guardian*, 24 September; 29 October 1887).

14   *Justice*, 16 February; 1 March; 24 May; 29 September 1889.
15   *Justice*, 21 June 1884.

unions tend to degenerate into benefit societies and mere wage raising organisations. Therefore, every social democrat's first and paramount duty is to strengthen the only social democrat organisation in Great Britain – the SDF – and to work vigorously for the overthrow of capitalism.[16]

II

Whether this intransigence any longer truly reflected the opinions of local militants must be doubted. Certainly it would be misleading to assume that the behaviour of the early years prefigured the SDF's later experiences in the North West. Quite the contrary, in fact, for by the turn of the century there had developed considerable pressure from social democrats for what had come to be known as the 'Labour Alliance'; in other words, the combination of socialist and non-socialist forces to create a political movement capable of expressing an independent labour point of view in local and national government. Furthermore, such pressure was accompanied by moves to establish the SDF as a permanent element in the labour parties that were springing up at this time. It is usual to think of this movement for independent labour as being inspired in varying measure by the pragmatic needs of trade unions coupled with the more far-seeing ideals of the Independent Labour Party (ILP): SDF involvement is generally regarded as having been at best opportunist, at worst destructive. In reality, SDF attitudes were neither of these, though the protean nature of social-democratic activity does tend to lay the movement open to charges of opportunism. It is certainly true that few branches displayed any consistency in policy during the 1890s, and that a wide variety of tactics emerged in the North West. Historians have found it useful to discuss these developments around the twin polarities of labour alliance and socialist unity but the point to be emphasised is that these positions were not mutually exclusive ones, and

16   *Ibid.*, 29 August 1891.

that in all the to-ing and fro-ing there appears to be a general tendency towards labour alliance.

The idea of a labour alliance may well have had its earliest manifestation in Salford during the early 1890s. It was evident as an SDF tactic throughout the moves to establish the Salford Labour Electoral Association in the summer of 1891 and in the subsequent creation of the Manchester and Salford ILP a few months later. As we have already seen, the SDF in Salford was one of the oldest social-democratic formations in Lancashire. It was based in the Ordsall area of the South Salford parliamentary division and by the early 1890s had acquired a rich political history.[17] Unemployment agitation continued to be a vital part of the group's activities, although Hunter-Watts, the 'rather anarchistic'[18] organiser of the 1887 campaign, had gone by 1889 and the direction of affairs had passed to a cadre of local men, prominent among whom were George Tabbron of the Brassfounders' Union, the gasworker Bill Horrocks, Alf Settle, a copper plate engraver of Irish descent and a former mineworker W.K. Hall. Under their aegis the branch made contact with other socialist groups, notably the Manchester Fabians, and became involved in the trade union struggle, playing a key part in the fight to form a branch of the Gasworkers Union at the Manchester and Salford Gasworks in the summer of 1889.[19] The effect was to draw the SDF into the orbit of the local trades council and thence into the confrontation between organised labour and the Manchester Liberal Union over the issue of municipal labour candidates that boiled up to crisis in July 1891. Thus was set in motion the whole train of events that resulted in the creation of the ILP.

Far from being, as is often supposed, a rival to the SDF the ILP in this context can be seen as an *extension* of social-democratic activities to

---

17   Including some interesting quarrels with the Socialist League, which can be followed up in the Socialist League Papers, SL 894/1–2, 2521/1–4. (International Institute of Social History, Amsterdam.)

18   The phrase is from H.W. Lee and E. Archbold, *Social Democracy in Britain* (London: Twentieth Century Press, 1935), 85–6.

19   *Justice*, 14 September 1889. Biographical details in *Workman's Times* (hereafter WT), 9 January 1892 and *Clarion*, 9 April 1892.

incorporate wider labour and, particularly, socialist interests. It was this feature of its parentage that largely accounted for the Manchester ILP's strongly 'leftist' pre-occupations, as N. Reid has shown in a recent article.[20] From the outset the SDF participated alongside many other labour groups in a series of meetings during the summer of 1891 on the subject of a local workers' political body. The unifying factor among an otherwise disparate collection of labour spokesmen was their common enmity towards official liberalism, stemming from the high-handed refusal of the Liberal Union to consider seriously Trades Council claims for municipal labour representation.[21] The SDF sought to maintain this sense of labour solidarity, endeavouring to foster a united labour party along the lines of the Bradford Labour Union, whose leaders (especially Bartley of the *Workman's Times*) the Salford people were in touch with. However, a mixture of personal rivalry and ideological incompatibility killed the Salford Labour Electoral Association at an early stage. The SDF probably made the mistake of seeking too strong a control of affairs and this, together with memories of the party's earlier intransigence, was sufficient to set socialists and non-socialists at loggerheads. At the Association's inaugural meeting, for example, Alf Settle struck a strident note by declaring that '… if he joined the Association he should endeavour to make it subservient to his Socialistic instincts … he would try to get it worked along the lines he advocated (but) if he found it went contrary to his opinions he would not support it'.[22] There seems also to have been personal friction between Settle and the radical secretary of Carters' and Lurrymen's Union, John Kelly, who was sponsored by his own union to oppose Settle's candidature in Ordsall Ward in the municipal elections of 1891, thereby splitting the labour vote and wrecking Settle's otherwise good prospects.[23] Such rancour spilled over into the selection of a Labour candidate to represent the Association in South Salford at the next General Election; initially it

20   N. Reid, 'Manchester and Salford ILP: a more controversial aspect of the pre-1914 period', *North West Labour History Society Bulletin*, 5, 25–31.
21   *WT*, 24 October 1890, 29 August 1891.
22   *Ibid.*, 21 August 1891.
23   *Ibid.*, 7 November 1891.

was to have been Thomas Harris of the Fabians but when he withdrew and was replaced by W.K. Hall the idea of a social-democratic nominee was totally unacceptable to many non-socialists.[24] In fact Hall's campaign, which was underway by the end of the year, was clearly designed to go some way towards a rapprochement: he stood essentially as an advanced Liberal, offering to promote political and social reform, Home Rule for Ireland, payment of MPs, and Old Age Pensions.[25]

It is interesting to see the SDF projecting itself in this way, under-playing its Marxism for the sake of labour unity. Hall was nevertheless roundly defeated in the General Election of March 1892, by which time the Labour Electoral Association seems to have become defunct. The for-mation of the ILP shortly afterwards was an attempt to restore something of the temporary labour unity of the previous year, though by 1892 it was more a unity of various strands of socialism – SDF, Blatchfordites, Fabians and the independent labour movement inspired by Joseph Burgess in the *Workman's Times*. As N. Reid has shown, social democrats were very much in evidence at the inaugural meeting of the ILP[26] and a good many of the ILP's early propaganda campaigns, notably its unemployment agitation of 1893, betrayed strong traces of social-democratic influence.[27]

The Salford experiment in Labour Alliance was by no means the only example of SDF moves in this direction. During the next few years groups at Accrington, Nelson and Blackburn all engaged in similar initiatives with varying degrees of success.[28] The SDF at Blackburn was probably the most successful, participating as it did in a triangular alliance with the local trades council and the ILP to form a labour party which by 1900 had out-stripped the Liberals as the chief opponent of a very powerful brand of local Toryism; it laid the basis for Philip Snowden's spectacular LRC

24 *Ibid.*, 12 March 1892.
25 *Ibid.*, 11 September 1891; *Manchester Guardian*, 3 November 1891; *Salford Chronicle*, 12 March, 9 April 1892.
26 Reid, 'Manchester and Salford ILP'; *WT*, 28 May 1892.
27 *Manchester Guardian*, 2 November 1893; E.S. Pankhurst, *The Suffragette Movement* (London: Longmans, Green, 1931), 95, 129–30.
28 *Rochdale Star*, 1 July 1892; *Justice*, 26 November 1892; *Nelson Chronicle*, 12 May 1893.

campaigns of 1900 and 1906 which finally broke the Tories' long-standing monopoly of parliamentary representation in the borough.[29]

The work of the SDF in Blackburn spanned the two poles of social-democratic activity, in fact, serving to illustrate not only the politics of the labour alliance but those of socialist unity as well. The co-operation of SDF and ILP in Blackburn, clearly outlined in the pages of their joint publication the *Blackburn Labour Journal*, exemplifies the willingness of most SDF branches in the 1890s and early 1900s to establish links with other socialists. In the late 1890s, perhaps as a symptom of the generally unfavourable conditions for working class politics at this time, socialist unity was a popular tactic throughout Lancashire. Much pressure was exerted on the national leaderships of both main socialist movements from rank-and-filers for a fusion of the parties. Littleborough, Droylsden, Preston, Bolton, Stockport, Liverpool and, of course, Blackburn all exhibited enthusiasm for such a move; at Stockport the members of the ILP actually withdrew from their parent body as a protest over the leadership's refusal to implement fusion.[30] And despite the inability of the rival leaders to achieve a national reconciliation there is no doubt that socialist unity became a fact of life in many localities. Charles Higham of Blackbum ILP told his national conference in 1899, '... in Blackburn, Nelson, Rochdale, Ashton and several other places, the local branches of the ILP and SDF already work cordially side by side and for elections and many propaganda purposes are already virtually federated together'.[31] Socialist co-operation of this kind brought with it no particular tactical imperatives during these years, indeed a variety of approaches was manifested by the groups concerned. At Blackburn, as we have seen, the outcome was a lively socialist-labour party, whereas at Rochdale by way

---

29   For details of Blackburn see *Blackburn Labour Journal*, July, October and November, 1899; *Northern Daily Telegraph*, 3 November 1903; 29 March 1904; P.F. Clarke, 'British Politics and Blackburn Politics, 1900–1910', *Historical Journal* XII (1969), 302–27.

30   ILP National Administrative Council Minutes, reports of 16 June, 25 June-16 July, and frequent reports of August–September, November–December, 1898. (British Library of Political and Economic Science, London.)

31   ILP, *Conference Report*, 1899, 9.

of contrast the emphasis was towards a Blatchfordian style of socialism with more interest in proselytising than in securing the return of labour candidates.[32] The result may have been, in this case, to drive a wedge between the socialist and labour forces in the town. This at least was the impression of the local trades council secretary who observed in 1902 that, '... if the principle of independent labour representation should have been completely divorced from socialism here in Rochdale, it is directly owing to the doctrinaire socialists of the SDF type who on every opportunity have vilified trade union candidates who did not happen to be socialists', adding, '... the ILP appears to have drifted into that exclusive position that characterises the SDF'.[33]

Such complaints about the SDF were not uncommon throughout its whole history and they made it difficult sometimes for social democrats to shed the image of single-minded intransigents. What was emerging on a broad front, though, was an open-minded, not to say pragmatic, form of social democracy in which a willingness to change, to dispense with dogma and, above all, to seek genuine contacts with the labour movement was clearly evident.

The latter point is well illustrated by the development of the SDF in Burnley, Here the movement was, to an extent, *sui generis*. By 1893 it had become the most dynamic SDF branch in the North West with an ambitious policy that sought to win for social democrats a hegemonic role in the local labour movement. What is more, the branch came near to succeeding, acquiring a measure of support in the locality that few other SDF groups were ever able to match. This success was in part due to the favourable circumstances in which social democrats found themselves in north-east Lancashire. Burnley and the surrounding district was an area of rapid and recent economic growth; in the 1890s business activity was still mushrooming and there was an accompanying influx of immigrant workers from the nearby Pennine Hills, like Philip Snowden's family who crossed

32   See *Rochdale Labour News*, July, September, December 1897.
33   Labour Party Letter Files, LRC 5/149, J. Firth to J.R. MacDonald, 28 December 1902. (People's History Museum, Manchester).

the border from the West Riding to settle in Nelson.[34] In the twenty or so years from 1890 the population of Burnley increased by almost 20 per cent, to over 106,000.[35] With so many immigrants from relatively close-by, the town acquired a well-organised chapel community and a predilection for liberalism and it was from among such quarters that Burnley's working class leadership was initially drawn, typified in the figure of the Weavers' Association President David *Holmes*. But being something of a 'new frontier', Burnley lacked an established set of working class institutions. The trade unions in both weaving and coalmining, the town's principal industries, had a fairly unstable history, especially in mining where it was only in 1888 that a secure branch of the Lancashire Miners Federation came into being.[36] The union leadership was unable fully to discipline its rank-and-file and there was plenty of grassroots discontent in the early 1890s over issues such as wages and working hours, which the SDF was able to exploit. Its speed in doing so can be explained by the fact that the branch, established in 1891, was organised by two experienced socialist campaigners: Dan Irving, who arrived by way of the socialist colony at Starnthwaite in the Lake District, and Joe Terrett (known as AG. Wolfe – '"Wolfe" a good fighting, somewhat ferocious name-and as for the "AG", well, they were the first two letters in agitator') who had worked for the SDF in some of its London strongholds.[37] Together they brought an aggressive approach to the branch, setting up a newspaper – *The Socialist and North East Lancashire Labour News* – and instilling a much-admired discipline into party organisation:

> A committee of thirty-six members was appointed and this committee was divided into twelve threes: three for each ward of the town. The duty of these three members is to go to private addresses of each member of the Party in the ward to collect his weekly subscription and to leave his copy of Justice. Incidentally, a deal of information is obtained. Each collector is provided with a book in which he notes

34 W. Bennett, *The History of Burnley* (Burnley: Burnley Corporation, 1951), Part IV, Chapter VI; P. Snowden, *An Autobiography* (London: Ivor Nicolson and Watson, 1934).
35 HMSO, *Census of England and Wales*, 1891 and 1911.
36 Bennett, *Burnley*, ch. VII.
37 Biographical details from *The Social Democrat*, III, 1899.

whether the subscribing member is a member of the Weavers' Association or the Co-operative Society. By means of this information and industriously whipping up the members, the SDF has been able to place Socialists upon the Committee of the Weavers' Association and also upon the Committee of the Co-operative Society.[38]

Although Terrett left Burnley for Sheffield around 1894, Irving was able, during the next few years, to take the Burnley branch through the full gamut of socialist experience, cultural as well as political,[39] always sure of being able to draw on a residuum of support from trade unionists in mining and weaving. This originated in the SDF's Eight Hour Day campaign of 1892, which earned the movement a reputation for championing the cause of the ordinary worker at a time when the union leaders and employers seemed to be conspiring against him. In the face of poor trade and threatened wage reductions, the SDF had urged a curtailment of working hours as a means of reducing overstocked markets and stimulating demand, but the employers, supported by Holmes in particular, argued that such a move would jeopardise Lancashire's trading position against its Far Eastern competitors.[40]

Nevertheless, the SDF won round the membership of both the Burnley and Nelson Weavers' Associations sufficiently to secure the passage of Eight Hour Day resolutions in 1892.[41] In the following year Terrett campaigned among the miners, exploiting the class conflict inherent in the lock-out of 1893, and established yet another hardcore of support. The *Workman's Times* (usually pro-ILP) commented: 'Comrade AG. Wolfe took advantage of the miners' holidays by holding afternoon meetings, and so popular and effective (sic) has he permeated socialism in the miners that they not only voted for us but worked with an enthusiasm and determination never excelled'.[42] With mills closed through lack of fuel, frustration was

---

38   *WT*, 12 August 1893.
39   On the cultural activities of the SDF in Burnley see C. Tsuzuki, *The Life of Eleanor Marx 1855–1898: A Socialist Tragedy* (Oxford: Clarendon Press, 1967), 276.
40   *Justice*, 6 October 1892; *Cotton Factory Times*, 24 June 1892.
41   Burnley Weavers' Association, Ms Minute Book, 11 May, 24 September 1892 (DDX 1274, Lancashire County Record Office [LCRO], Preston). *Nelson Chronicle*, 19 August 1892.
42   11 November 1893.

also running high among the weavers. In the municipal elections of 1893 the SDF sponsored five candidates on a platform of comprehensive social reform and independent labour. 'THE TWO POLITICAL PARTIES HAVE COMBINED', proclaimed *The Socialist*, 'to prevent the return of Labour candidates ... we hope you will at once become alive to this fact and AS WORKERS ALSO COMBINE to further YOUR interests, and send men pledged to a definite Labour programme'.[43] Two candidates were successful, John Sparling of the Miners and John Tempest of the Twisters' and Drawers' union, their election to the town council completing a rewarding year for the SDF which had earlier seen Sparling become an official of the local miners' branch and two other members – John Markham and James Roberts – secure election to the executives of the Weavers Association and the Trades Council respectively.[44]

On the strength of these early victories the SDF moved directly into a confrontation with Lib-Labism. The main objective was to capture the Weavers' Association as a base for labour representation. By assiduous 'whipping' of the social-democratic membership it proved possible in 1894 to secure the passage in the Weavers of an SDF resolution supporting the policy of local labour representation, thereby gaining access to an important financial source. At the same time the SDF was able to remove from the control of the Liberal-inclined Executive Committee of the Weavers the choice of the Association's delegates to the TUC, in this way directing the nature of the involvement of the Weavers in wider political circles.[45] But these moves were less striking than they seem. They had the effect principally of stimulating a Lib-Lab counter-attack which revealed just how strong were the anti-socialist forces in the town. Taking a leaf from the SDF's book and in like manner packing the meetings of the Weavers, the old guard was able to nullify most of the SDF's gains. A measure of the disunity this caused was in 1894 when, though no fewer than ten labour candidates appeared at the polls in the municipal elections, there was no

43   *Socialist*, 14 October 1893.
44   *WT*, 8th July 1893; *Socialist*, 4 November 1893.
45   Weavers' Minute Book, 1 and 10 August 1894; *Burnley Gazette*, 4 August 1894.

concerted action and none was successful, though ironically a member
of the Lib-Lab leadership – Robert Pollard – standing as a Liberal in
Stoneyholme did get in.[46]

    This period of confrontation in Burnley is interesting not only for
indicating the strength of the two sides but also for establishing the pattern
of Burnley working – class politics in the period up to the First World War.
There was never any effective unity of purpose during this time. This was
never more clearly illustrated than in the General Election of 1906 when
there were, in fact, two Labour candidates competing for the working class
vote – Hyndman for the SDF and Fred Maddison of the Liberals. Tension
between these two wings was never far below the surface, though it is
worth noting the extent to which it was the SDF that sought to heal the
breach. For a time between 1904 and 1906 Dan Irving succeeded in creating a local Labour Representation Committee which mounted a united
Labour campaign in the Board of Guardians election of 1904 and in the
municipal contest of the following year, though in 1906 its chief financial
support – the Weavers' Association – was lost following further disagreements between socialists and Lib-Labs, this time over the question of
religious education in schools.[47]

III

By the beginning of the twentieth century probably the most marked feature
of SDF tactics in Lancashire was their flexibility. This did not necessarily
mean that continuity with the early years had been lost – there was still
a strong emphasis on the politics of unemployment and this if anything

46   *Burnley Gazette* 3 November 1894.
47   For details, *Burnley Gazette*, 2, 12 September 1903; 21 October 1905; *Cotton Factory
    Times*, 9 February 1906; Burnley Textile Trades Federation Minute Book, sub-
    committee reports 6, 21 February, 1905, (DDX 1274, LCRO).

increased in the early part of the twentieth century with the inauguration of the SDF's national 'right to work' campaign. In all the areas where the Federation had branches there were marches, demonstrations and May Day rallies on the issue of unemployment. But much else had also been taken aboard, notably an interest in electioneering and the formation of electoral pacts with trades councils and the ILP. Professor Tsuzki, indeed, has sought to classify the Lancashire members of the SDF – 'many of whom were unionists in the cotton towns, anxious to maintain the SDF link with the trade unions through the Labour Representation Committee'[48] – as belonging to the 'right' of the Federation, in contrast with those of other areas who took a more revolutionary line. There is clearly some validity in the claim though it is perhaps too rigid a characterization and fails to capture the degree of fluidity in local activity. Nevertheless, it is true that many Lancashire branches favoured the SDF's national co-operation with the Labour Alliance and strongly opposed the decision taken in 1901 at the Birmingham conference to withdraw from the LRC.[49] Nelson social democrats, supported by those of nearby Burnley, argued that such a move would shut the SDF off from local labour developments to the detriment of the Federation's own development.[50]

And so it did prove in Nelson itself, where between 1902 and 1905 the local Labour forces not only secured the by-election victory of David Shackleton at Clitheroe but the more important (in some respects) capture of Nelson Town Council in 1905, the first Lancashire council to fall to Labour. It was in order to be able to participate in such developments that many Lancashire members campaigned within the Federation to keep the contact with the LRC. 'All over the country', claimed J.H. Thornton of the Burnley branch in a letter to *Justice*, 'the SDF rank-and-file are joining and working as LRCs for local purposes.'[51] The sentiment was reiterated by John Moore of Rochdale, one of the less isolationist members of his

48   C. Tsuzuki, *H.M. Hyndman and British Socialism* (Oxford: Oxford University Press, 1961), 135.
49   *Justice*, 10 August 1901.
50   *Ibid.*, 5 April 1902.
51   *Ibid.*, 4 March 1905.

branch, who noted that, '… in every direction I go I find the opinion of
the majority of SDF members I come into contact with is in favour of re-
joining the LRC'.[52] Moore in fact made a strong bid, with the support of
Blackburn and Burnley, to secure re-affiliation at the 1905 SDF conference,
though his motion was eventually lost by a large majority, as was a similar
one put the following year by the East Liverpool branch.[53] Nevertheless,
the idea remained a potent one for many social democrats and their views
were summed up in this comment from Thornton:

> Either we believe this Labour Representation movement is one that is tending towards
> the emancipation of the workers from capitalism and wage slavedom or it is a mere
> game of blind man's bluff and will lead the workers into a mere political quagmire.
> If it is the former, we feel that it is the duty of the Social Democrat to be inside the
> movement, helping it on the right channel to its ultimate goal. If the latter, then our
> duty is plainly to oppose it for all we are worth.[54]

There was little doubt where Thornton's preferences lay, but equally there
were social democrats who saw it as their duty to oppose the Labour
Alliance. Very often these people came from branches with a tradition of
socialist unity. In the 1890s, when the tactic of socialist unity had come
into being, it was frequently a spontaneous response to circumstances.
By the early twentieth century, however, circumstances had changed and
socialist unity had in some cases become a far more assertive tactic with
far-reaching implications for the duties of the social democrat. This seemed
particularly true of branches in the Manchester area, which by the early
1900s were heavily involved in the Federation's 'right to work' agitation.
Between 1904 and 1906, at the time when in Burnley Irving was working
for a united Labour party, Skivington and Watson were similarly engaged
in co-operation with other labour forces to prepare a draft parliamentary bill on unemployment and to get Skivington elected to the Board of

52   *Ibid.*, 11 March 1905.
53   *Ibid.*, 29 April 1905; 21 April 1906. East Liverpool's proposal of 1906 received more
     support than did Moore's of the previous year, the voting being 55–11 (1905) as against
     55–29 (1906).
54   *Ibid.*, 5 May 1906.

Guardians.[55] But over and above this 'respectable' activity they were taking to the streets to protest over the Government's failure to effect legislation and clashing with the police in some turbulent battles. In 1906, to publicise the idea of 'the right to work', the SDF seized control of uncultivated private land in Levenshulme, setting unemployed men to work on it and getting into further trouble with the police and authorities.[56] In one sense this activity chimed well with the idea of labour representation since progress on unemployment could be assisted by municipal election successes. Skivington profited in some ways from his election as a Guardian in 1905 for it enabled him to fight in the Board for an improved distribution of poor relief. No doubt the SDF's attachment to the Manchester Labour Party was guided by similar motives.[57]

But in another sense the exponents of unemployed agitation were finding themselves distanced strategically from the labour-alliance principle. This was especially so after 1906 with the disappointing, not to say obsequious, showing of the Labour Party at Westminster where it adopted a quietly subordinate role in relation to the ruling Liberal Party. The alliance of Liberals and Labour seemed a most unpromising vehicle for the kinds of solutions on the unemployment issue that many socialists had come to expect, solutions which demanded radical new measures in land nationalization and public spending. In the emerging philosophy of New Liberalism such ideas found little sympathy and for many social democrats it must have seemed that an accommodation with the political powers-that-be would lead only up a blind alley. Consequently confrontation became, for such socialists, the order of the day: confrontation not only with the Liberal Party but with its Labour allies also. In other words the way ahead lay with socialist unity rather than labour alliance. It was no coincidence either that much of the stimulus for this kind of politics came from Manchester, which had been the hub of the unemployment

55   *Ibid.*, 21 January, 4 February 1905.
56   *Ibid.*, 21 January, 8 April 1905; 21 July, 18 August 1906. See also K.D. Brown, *Labour and Unemployment 1900–1914* (London: David and Charles, 1971), 44, 59, 76.
57   The SDF was affiliated to the Manchester LRC at its inception in 1903 (*Justice*, August 1903).

agitation as far as the North West was concerned. It was from Manchester that a number of national moves were set in motion to activate socialist unity; the issuing of the 'Green Manifesto' to reform the Labour Party in 1910, the establishment of Socialist Representation Committees and the formation in 1911 of the British Socialist Party out of the SDF and the more 'left' elements of the ILP.[58] With such developments the diversity of social-democratic politics in the North West was maintained, carrying through to the First World War and the eventual fragmentation of the Federation under the impact of wartime pressures.

IV

Limitations of space have prevented a fuller treatment of the local activities of the SDF in this important region, though the essay has served to emphasise some of the key aspects of the movement's development there. What has become abundantly clear is that, on the whole, theory did not play as large a part in the thinking of local militants as it perhaps did in the minds of the national leadership. The very variety of local action is in itself a demonstration of the absence of any hidebound attitudes. Social democrats do not emerge, at the local level, as the single-minded sectarians they are sometimes portrayed as being. In fact there often seems little to distinguish the SDF from the ILP in terms of tactics. Branches clearly enjoyed a good deal of freedom of action and their political experiments seem to have been guided by the 'sound instincts' of local leaders, to use Hobsbawm's term.[59] In this sense a valuable parallel may be drawn between the SDF and the French Marxists of the POF who, as Willard has shown,[60]

---

58   See Reid, 'Manchester and Salford ILP'.
59   E.J. Hobsbawm, *Labouring Men: Studies in the History of Labour* (London: Weidenfeld and Nicolson, 1968 edn), 231–8.
60   Willard, *Les Guesdistes*, 595–602.

were similarly affected by regional autonomy which produced local diversity and a marked contrast in style between the 'centre' and the 'periphery'. It may well have been this feature of the SDF's make-up that reduced its impact in the British labour movement. Though on the one hand local autonomy was a source of strength in that it allowed social democrats to adapt to their immediate environment, on the other hand it produced a movement notoriously prone to internal divisions over strategy, and one which ultimately was unable to preserve its identity as a unified socialist force.

CHAPTER FOUR

Manchester and Salford Politics and the Early Development of the Independent Labour Party

The grass-roots activities of the Independent Labour Party have been the subject of increased scrutiny from historians over the past few years.[1] Consequently we can now be a little surer about the contribution of the party to the development of an independent labour movement in Britain at the end of the nineteenth century, though with every fresh case study a different local strategy seems to come to light. The one outstanding profile in this field is the closely observed account of the ILP in Bradford by J. Reynolds and K. Laybourn, who identify several key features in the party's growth in that city, notably the reformist nature of ILP socialism and the close associations with local trade unionism. 'From the outset', they tell us, 'Bradford trade unionism and the Bradford ILP were seen as two aspects of a single homogeneous labour movement aimed at the emancipation of the working class from poverty and exploitation.'[2] But how far this pattern of development was repeated elsewhere is a different matter. David Rubinstein's account of the ILP's intervention in the Barnsley

---

1   In the *International Review of Social History*, for example: Deian Hopkin, 'The Membership of the Independent Labour Party, 1904–1910: A Spatial and Occupational Analysis', XX (1975), 175–97; J. Reynolds and K. Laybourn, 'The Emergence of the Independent Labour Party in Bradford', XX (1975), 313–46; David Rubinstein, 'The Independent Labour Party and the Yorkshire Miners: The Barnsley By-Election of 1897', XXIII (1978), 102–34. In the *Bulletin of the North West Labour History Society* (Manchester): S. Carter, 'The Independent Labour Party in Ashton-under-Lyne 1893–1900', No 4 (1977–1978), 63–91; N. Reid, 'Manchester and Salford ILP: A more controversial aspect of the pre-1914 era', No 5 (1978–1979), 25–31.

2   Reynolds and Laybourn, 'Emergence of the Independent Labour Party in Bradford', 346.

by-election of 1897, for example, reveals that the ILP in this area did not take up a Bradford-style policy of labour alliance until the late 1890s, and suggests that this was the case far the ILP as a whole.[3] Yet studies of the party's activities on the other side of the Pennines indicate a different story still. N. Reid's short essay on the ILP in Manchester points to a continuing socialist tradition among ILPers in that city which frequently brought them into conflict with their comrades in other areas, whilst S. Carter's analysis of nearby Ashton-under-Lyne allots a very minor role indeed to the ILP in the development of independent politics.[4]

The present essay is offered as a means of taking this question of ILP strategy further by investigating the ILP's part in the politics of Manchester towards the end of the century. In one sense the essay simply seeks to extend our knowledge of the ILP in that city: considering Manchester's significance in the early socialist movement, especially as the birthplace of the Clarion, it has been surprisingly neglected. But additionally it is hoped that the following pages will help to complement the study of Bradford by Reynolds and Laybourn, and thus provide a comparison of ILP strategy and ideology between what were probably the two most important centres of socialism in the North of England at this time.

I

By 1910 Manchester possessed one of the most effective centralised labour parties in the country: in municipal and parliamentary politics labour was a force of some significance. The rise of labour to this position had been a comparatively rapid process, with few signs in the 1880s that an independent working-class party would develop and pose a threat to the

3   Rubinstein, 'Independent Labour Party and the Yorkshire Miners'.
4   Reid, 'Manchester and Salford ILP'; Carter, 'Independent Labour Party in Ashton-under-Lyne'.

established alignment of forces. Manchester's reputation as a radical city had seemed at that time to be in danger of melting away: from the 1850s the city where Stephens had preached Chartism to multitudes on Kersall Moor and where, according to Engels, was to be found 'the seat of the most powerful Unions, the central point of Chartism [and] the place which numbers most Socialists'[5] had acquired a docile appearance. In place of its working-class radicalism and the strident bourgeois philosophy to which Manchester had given its name, the city had become increasingly noted for its Toryism both among the bourgeoisie and the workers. 'Manchester', observed the *Methodist Times* in 1895, with a somewhat exaggerated sense of nonconformist gloom, 'seems to be completely under the thumb of liquor and clericalism.'[6]

To some extent this transformation in the city's political temper was an effect of its changed economic character, a change that wrought contra-dictory pressures on the working-class community. W. Cooke Taylor had noted in the 1840s that Manchester was 'becoming daily more and more a commercial depot',[7] ceasing to be a major manufacturing centre for cotton; from the middle of the century it was developing into the hub of a pulsating metropolitan conurbation that spread along the Irwell and Mersey valleys, creating a huge commercial zone. With the opening in 1894 of the Ship Canal the area's potential for growth seemed unlimited, and one observer dared to predict (not entirely inaccurately) that 'eventually along its banks will be an unparalleled concentration of works transferred there on account of the economy of production.'[8] But in the 1890s Manchester's develop-ment as a modern industrial base was only partially completed. The city represented in itself a case of uneven economic development: the old work-shop trades of Ancoats and the Jewish tailoring shops of Strangeways still

5   Frederick Engels, *The Condition of the Working Class in England* (introduction by E.J. Hobsbawm, London: Panther Books, 1969), 266.
6   *Methodist Times*, 18 July 1895.
7   W. Cooke Taylor, *Notes of a Tour in the Manufacturing Districts of Lancashire* (London, 1842), 19.
8   Lord Egerton of Tatton, 'The Manchester Ship Canal', *Nineteenth Century*, XXXV (1894), 19.

remained alongside the coalmines of Bradford and the even more modern engineering works developing in Salford. In fact Manchester experienced a proliferation of diverse occupations in the 1890s and this brought about a fragmented labouring community; the monolithic occupational pattern of neighbouring towns like Oldham and Bolton – the result of dominant staple trades – was entirely absent.[9] So too were the bases for the strong and extensive trade-union memberships characteristic of the cotton towns. Manchester trade unionism, despite the impetus of the 'new union' boom in the early 1890s, was never very strong before the First World War. Added to this was a further aspect of economic change that tended towards the fragmentation of the labouring class, namely the presence in the city of a number of immigrant communities: Germans, Lithuanians, Jews all gravitated from Europe into Manchester during the late nineteenth century to form their own self-contained districts. But most notable of all were the Irish – some 80,000 of them – packed into the densely populated streets of Hulme, in the South-Western part of the city, and in the district of St Michael's between the Oldham and Collyhurst roads.[10] Here were some of the most overcrowded parts of an already overcrowded city.[11]

But if growth fragmented the working class, it also had important effects upon the relationships between classes. Manchester's commercial functions created a significant population of middle-class businessmen and lower-middle-class black-coated workers, both spatially segregated from the proletarian communities. This process had started in the middle years of the century as the encroachment of factories, and warehouses had begun to threaten the fashionable bourgeois quarters of the city centre such as Upper Brook Street and Ardwick Green. From the mid-century the wealthy Mancunians began to move out, initially into

9   See Appendix I.
10 John Denvir, *The Irish in Britain, from the earliest times to the fall and death of Parnell* (London: Kegan, Paul, Trench, Trubner and Co, 1892), 432; *Manchester Guardian* (*MG*), 16 November 1885.
11 See John Tatham, *Report on the Health of Greater Manchester, 1891–1893* (Manchester: Manchester City Council, 1894), and T.R. Marr, *Housing Conditions in Manchester and Salford* (Manchester: Sherratt and Hughes, 1904).

suburbs like Rusholme and Stretford, and later further south still into select Cheshire villages, commuting to business by train.[12] With the introduction of the telephone it even became possible to conduct one's affairs from St Anne's-on-Sea, forty miles away on the Fylde coast.[13] This exodus of the Manchester business elite, perceptively chronicled by Katharine Chorley in her classic book *Manchester Made Them*, was complete by the end of the century: 'the process spoilt the character of Manchester', says Mrs Chorley, 'because if left her without her natural leaders.'[14] But the same concerns also created vast tracts of suburbia for the less opulent bourgeoisie: Withington, Burnage, Didsbury and Levenshulme were all new residential areas incorporated into Manchester's boundaries by the time of the First World War.[15] And for every suburb of this type there were many more pockets of less wealthy but equally unproletarian life dotted about the two cities.

The separation of the classes in this way affected politics, since the placing of a physical and social barrier between the leadership of the two established parties and their potential working-class followers removed some of the bases for a shared political culture. Of the two the Liberals seem to have been more disadvantaged by this. Not only were their middle-class supporters all too frequently switching allegiance to the Conservatives, a feature noted by Katharine Chorley,[16] but the Liberals were failing to attract popular support in sufficient quantities at election times. The decline of Liberalism as an electoral force was strikingly illustrated in the General Election of 1885 when, in defiance of the pre-poll optimism of the Liberal *Manchester Guardian*[17] the Tories swept the board in the newly created working-class divisions of Manchester and Salford, thus prefiguring what

---

12 Katharine Chorley, *Manchester Made Them* (London: Faber and Faber, 1950), 137–8.

13 In the case of Sir Charles Macara, see P.F. Clarke, *Lancashire and the New Liberalism* (Cambridge: Cambridge University Press, 1971), 30.

14 Chorley, *Manchester Made Them*, 138.

15 Shena D. Simon, *A Century of City Government: Manchester 1838–1938* (London: George Allen and Unwin, 1938), map facing 112.

16 Chorley, *Manchester Made Them*, 234, 236.

17 See *MG*, surveys of 14–25 November 1885.

was to be a near Tory hegemony in this area during the next fifteen or so years.[18] Exactly why the Tories should have so bettered their rivals in the working-class districts is difficult to explain. Of course, given the limited size of the late-Victorian working-class electorate it is likely that even in predominantly proletarian constituencies the weight of middle-class votes would have been disproportionately heavy, so that Tory victories may have been less dependent upon the support of the labouring population than at first sight they appear.[19] Nevertheless, the Tory Party probably enjoyed superior financial resources with which to mount electoral campaigns,[20] whilst the Liberals were additionally penalised by their association with the Irish Question, hardly an election-winning issue in the '1880s and early '1890s. Moreover Manchester, no less than other parts of Lancashire, presented the Tory Party with a congenial cultural environment in which to operate; the nationalist, or more precisely xenophobic, instincts induced among the native working class by the Irish immigrant presence were an essential part of Tory ideology.[21] The Irish community, its already separate ethnic identity doubly underlined by the energetic shepherding of the Salford Catholic diocese,[22] was always likely to produce a conservative

18   See Appendix II. Of the eleven constituencies in the immediate area of Manchester and Salford only Manchester North – West, containing the business vote, and Manchester South, and to a lesser extent Salford North and Stretford, were middle-class in character.

19   Cf. Paul Thompson, *Socialists, Liberals and Labour: The Struggle for London, 1885– 1914* (London: Routledge and Kegan Paul, 1967), 69–70.

20   For the development of 'New' Toryism in Manchester and its personnel see H.J. Hanham, *Elections and Party Management: Politics in the Time of Disraeli and Gladstone* (Hassocks: Harvester edn, 1978), 314–22.

21   For a fuller discussion of these issues see Clarke, *Lancashire and the New Liberalism*, chs 2 and 3, and Jeffrey Hill, 'Working Class Politics in Lancashire, 1885–1906: A Regional Study in the Origins of the Labour Party' (unpublished PhD thesis, University of Keele, 1971), chs 5 and 6.

22   'There is perhaps no diocese in England better provided in respect to its parochial schools', recorded Herbert Vaughan on the work of his predecessor, Bishop Turner of Salford. Vaughan himself supervised major advances in school building and teacher training. See John Snead Cox, *The Life of Cardinal Vaughan* (2 vols; London: Herbert and Daniel, 1910), I, 252, 270, 374, 380, 390 and 414.

backlash among indigenous voters to the benefit of the Tories; this was especially so when such feelings were primed by an active and latitudinarian Established Church.[23] The Tory position on the drink question also won the party support from working people, as it did in many other parts of the country.[24]

In this atmosphere nonconformity, Liberalism's strongest *point d'appui* with the labouring classes in many other towns, possessed little relevance as a popular movement. As Benjamin Nightingale's extensive survey reveals, Manchester nonconformity tended to be concentrated in the suburbs[25] with the poorer districts starved of chapel patronage, a fact recognised but not overcome by the Methodists.[26] There was little evidence, apart from one or two cases where charismatic preachers drew good support,[27] of the vital chapel society with strong roots in the working class that was so characteristic of, say, Bradford. Nevertheless the Liberal Party did retain one element of loyalty from a section of the working class and this came from the small, artisan-based organised labour movement. Among the craftsmen in the 'respectable' trades – bookbinding, printing, engineering and tailoring, for example – there seems to have been little attraction to the Tory ethic. The Manchester and Salford Trades Council, established in 1866 and recruited almost exclusively from the skilled artisans until the later 1880s, was a stronghold of Lib-Labism, the traditions being maintained by leaders like Peter Shorrocks of the Tailors, an executive council member of the Manchester Liberal Union, and Henry Slatter of the Typographical Association, who in 1885 became Manchester's first JP to be drawn from

23   Thomas Hughes, *James Fraser, Second Bishop of Manchester. A Memoir. 1818–1885* (London: Macmillan, 1888), 246–57; *MG*, 23 September 1885.

24   See Clarke, *Lancashire and the New Liberalism*, 34–6.

25   Benjamin Nightingale, *Lancashire Nonconformity* (6 vols; Manchester: J. Heywood, 1890–1893), V, 62ff.

26   *Methodist Monthly*, February 1900.

27   For example S.F. Collier at Central Hall and the Wesleyan Mission in Oldham Street, and Mr Broxap at Gravel Lane. See George Jackson, *Collier of Manchester: A Friend's Tribute* (London: Hodder and Stoughton, 1923), and *Methodist Monthly*, February 1900.

the ranks of labour. By the mid 1880s these and other men were being succeeded by a younger generation of leaders schooled in the same traditions: Richard Watters, also of the Typographers, Matthew Arrandale, an engineer, and G.D. Kelley of the Lithograph Printers Society were the most prominent.[28] Among organised workers of this type, for whom representation in Liberal Party counsels was a mark of status, Liberalism was an active creed capable of sustaining working men's clubs in a number of districts in the city.[29]

It was the political attachment of this section of the labour force that gave the Liberal Party, despite its poor electoral performances, a crucial role in Manchester working-class politics after 1885. Although the Tories made some efforts to capture the loyalty of this group, they were certainly never able to speak as the authentic voice of the politically conscious and motivated workers, and for this reason were never a factor of real significance in the politics of the organised working-class movement. The Liberals were, however, and it was their liaison with what was in many ways the vanguard of the working class that made them potential gainers from any extensions in the boundaries of the trade-union movement. This issue became especially important in the late 1880s and early 1890s with the launching of new industrial organisations among the labouring and semi-skilled sections of the local labour-force, which was accompanied by increased pressure for labour representation as a means of achieving an expanded programme of industrial and social reform. The question of the Liberal Party's ability, and willingness, to respond to this pressure assumed critical significance at this time, not merely for the party itself but for other political groupings hoping to capture working-class interest. For the socialists of the ILP in particular the presence of a Liberal party with close attachments to a section of the labour movement raised important questions about future developments.

28   See Leslie Bather, 'A History of the Manchester and Salford Trades Council' (unpublished PhD thesis, Manchester University, 1956), 89ff.
29   *MG*, 17, 19, 20 and 25 November 1885. Radical working-men's clubs were active in Hulme, Newton, Pendleton and Bradford, among other places.

II

The formation of the Manchester and Salford ILP in May 1892 came after almost three years of active working-class politics throughout the entire area of South-East Lancashire. Whatever the implications of this activity (and we shall see later where its main thrust lay), there can be little doubt that at the outset the ILP represented a markedly socialist political initiative. To say that the party was wholly concerned with implanting the ideals of socialism among the masses rather than seeking independent labour representation would, perhaps, be misleading. Both objectives were written into the party's Constitution, though the order of priority was not insignificant:

> That the programme of the party be 'The nationalisation of the land and other instruments of production';
>
> That the party shall devote itself to securing the election of members to all representative bodies for the purpose of realising the programme of the party.[30]

Among the group of intellectuals who had been instrumental in launching the ILP, however, there was undoubtedly a very strong leaning towards socialist proselytising. John Trevor, for example, the former Unitarian minister at the Upper Book Street Chapel, established the Labour Church as a means of bringing socialism to the inner man: 'the Emancipation of Labour', he proclaimed, 'can only be realised so far as men learn both the Economic and Moral Laws of God, and heartily endeavour to obey them.'[31] Similar ideas about educating people into thinking differently about their condition before attempting a structural transformation of capitalist society could be found in the writings of journalists like Alex Thompson of the *Clarion* and the Cambridge graduate Fred Brocklehurst. They found their most powerful expression of all, however, in Robert Blatchford.

30 *Workman's Times (WT)*, 28 May 1892.
31 *Labour Prophet*, February 1892.

Blatchford exercised a profound influence over the early ILP in Manchester. He was its first president, from 1892 to 1893, and at least until the *Clarion* ceased to be a purely Manchester-based paper the ILP was popularly known in the district as 'Blatchford's Party'.[32] His socialism was clear, simple and emotional. 'The policy of *The Clarion*', he declared in his first issue, 'is a policy of humanity',[33] and, casting himself as its 'recruiting sergeant', he sought to make it the ideology of a mass movement. His indictment of industrial capitalism, *Merrie England*, sold three quarters of a million copies within a year of its publication in 1893, and helped to spawn a whole clutch of Clarion clubs for cycling, singing, scouting, rambling and other pursuits in which was nurtured a distinctive socialist culture. As an instrument in opinion forming Blatchford believed infinitely more in the power of the press than of Parliament: 'Parliament follows public opinion', he argued, 'it does not lead',[34] and this meant that the *Clarion* adopted a low-key approach to the electoral ambitions of the ILP. It was envisaged that the party 'would be more than a mere electoral club, but would educate and expose injustice'.[35] As far as electioneering was pursued, moreover, Blatchford urged an uncompromising stance, realising that in Manchester a party aiming for a genuinely working-class image would need to challenge not only the Liberals, as in other areas, but also the Tories: 'both parties are our enemies and our object is to defeat both.'[36] This position was enshrined in the celebrated Fourth Clause of the party's Constitution, which prevented ILP members from voting at elections for the candidates of any other political party.

Influenced by such a passionately socialist propagandist, then, it is perhaps not surprising that the Manchester ILP began its political life with a strategy that often brought the party into conflict with other ILP groups in the North. But it was not only Blatchford's hand that guided the Manchester movement. One of the most active sources of support for

32   See article by Alex Thompson in *MG*, 1 January 1944.
33   *Clarion*, 12 December 1891.
34   *Clarion*, 11 February 1893.
35   *Clarion*, 28 May 1892.
36   *Clarion*, 11 February 1893.

the creation of an ILP in this area, and one which historians have tended to overlook, was the Social-Democratic Federation. The SDF had been established in Manchester since the mid 1880s and by the time of the ILP's formation had served a testing apprenticeship in a hostile environment. It had always been a small party (possibly fifty members were attached to its main branch in Salford) whose energies had been dissipated in early days by the adoption of a too revolutionary stance. But some success was experienced by Social Democrats in 1886 and 1887 through leading a series of campaigns on the problem of unemployment, a real issue among the working class in the heart of Salford. Under the direction of John Hunter-Watts the SDF organised hunger marches, open-air demonstrations, processions and petitions to the Salford City Council, demanding a public-works programme to relieve the unemployment in the area.[37] These campaigns, centred on the populous and deprived districts of Ordsall and the Eccles New Road, created a fresh dimension in street politics and provided propaganda techniques that were to be incorporated in to later ILP work. On the whole the Social Democrats had eschewed formal politics, believing electioneering to be the first step towards compromise with the established system. This view was especially strong in the speeches and writings of the SDF's national leader, H.M. Hyndman, whose influence over provincial branches at this time was profound. 'Let us only recognise', Hyndman asserted, 'that political action is [...] more in the interests of the possessing classes – as likely to save them from attempts at violent revenge – than of the proletariat.'[38] The same attitude characterised the SDF's relationship with trade unions, which were regarded as sectional institutions incapable of reflecting the aspirations of the whole working class.

In the course of time, however, local branches of the SDF began to establish their own autonomy, and this enabled them to adopt a less intransigent policy towards other manifestations of popular action. By the end of the 1880s, for example, the Salford SDF was directing its attention to the question of 'new unionism' among the unskilled labourers of the area and

37   For example, *Justice*, 19 January, 12 February and 10 December 1887.
38   *Justice*, 1 January.

beginning to offer practical assistance in strikes. Bill Horrocks, W.K. Hall and George Tabbron, all leading Social Democrats from Salford, were involved in the struggle of the Gasworks labourers to win better conditions from the local Corporation,[39] whilst Leonard Hall, a veteran of both the SDF and the Socialist League (and later President of the ILP), set up the *Navvies' Guide* as a recruiting news-sheet for labourers, and later formed the Lancashire and Adjacent Counties Labour Amalgamation.[40] By this time the SDF had shed much of its earlier sectarian outlook and was willing to co-operate with other labour groups. In the spring of 1892, for example, W.K. Hall stood as Parliamentary candidate in the South Salford constituency, adopting as a means of capturing working-class support a programme of radical measures that were little different from those of his Liberal opponent.[41] The ultimate example of the SDF's readiness to liaise was provided in May of the same year when, at the inaugural conference of the ILP in the St James Hall, five Social Democrats were prominent on the platform.[42]

The SDF's involvement in the new party brought a Marxist legacy, which fused with the less precise but no less vigorous socialism of the Blatchfordites – derived, according to Blatchford himself, from Hyndman, William Morris and (an anonymous demotic influence) 'a poor devil of a workman'.[43] For the next decade or so the SDF was to remain an essential element of the ILP with co-operation between the two bodies a marked feature of propaganda. At times their organizations became so close as to make any distinctions between them almost imperceptible, and it was no doubt this liaison which inspired and strengthened the tendency towards the idea of socialist unity in the Manchester ILP. Blatchford was a stubborn advocate of this at both local and national levels; it accounted partly

---

39   *Justice*, 10 November 1888, 6 April and 14 September 1889.
40   *Labour Prophet*, February 1894.
41   *Salford Chronicle*, 12 March and 9 April 1892. Hall propounded Home Rule for Ireland, old-age pensions and payment of MPs as his main policies.
42   *WT*, 28 May 1892. They were Leonard Hall, W.K. Hall, Tom Purves, Alf Settle and G. Evans.
43   Robert Blatchford to G.B. Shaw, 18 August 1892, Shaw Correspondence, Series I, British Library, Add. Mss 50512.

for his quarrels with Keir Hardie and for the tension that existed between Blatchford and other Manchester members like Brocklehurst and Leonard Hall, who were on the National Administrative Council of the party. But the success of the Clarion movement ensured that Blatchford's influence always had a residual place in the Manchester ILP even after Blatchford resigned his presidency in 1893 and took the *Clarion* off to Fleet Street. Consequently, as Reid has shown, there was a fairly permanent socialist polarity in the party, which pulled against the development of a Bradford-style labourism in Manchester.[44]

But how representative of local working-class opinion was the ILP? It was formed at a time when the general climate of labour thinking was being stimulated by the trade-union revival, which brought in its wake a far greater awareness than before of the virtues of collective action through both industrial and political methods. Manchester saw a cascade of new industrial formations in the early 1890s encompassing a variety of previously unorganised trades: navvies, tramway workers, carters and lurrymen, paviours, hairdressers, quarrymen, cab-drivers, porters, watermen and many others all came under the influence of industrial organization to a greater or lesser extent. But the impact of these developments was often less than at the time was anticipated. Initially many unions, taking their cue from the success of the Gasworkers in the summer of 1889 when these were organised into a branch of Will Thorne's national union and secured eight-hour shifts from the Corporation, took up their specific grievances and met with early triumphs. John Kelly's Carters and Lurrymen of Salford, for instance, quickly managed to improve the rates of pay for coal carters,[45] and similar early successes came the way of the Shop Assistants, led by the socialist William Jackson, and the Tramway Employees organised by his namesake G.T. Jackson. But setbacks were also common. At the end of 1889, only six months after their triumphal emergence, the celebrated Gasworkers suffered a disastrous defeat in attempting to enforce the principle of 'every man with a ticket' upon an unwilling Gas Committee. Employer resistance

44   Reid, 'Manchester and Salford ILP', 26.
45   *WT*, 11 September 1891.

of this kind, together with poor management and inter-union rivalry, accounted for many failures especially with the return of bad trade by 1892. The numerical impact of the new unions in Manchester and Salford is difficult to estimate, therefore; national unions like the Dock Labourers and the Tramway Employees (who absorbed the Carters and Lurrymen of Salford) recruited well, whilst of the specifically Manchester-based unions the Quay and Railway Porters and the British Labour Amalgamation (a reorganization by the socialist Tom Fox of Leonard Hall's original Labour Amalgamation) probably exercised the most influence locally during the 1890s.[46] Of the smaller bodies, whose memberships rarely rose above a few hundred (the Women Workers' Federation, the Jewish Tailors and the Shirt and Jacket Cutters are good examples), the majority made their contribution to the labour movement through the Trades Council; its increased membership at this time in fact reflected the growing numbers of new unionists – from 1892 its membership reached some 25,000 with about 100 affiliated societies and this figure was generally maintained during the remainder of the 1890s.[47] So, whilst we should be careful of overestimating their strength, it seems that the new unionists achieved an extension of the organised working class of some significance.

As far as the political implications of this development are concerned, however, there is little evidence to suggest that new unionism brought about a radical change in the direction of working-class political allegiances. The membership was undoubtedly composed of 'outsiders' who had not shared in the creation of Lib-Labism, but, on the other hand, they were not necessarily automatic supporters of socialism. Where links between the new unions and the ILP can clearly be established is among the leadership: a whole cadre of new-union organisers – among whom were such people as Leonard Hall, James Heaviside, John Harker and Tom Fox – achieved

---

46   The principal new unions in the Manchester area by 1900 were; Dock Labourers (total national membership 14, 493), Labour Amalgamation (1,608), Tramway Employees (national, 7,536), Quay and Railway Porters (3,400). Board of Trade, Labour Department, *Report on Trades Unions in 1899* [Cd 422].

47   Manchester and Salford Trades Council (MSTC), *Annual Reports*, 1892, 1895, 1897–1899 (Manchester Public Library).

positions of prominence in the ILP during the 1890s; but whether their views and influence extended down to their memberships is a different matter. The essential point perhaps is that the radicalism of these men had not been formed as a result of their specific experiences as new unionists so much as it was a consequence of general social pressures. A good example of this type of leader was J.R. Clynes, the later Labour Minister who, although based in nearby Oldham in his early career, nevertheless had many contacts with Manchester, for which he became an MP in 1906.[48] Clynes was the son of an Irish labourer and was brought up in Oldham, where he attended a local Catholic School. He left at the age of ten with some unhappy memories and went to work in a cotton mill as a 'little piecer', soon rebelling against the harsh discipline and low wages of his trade. As an adolescent he was writing letters to local newspapers to publicise the piecers' conditions and in the mid-1880s, when he was no more than sixteen or seventeen, he organised a trade union for his fellow workers in an attempt to force better treatment from the spinners (in Clynes's own words 'it did not last very long'). His political initiation was through the Irish National League, and philosophically he cultivated an eclectic code through reading Ruskin, Carlyle, Mill and Emerson. Shortly after the Manchester gas strike of 1889 Clynes was enlisted by Will Thorne to act as an organiser for his union in the North West and thus began a long association with the labour movement. Soon after his transfer from mill to trade union he joined the ILP. Looking back, Clynes was able to connect his union and socialist activities quite naturally.

> It soon became obvious that Unions acting only in the affairs of the workshop could never attain their objects satisfactorily. These objects went further than mere isolated protests against unfair conditions in specified trades; they aimed at an eventual state when the whole of Britain should accept as a working axiom the Biblical assurance that 'A labourer is worthy of his hire'. We wanted the men who made the profits to share the profits to a larger degree.[49]

48   On Clynes see J.R. Clynes, *Memoirs* (2 vols; London: Hutchinson, 1937); Edward George, *From Mill Boy to Minister* (London: T. Fisher Unwin, n.d.), chs V–VIII; Will Thorne, *My Life's Battles* (London: George Newnes, n.d.), 114–16.
49   Clynes, Memoirs, I, 69.

Clynes was typical of the younger rebels whose aggressive awareness of social and economic injustice caused them to seek a new means of emancipating the working class, and their search took them into industrial and political channels. But the new-union thrust was not invariably in this direction. Some unions, Kelly's Carters and Lurrymen was a good example, never took to socialism, whilst others assumed a political stance for the same reasons that accounted for a change in the policy of craft unions at this time. Indeed, the artisans probably exercised an important influence over new-union growth in the early 1890s. G.D. Kelley had actively sought, as secretary of the Trades Council, to recruit new members, and frequently had taken the lead himself in offering advice and assistance to groups, like the Brushmakers or the Cloth Hat and Cap Makers, who were endeavouring to organise for the first time.[50] Kelley's policy was not wholly altruistic, moreover, for by extending the bases of the local labour movement in this way he was also helping to fortify the position of the craftsmen themselves. By the late 1880s most craft trades were being threatened nationally by advancing technology combined with foreign competition, and steps were being taken by the unions in the engineering, boot and shoe, printing and many other trades to ward off unemployment and the undermining of wage levels. In this atmosphere Manchester opinion could hardly have been unaffected by an alarming manifestation of the dangers facing skilled men in the form of a lengthy and violent strike over wage rates in the nearby town of Bolton in 1887. Here the engineering trade had been convulsed by a six-month stoppage during which the employers, acting on a co-ordinated, national basis against the local efforts of the workers, had used systematic mass importations of blackleg labour backed by large formations of police and military to break the engineers' resistance.[51] In the light of this it is not surprising that the Trades Council leadership in Manchester and Salford sought to strengthen the local working-class movement by union building and, at the same time, to fashion other weapons of

50 *WT*, 5 September 1890 and 17 March 1894.
51 *Bolton Weekly Guardian*, 2 and 9 July 1887; James Clegg, *Annals of Bolton* (Bolton: Bolton Chronicle, 1888), 227.

self-defence, notably political ones. During 1890 the Trades Council formulated a programme of demands for legislative action on Fair Contracts and Eight Hours, and stepped up pressure on the Liberal Party for labour representation.[52] By methods such as these the traditional craft leadership of the Trades Council not only maintained its control over the local labour movement, but managed to avoid any serious confrontations between the old and new unions. Harmony on the whole characterised inter-trade union relations in Manchester, in contrast to the internecine quarrelling often evident in other towns.

A further key influence in the formation of a labour, rather than socialist, consciousness was that exercised by the *Workman's Times* and its editor, Joseph Burgess. Burgess, a local man born at Failsworth in 1853, was a campaigning journalist who had long been associated with independent newspapers. When his own *Oldham Operative* failed after a short spell in the mid-1880s, he had joined the staff of the influential trade-union journal the *Cotton Factory Times* and thus sharpened his knowledge of industrial affairs.[53] From 1890 to 1894 he edited the *Workman's Times*, assisted by James Bartley, who ran the Northern edition when Burgess himself moved to Fleet Street in 1891 to extend his operations. The paper became a vademecum for trade unionists in the North and Midlands, providing a wealth of information and practical help as well as moral support. In Burgess's hands the *Workman's Times* endeavoured to canalise industrial struggles into political confrontation with the established parties, thus pointing the way towards independent politics. This was the hallmark of Burgess's message: he called for the workers to fashion their own weapon which would defend their interests in a way the parties of the bourgeoisie never could.

> it would not, we know, be a difficult matter to show that the Liberal Party had done a good deal for the working man. But neither would it be hard to prove that the Conservative Party had also done a good deal for him. That, however, is not the

52   *WT*, 26 September and 24 October 1890.
53   Joseph Burgess, *A Potential Poet? His Autobiography and Verse* (Ilford: Burgess Publications, 1927).

question. It is not what either party has done but what they have not done that we
are most concerned for.[54]

For this reason Burgess opposed organisations like the national Labour
Electoral Association, which operated under the auspices of the Liberal
Party. It was he, appropriately, who first began to use the term 'independent labour party' to express his principle – 'it is to assist in the creation of
such a party that we dedicate our best efforts', he told his readers.[55] Though
a socialist, Burgess exuded little of the passion associated with Blatchford
and the *Clarion*. In later years he became a keen supporter of Keir Hardie,
but in the early 1890s his main interests were in labour representation. Of
his scheme for an independent party he wrote:

> Its main object is the formation of a healthy public opinion in connection with
> working-class questions. This public opinion can be created in no way so speedily
> as by bringing Independent Labour candidates into the political arena, and running
> them on really independent lines.[56]

This 'healthy public opinion' involved for Burgess, in contrast to Blatchford,
no attempt to formulate a serious anti-capitalist ideology. Although he frequently attacked the Liberals and their labour allies like Matthew Arrandale
('he has "hob-nobbed" with party politicians',[57] complained Burgess on one
occasion), his philosophy scarcely extended beyond the ideological bases
of popular radicalism.

The views of Burgess and the *Workman's Times*, however, seemed
to reflect well the general aims of the labour movement at this time in
Manchester. With trade unionists both old and new turning more readily to
the notion of legislative solutions to industrial problems, the issue of labour
representation was very much alive. The Trades Council had become affiliated to the national Labour Electoral Association with G.D. Kelley taking
a leading part in pressing the Liberals for more consideration to labour.

---

54   *WT*, 3 April 1891.
55   *WT*, 3 April 1891.
56   *WT*, 16 January 1892.
57   *WT*, 27 March 1891.

Locally pressure was building up from trade unionists on the Manchester Liberal Union for more working men candidates in municipal elections. By 1891 the Liberal Party's traditional role as the champion of organised labour was under close examination.

III

As for the Liberal leadership, it was slow to respond to the challenge from below. The party had fallen under the dominance of a social elite. The party machinery, re-fashioned in 1885 on a divisional basis to correspond to the new electoral system, had quickly become reliant upon the middle-class suburban associations. They provided the real source of party finances, channelling their money through the central treasury to maintain the impecunious organizations in the working-class districts. But by thus paying the piper the wealthy element was able to call the tune on policy, and it generally favoured Constitutional issues such as Home Rule as against the industrial reforms or labour representation which interested organised Labour.[58] When the Trades Council began to press for what amounted to a louder voice in Liberal Party affairs, the Manchester Liberal Union was largely unsympathetic. In 1890 a groundswell of rank-and-file discontent was evident in the Trades Council and it was only a matter of time before it erupted. This happened when J. Jenkins of the Bakers' Union, a self-confessed 'rabid radical', led a move to force Kelley, Arrandale and Watters into a more determined position on labour representation; Jenkins's well-supported resolution contained a thinly veiled threat to the Liberal Party 'that it be an instruction to the Executive Committee [of the Trades Council] to consider and report to the Council the best means to

58   Manchester Liberal Union(MLU), Minute Book of Liberal 1200, 29 April and 27 July 1886 (Offices of Manchester Liberal Federation).

adopt to secure the representation of labour on the city council'.[59] In the following year Kelley was in fact elected to the Manchester City Council as a Lib-Lab, although at the same time the Manchester School Board Liberal Candidates Committee rejected all but one of the names submitted to it for the School Board elections by the Trades Council. This snub was rendered more injurious when the Council's written request for further talks about the proposed candidatures was ignored. After waiting for almost two months during the summer of 1891 for a Liberal response, the Trades Council finally informed the MLU that there would be no further dealings between the two bodies over labour candidates. Though the Liberals soon afterwards relented and invited the Trades Council to submit nominations for a Free Board School Party, the Council stood firm on its previous decision.[60]

It was in this context that the Salford Labour Electoral Association was formed at a series of meetings held during July and August in the Trafford Hotel. The Association, or 'Labour Union' as it was more commonly referred to, derived much of its inspiration from the Bradford body set up earlier in the year and, indeed, James Bartley of the *Workman's Times*, a pioneer of the Bradford ILP, attended the inaugural meetings in Salford to address the delegates on events in the West Riding. In the words of John Kelly, secretary of the Carters' and Lurrymen's new union, the Salford Labour Union 'would embrace all shades of political opinion,'[61] and for a short time it certainly proved capable of drawing together a diverse group of people all hostile in varying degrees to the established political parties.

In addition to Kelly, a new-unionist radical grown disillusioned with both the Liberals and the Tories (neither, he asserted, 'care three ha'p'orth of common gin' for the working man[62]), the Labour Union was supported by all shades of opinion: Richard Watters and George Rogerson, both members of long-established craft unions and leaders of the Trades Council, attended

59   *WT*, 24 October 1890.
60   For details *WT*, 28 August 1891.
61   *WT*, 7 August.
62   *WT*, 18 September.

its meetings alongside, for example, Alf Settle, the Marxist copper-plate engraver who had worked with the SDF in Salford, and his socialist friends George Tabbron of the Brassfounders and G.T. Jackson of the Tramway Employees. Prominent also were James Heaviside and J. Jenkins, whose resolution of 1890 had helped to precipitate the organization.[63] As such, the Labour Union was the first real manifestation of independent labour politics in the Manchester area. But its experiences were very different from those of its counterpart in Bradford, where the Labour Union provided the foundations for a united labour alliance soon to be transformed into the ILP.

In Manchester it proved impossible to sustain the unity of 1891. Socialism became the major stumbling block. Early disagreement over the nature of the Union prefigured this, some people looking for a party that would serve as an organizational vehicle for independent labour representation whilst others, more ambitiously, sought to build a movement with individual membership and a strong ideological commitment. It was Alf Settle who brought the entire issue to the point of confrontation in a meeting during August by declaring that 'if he joined the association he should endeavour to make it subservient to his Socialistic instincts'; as a further challenge he added that he 'would try to get it worked along the lines he advocated; but if he found it went contrary to his opinions he would not support it.'[64] Settle's intervention in this manner caused conflict within the Union to rage divisively, nowhere more so than in the municipal elections of that year, in which Settle himself figured. There were two labour candidates in Salford sponsored by the Union: George Rogerson in Regent Ward and Settle at Ordsall, where he had polled well for the SDF in 1890. Rogerson's chances were thin and indeed he was defeated, but Settle might well have been successful had it not been for the intervention of John Kelly in the contest, sponsored by his union as a candidate to fight specifically against the influence of socialism. Kelly regarded Settle, who was not a trade unionist, as an opponent of Liberalism and therefore opposed him in the guise of a truer representative of labour. As a result the working-class vote

63   *WT*, 7 August.
64   *WT*, 21 August.

was split and the Tory candidate, Rudman, easily topped the poll.[65] Further illustrations of this endemic conflict were provided during the winter, when quarrels arose over the selection of another socialist, W.K. Hall, as a Labour Parliamentary candidate for South Salford: the choice upset a good many non-socialists, and this no doubt contributed to Hall's poor performance in the General Election of 1892.[66] By the spring of that year the Salford Labour Union appears to have become practically defunct, the labour unity it had momentarily enshrined shattered by ideological dispute.

There is, therefore, considerable value in the notion of two traditions, a 'socialist' and a 'labourist', in Manchester working-class politics at this time, the gap between them being probably wider than that in Bradford between the ILPers and the Lib-Lab old guard. Socialism in 1891–1892 clearly had little chance of becoming the complete expression of Manchester working-class opinion: for one thing the ideology of the SDF and the *Clarion* was probably more adventurous than the reformist perspectives of the Bradford ILP, whilst for another there was less of a sense of class confrontation in Manchester. The MLU's attitude was certainly not encouraging for labour but Manchester Liberals appeared to exhibit little of the outright aggression towards the idea of independent labour representation evinced by their Bradford counterparts. Moreover, the absence of an issue equivalent in magnitude to the Manningham Mills strike meant that questions of an industrial-relations nature rarely came to be generalised into issues of class and power, which might have lent credence to socialist thinking. For these reasons, then, the formation of the Manchester and Salford ILP in 1892, far from heralding the arrival of an angry and coherent mass labour movement, represented little more than a union of socialists. Its relatively humble origins were perhaps best symbolised in the description given by one of its early adherents, Sylvia Pankhurst, of the party's meeting place: 'a poorly lit, evil-smelling room over a stable, in a side-street off Oxford Road'.[67]

65   *WT*, 7 November.
66   *WT*, 12 March 1892. Hall received 553 votes, less than 8 per cent of the poll.
67   E. Sylvia Pankhurst, *The Suffragette Movement* (London: Longmans, Green, 1931), 128.

With working-class politics in retreat at the time of its formation the ILP's future was problematical. As befits a new group of political militants, the party's own estimation of its prospects were optimistic: 'it will grow', predicted Blatchford, 'it will spread out its roots over the country.'[68] The early proliferation of branches throughout the North in 1892 and 1893 appeared to vindicate this view as the ILP soon achieved parity with the SDF and probably surpassed it in most places. But this achievement was of marginal value when set against the fact that, despite its often considerable propagandist efforts, the ILP neither had much of an electoral impact nor secured a particularly high membership.[69] It could certainly not claim to be a mass party. The realization of this fact caused most ILP groups in the North to seek an alliance with trade unions sooner or later: in Manchester the pressures for 'labourism' were especially strong and can be seen from a relatively early stage in the party's development. One of the most compelling reasons for this lay in the threat of a Liberal revival amongst the organised working class in the mid 1890s.

IV

Following the repercussions of the MLU's lukewarm response to labour demands in 1891, the party began to reconsider its relationship with the Trades Council. Without a more positive initiative the prospects for a continuation of the traditional Lib-Lab alliance were undoubtedly very dim, and by 1893 a radical element had come to prominence in local Liberal

---

68 *Clarion*, 28 May 1892.
69 There were 26 branches of the ILP reported in Lancashire in January 1894, 45 the following year, (*WT*, 13 January 1894; *Labour Annual*, 1895, 103ff). In February 1894 the SDF reported 27 branches in Lancashire (*Justice*, 19 May 1894). The ILP *Directory and Branch Returns* for 1897 listed membership of branches in the Manchester district at 693. In 1898 the financial membership of the Manchester and Salford ILP was estimated at 268, by March 1899 at 401 (*Manchester*, December 1900).

circles advocating an active programme to recoup labour support. The appearance of the ILP in 1892 and its early ambitious attempts to become an electoral force – twelve candidates were put forward by the socialists in 1893, though none was actually elected – enabled this radical element to goad the Liberal Union into action. It is clear from reports in the districts that Liberals regarded the ILP as a real threat at local and parliamentary levels, and it was to consider ways and means of withstanding such a challenge that the MLU convened a special meeting in November 1893.[70] But it soon became apparent at this meeting that even the radical group of Liberals were divided over the most suitable methods to employ. Broadly speaking two views emerged. On the one hand a faction led by Alderman Edwin Guthrie and his friend C.P. Scott, editor of the *Manchester Guardian*, favoured a policy of increased labour representation as a means of courting the non-socialist elements of the labour movement; their feeling was that such a manoeuvre would serve to outflank the ILP and arrest any drift towards socialism. But, on the other hand, there was strong feeling in the MLU about conceding power and influence to the working class, and it was in order to appease these sentiments that J. Harrop proposed a counter-measure: to steal the ILP's clothes by coming out with a strong measure of social reform. As Harrop put it, the Liberals should 'adopt so much of the Labour Party's programme as is possible' and by these means avoid the humiliating experience of going 'cap in hand' to organised labour.[71] What in all probability decided the issue was the fact that the Guthrie-Scott group overplayed their hand; given the traditional social configurations of Manchester Liberalism the prospect of a radical devolution of power to the organised working class was difficult to accept, even when proposed in such diplomatic terms as T.G. Ashton's, 'that the Manchester Liberal Union recommends each division of Manchester to carefully consider the advisability of recommending certain wards in their division to adopt representatives of labour as candidates in the next municipal vacancies.'[72]

70   MLU, General Committee Minutes, 17 November 1893, letter of 16 November.
71   MLU, Minutes, 17 November 1893.
72   MLU, Minutes, 17 November 1893.

In the face of this members preferred to embrace Harrop's scheme, and the Committee eventually agreed to frame 'an advanced municipal programme for Manchester' in consultation with Liberal City Councillors. In the following spring a Programme Sub-Committee reported with a provisional list of some twenty reforms, included in which was a rather obscure and vague reference to 'more labour representatives'. In July 1894 the full committee of the MLU adopted this scheme as the Progressive Municipal Programme.[73]

As P.F. Clarke has shown, Guthrie and Scott did not rest content with this decision, but continued to pursue their objectives by exploiting the reference to labour representation.[74] Guthrie, in fact, took up the issue with both the Prime Minister, Lord Rosebery, and with leaders of the National Liberal Federation, arguing that it was imperative to outmanoeuvre socialism by 'adopting a considerably increased number of working men' in Manchester.[75] Contact was also made with three influential local union leaders, Francis Chandler, Matt Arrandale and G.D. Kelley, all of whom appeared favourably inclined to the new Liberal attitude, and obligingly offered recommendations for labour candidates in City Council and School Board elections.[76] At this point, therefore, it seemed likely that Guthrie's initiative might have effect and that Manchester Liberalism might indeed forge an alliance that would re-unite the working class with the bourgeoisie. But a combination of factors conspired against such an eventuality. For one thing no encouragement was forthcoming from the party's national leadership; Rosebery failed to take a lead and the National Liberal Federation eventually pronounced that such a scheme involved too many difficulties, 'both financial and of other kinds'.[77] Furthermore the ILP's electoral assault, so vividly imagined in 1893, was seen two years later to have been only a turnip ghost.

73   MLU, Programme Sub-Committee Minutes, 2 March, 28 May and 13 June 1894; General Committee Minutes, 5 July.
74   Clarke, *Lancashire and the New Liberalism*, 164–5.
75   MLU, General Committee Minutes, 26 July 1894.
76   MLU Minutes, 1 and 14 August 1894.
77   MLU Minutes, report of sub-committee meeting, 19 December 1894.

By this time the ILP's municipal successes in Manchester were limited to the return of J.E. Sutton as City Councillor for Bradford Ward, whilst in the General Election ILP candidatures in the Manchester area had been a disastrous failure.[78] With its earlier fears shown to have been unfounded as far as ILP socialism was concerned, therefore, the MLU felt able to forget about labour representation and rely on the Progressive Programme to win working-class votes. The practical extent of Guthrie and Scott's proposals was limited to the election of Matt Arrandale to the City Council, where he joined Kelley in 1895. Discussion on the subject of labour candidates continued in Liberal circles in the later 1890s, but without producing any significant achievements. Opposition to campaigns for labour representation, as occurred in 1899 at Harpurhey and St Marks for example,[79] still tended to outweigh efforts to co-operate with them, and for this reason advocates of labour representation were driven into the arms of the ILP.

What might have resulted from a wholehearted pursuit of the Guthrie-Scott plans is hard to judge. It is, however, difficult to believe that liberalism was at this time facing an objectively hopeless situation or that had the Liberals revealed more determination to throw off their social prejudices the advocates of labour representation could not have been contained within the established party framework. But the failure to act more positively certainly had some obvious effects. By the end of the decade the Trades Council was engaging in increasing electoral activity with the ILP, whose reformist municipal politics offered everything included in the Liberal programme and more besides. Moreover, in many of the poorer districts of the city the absence of active working-class participation in Liberal Party organization caused morale to evaporate almost

78   The ILP put up two candidates in the immediate area of Manchester and Salford. R.M. Pankhurst, an erstwhile Liberal, received 4,261 votes at Gorton, but had no Liberal opponent; James Johnston at Manchester North-East received only 546 votes, whilst in nearby Ashton-under-Lyne and Hyde ILP candidates similarly posed badly, less than 500 votes in both cases.

79   *Manchester*, July and October 1899; MLU, General Committee Minutes, 17 June and 6 October 1898.

completely. When Herbert Gladstone, as Liberal Chief Whip, intervened in Manchester affairs in 1902, he found Liberal organization badly in need of re-invigoration, and it was largely through his inspiration that the MLU was reformed in 1903 as the Manchester Liberal Federation. This new structure overcame some of the old autonomy of the Divisional Associations, which in the past had been a conservative influence in the party, and enabled Liberals to adopt a more realistic approach to labour.[80] But it was ironic that the establishment of the MLF coincided with the formation of a Labour Representation Committee for Manchester and Salford based on the local trade union and socialist movements. Never could the aphorism 'too little, too late' have been more appropriately applied to Liberal endeavours.

V

Liberalism's failure arose from a fundamental misreading of the local political situation. In short, the MLU overestimated the challenge of the ILP, and by so doing overlooked the legitimate and on the whole non-socialist claims of organised labour. For its part the ILP was quick to respond to this, and there was considerable dexterity in the way ILP organisers managed to align the party's development with that of the labour movement in general and the Trades Council in particular.

In doing this, however, they had to overcome the strong tendencies towards socialist, as against labour, politics, which were best represented by Blatchford. Blatchford's resignation as president of the Manchester ILP in 1893 was an important step in this development, for it marked his gradual removal as the central figure in the local party. Initially his resignation seems to have been brought about by an aversion on his part to the

80 Details in Viscount Gladstone Papers, British Library, Add. Mss, First Series, 46105, 46106, 46454.

notion of 'leadership', his dislike of which became more intense in 1894 with the election of Keir Hardie as president of the national movement.[81] Additionally, however, Blatchford had touted the cause of socialist unity during 1893 and 1894, and this not only produced conflict with other local groups, but unsettled relations in Manchester. Burgess opposed Blatchford on the issue from the beginning, accusing him of 'scuttling the ship',[82] and Leonard Hall and Fred Brocklehurst became increasingly sceptical of the policy after their election onto the ILP's National Administrative Council. Disagreements over policy grew during 1894 with Blatchford fanning the flames by making personal attacks on Leonard Hall, who had succeeded him as president in Manchester. Hall eventually resigned the post himself, soon after renouncing the Fourth Clause and dropping his intended candidature for the Parliamentary seat in North-East Manchester.[83] Personal rivalries of this kind did not help to prepare the party for the General Election of 1895, in which two ILP candidates were put forward in the Manchester area; it is not surprising that they fared poorly.

But the removal of Blatchford and other members of the original intellectual group from influential positions in the party meant that by the mid 1890s a body of less well-known leaders was coming to exercise more control over party policy. Many of them were trade unionists: Sutton of the Miners, Harker of the Shirt and Jacket Cutters, Nuttall of the Block Roller and Stamp Cutters, Fox of the Labour Amalgamation, and, later, Doyle of the Concreters and Purcell of the French Polishers. Between them they were able to form links with the Trades Council. What is interesting in this is the way the ILP allowed its policies to dovetail with those already taken up by the Trades Council well before any strong socialist representation became evident in its leadership. In the early 1890s the Trades Council, still firmly in the grip of its artisan leadership, had launched progressive campaigns for an eight-hour day, the nationalization of land and railways,

---

81   In 1893 he wrote: 'We want no leaders, and should be ill-advised to tolerate any', a
      remark ostensibly prompted by his distaste for C.S. Parnell, the Irish Nationalist
      leader, but implicitly referring to Keir Hardie. (*Clarion*, 11 February 1893.)
82   *Clarion*, 11 August 1894.
83   For details see *Clarion*, 25 August, 24 November, 1 and 8 December 1894; 29 June 1895.

and public-works schemes for the relief of unemployment. Allied to these were assertive claims for labour representation at municipal and national levels.[84] It is in the light of this that we should view the ILP's twelve independent candidates in the municipal elections of 1893 – quite apart from the total failure of the campaign in electoral terms a valuable demonstration of the party's independent labour stance – and the equally important series of demonstrations, hunger marches and soup kitchens organised by the party in the same year on behalf of the unemployed.[85] Moreover, during the mining lock-out of 1893 R.M. Pankhurst, a notable local radical who had recently been converted to the ILP, toured the pit districts of Bradford and Clayton in the eastern part of the city lecturing on the principles of nationalization in the mines,[86] a socialist measure but one likely to appeal to miners with a strong sense of grievance about their employers' conduct. Shortly afterwards Joseph Burgess and three local ILP activists, Bilcliffe, Harker and Heaviside, took the issue further by setting up the *Colliery Workman's Times* as a weekly journal to promote 'the nationalisation of the mines by and through the independent representation of labour in Parliament',[87] thus neatly combining the socialist and independent-labour aspects of the ILP's constitution.

The efforts were in fact a great success. Not only was an ILP branch formed among the colliers in Bradford, but their local secretary, J.E. Sutton, was converted and thus began a distinguished career with the party, on whose behalf he was elected to the City Council in the following year.[88] Through such activities and contacts the ILP was able to establish a close rapport with the Trades Council and it was only a matter of time before ILP members were elected, in their capacity as trade union leaders, to the Executive Committee. In 1895, for example, Sutton himself together with John Harker and the old social democrat George Tabbron took their places on the Committee of the Trades Council. More socialists were to

84 MSTC, *Annual Reports*, 1892 and 1895.
85 *MG*, 2 November 1893; Pankhurst, *Suffragette Movement*, 95, 129–30.
86 Pankhurst, *Suffragette Movement*, 125.
87 *Colliery Workman's Times*, 9 December 1893.
88 *MG*, 2 November 1894.

follow in later years. Even before this, though, the convergence of ILP and Trades Council interests could be seen in joint election work. In 1894 the two bodies co-operated in the School Board Elections under the auspices of a United Labour Party, whilst the seven ILP candidates for the municipal-council elections in the Manchester area were all given the official blessing of the Trades Council.[89]

By the middle of the 1890s, then, there was something of a 'good neighbour' policy operating between the two bodies. It remained to be seen though, whether this could be translated into a more concrete political formation that would embody the principle of independence. Progress towards this was certainly assisted by the failure of the Liberal initiative, which removed a considerable obstacle from the path towards a labour alliance, and by Blatchford's increasing attention in his journalism to national rather than Manchester issues. By the later 1890s the ILP was able to further Clause Two of its Constitution by making a bid to become a really effective electoral organization. As early as 1893 the party had elaborated an election programme of great comprehensiveness. The Municipal Programme, as it was called, detailed a host of reforms in the administrative and political structures of local government. It owed much, in fact, to previous SDF schemes for creating a more civilised environment for working people in the big industrial cities: the abolition of slum dwellings and provisions for the building of healthier homes, cheap transport for workmen, an eight-hour day for Corporation employees, pensions for those employed by the Municipality, equal pay for men and women, and free food and clothing for needy schoolchildren were among the more prominent demands. The programme was designed to give local authorities greater power to improve the environment, and this involved sweeping away some of the obstacles to change such as the Aldermanic Bench, the rating system and the Poor Law. As such the ILP's Municipal Programme went much farther than the Liberals' response to it of the following year, and could therefore be seen either as a root-and-branch reform of the foundations of local government

89   MSTC, *Annual Report*, 1896; *MG*, 2, 3, and 20 November 1894; *Clarion*, 27 October; Pankhurst, *Suffragette Movement*, 119.

or simply as a series of useful changes, anyone of which would bring some immediate improvement in social conditions.[90]

The Municipal Programme, then, served as a manifesto for a wide range of voters. To complement these ideological initiatives, however, the ILP needed to equip itself with an electioneering machine and, in this context, the administrative changes set in motion by the party secretary Joe Nuttall from about 1896, and completed by his successor Thomas Gunning shortly after 1900, formed an important part of ILP electoral development.[91] Not that the changes brought about any immediate increase in socialist representation; in the later 1890s the ILP could support only two City Councillors in Manchester (Sutton and Brocklehurst) and normally one (G.T. Jackson) in Salford; as such it never seemed likely to become an independent electoral force of any real power. More significant, however, was the fact that Nuttall's and Gunning's reforms created a party machine that, given the opportunity, could be adapted to form the basis of an independent working-class party. This indeed happened when the Manchester and Salford Labour Representation Committee was created in 1903.

The formation of this party, which re-created the labour unity that had been temporarily apparent in 1891, owed something therefore to the efforts of the ILP. Following the failure of Liberal reforms in the mid-1890s, perhaps it was only a matter of time before the organised working class of Manchester kicked over the traces of its Liberal tutelage and became independent, but the ILP's coaxing clearly had some effect. Its willingness, for example, to arrange ad hoc electoral alliances with other labour forces prepared the way for a more permanent relationship, especially since the co-operation had often been successful. In 1900 the United Workers' Municipal Election Committee, organised by Tom Gunning, helped to achieve harmony between the two wings of the labour movement, whilst the launching by the ILP of a monthly newspaper, *Manchester*, in 1899 served to provide a forum for labour interests in the city.[92] And all this

90   *WT*, 5 August 1893.
91   *Manchester*, August and December 1900.
92   In 1897 the Trades Council-ILP alliance had returned Nuttall and Brocklehurst to the School Board, MSTC, Annual Report, 1897. The journal *Manchester* (from 1901

time ILP members were gaining prominence in the Trades Council: by the early 1900s Sutton, Harker and Tabbron had been joined on the Executive Committee by Tom Fox, Joe Nuttall and A.A. Purcell, so that left-wing resolutions received some encouragement from the top.[93] But it is doubtful whether the ILP could have precipitated such an effective labour alliance by itself. Favourable external developments were, in fact, of vital importance in explaining why the organised labour movement of Manchester should embrace the principle of independent labour representation at the very beginning of the twentieth century.

Of particular significance in this respect was the striking degree of solidarity that developed among workers at this time and which largely derived from the feeling that labour was under attack. Threats to the working-class position were seen, for instance, in the new Education Act, which had removed schools from direct popular control. Displeasure over this legislation was soon compounded by adverse decisions in the Taff Vale litigation, which was the prominent issue in a mass demonstration organised by the Trades Council on May Day 1902. Held in Gorton Park, the demonstration called for new measures to define the legal status of trade unions as well as demanding a scheme for old-age pensions and improvements in local housing conditions.[94] In the following year these problems, still unresolved, were augmented by the publication of Conservative proposals on Tariff Reform – 'a fresh attempt to grind the poor by the Food Tax', as G.D. Kelley described them.[95] In the face of what seemed like a concerted assault on working-class living standards a solution was increasingly sought through labour representation, which, more than at any previous time, became the overriding slogan of the labour movement, bringing together socialists and non-socialists, craftsmen and unskilled. Taff Vale was the crucial

The Social Reformer) was launched in the summer of 1899 to promote the idea of municipal socialism, and in October 1900 the United Workers' Municipal Election Committee arose out of discussions held the previous July among a wide range of local working-class groups.

93 MSTC, *Annual Reports*, 1900–1906.
94 MSTC, *Annual Report*, 1902.
95 MSTC, *Annual Report*, 1903.

turning-point, arousing the collective anger of the organised workers in a way that, as Kelley himself admitted, could 'only be appeased by the return of Labour men to the House of Commons'.[96]

It is interesting to note, moreover, that the Trades Council had become affiliated to the national Labour Representation Committee in 1901, although it had not been prepared to participate in the formation of a local LRC. The non-socialist Kelley attended the national LRC conferences of 1901 and 1902 as the Manchester delegate and seemed unwilling to become involved with the socialist element, a posture which suggested that there was still some distance between the two camps despite the joint electoral enterprises of previous years. From 1903, though, the situation changed radically. In that year the Council resolved that 'the time is now opportune for Labour to assert itself by advancing candidates at the next General Election for the purpose of securing Direct Labour Representation in the House of Commons and at least 2 constituencies in Manchester and one in Salford be selected'.[97] The Council then proceeded to nominate John Harker and G.D. Kelley, thus dividing the proposed candidatures between the socialist and non-socialist elements. From this point it was a short step to the formation in the summer of 1903 of a local LRC comprising 55 trade societies from the Trades Council together with 5 ILP and 2 SDF branches.[98] It was through this body that the ILP's party structure and programme, evolved during the 1890s, became the structure and programme of the new local labour party, whose principal officers were all ILP men.

The final rejection of Lib-Labism by the skilled elite of the Manchester working class was clearly embodied in the attitude of G.D. Kelley. When Kelley eventually joined the Labour Party at some point between late 1903 and early 1904, he severed an attachment to the Liberals that had been formed some half a century earlier when he was beginning to make his way in the service of his union. As a self-educated artisan Kelley had spent most of his adult life as an official of the Lithograph Printers'

96   MSTC, *Annual Report*, 1903.
97   MSTC, *Annual Report*, 1903.
98   *Justice*, 8 August 1903.

Society; he had been its general secretary since 1878 and the secretary of
the Manchester and Salford Trades Council since 1881, always behaving
as an impeccably respectable radical, pursuing the goal of labour representation within the framework of a populist Liberal movement. He
himself had been relatively successful, acquiring prestige in Manchester
as a City Councillor and JP by the 1890s. But the failure of the Liberal
Party as a vehicle for general working-class advancement had become
steadily more apparent to him. First the Labour Electoral Association
had been suffocated through lack of encouragement, and then the MLU
had turned its back on labour representation, whilst repeated electoral
failures had left the party in no position to defend the interests of working men by the early 1900s. Kelley was forced to admit that the Liberals
had been unable to do 'all a workman had a right to expect from them,'[99]
and was left to inveigh against the 'rich men and great landlords' of the
Tory Party – 'a party of privilege and monopoly'[100] – as it attacked the
foundations of the trade-union movement. It was hardly surprising that
he was to be found by 1903, when the full force of the Taff Vale judge-
ment hit the labour movement, pleading in his Trades Council report
for 'a sinking of petty differences, whether of personal feeling or political creed […] to aim for the goal of labour representation'.[101] It was more
or less at this point that G.D. Kelley left the Liberal Party and joined
forces with his former adversaries, the socialists of the ILP, in the newly
fashioned Manchester and Salford LRC.

No doubt many members of the trade societies which became affiliated at this time shared Kelley's views and welcomed the opportunity
to articulate their interests through a new organization fully committed
to working-class advancement. For Kelley himself the change of allegiance was timely, for it brought him the prize that previously had eluded
his grasp: within two years he was a Labour Member of Parliament for
Manchester.

99   Cited in Bather, 'A History of the Manchester and Salford Trades Council', 166.
100   MSTC, *Annual Report*, 1903.
101   MSTC, *Annual Report*, 1903.

VI

The advance of the Manchester and Salford Labour Party over the next few years was sufficiently rapid to confirm the support for such an organization and thereby to vindicate the labourist tendencies within the ILP since the mid-1890s. The party quickly acquired the broad-bottomed appearance of what, in later years, came to be called a 'model party' by Labour organisers; that is to say it managed to blend the trade-union interest, which assured extensive financial support, with the ideological vision of ILP socialism. Together these gave the party the necessary endowments with which to challenge for power in municipal politics.

The Manchester Labour Party opened its doors to trade unions, trades councils, co-ops, socialist societies and 'all other Labour or socialist organizations that are willing to work for the objects and conform to the rules of this Committee and the National Labour Party'.[102] The backbone of the party was its trade-union affiliations, numbering over 17,000 by 1910, and this naturally gave the union element a preponderance on the Committee. But a generous representation of two delegates for every 200 members (and three for higher membership) meant that the socialist societies were assured of an important influence in the Labour Party's controlling counsels.[103] This influence was in fact enshrined in the broad, socialistic programme by which the party identified itself for electoral purposes: based upon the ILP Municipal Programme of 1893, but well larded with practical industrial issues of special concern to trade unionists, the Labour programme ranged from the nationalisation of land and railways, through free trade and free education from elementary to university level, to workmen's compensation, the eight-hour day and 'national efficiency'.[104] Moreover, a highly centralised and efficient system of electoral management produced some promising results quickly in municipal politics. By 1910, for example, Labour could

102 Manchester and Salford Labour Representation Committee (MSLRC), *Annual Report*, 1906, (Manchester Public Library).
103 MSLRC, *Report*, 1905, 1908, 1910 and 1912.
104 MSLRC, *Report*, 1906; *Cotton Factory Times*, 6 November 1903.

mobilise 15 representatives in the Manchester City Council and never fell below this strength before the First World War.[105] The foundations were thus established for the Labour Party's speedy advance after the war as the natural party of the working class in Manchester.

In considering the development of the ILP in Manchester and Salford we are faced with a process that was at once less dramatic and more gradual than that of Bradford. There was an obvious social and economic difference between the two cities in that the class polarization of Manchester – well established in spatial terms by the end of the nineteenth century – was hardly evident at all in Bradford before 1914. Paradoxically, though, this does not seem to have made for more intransigent political relationships in Manchester, as might have been expected. On the contrary, it was Bradford which witnessed an intense confrontation in its political development at the beginning of the 1890s. Bradford's social admixture and its (consequent) strong popular nonconformity appears to have engendered in the mind of the Liberal manufacturing elite a sense of confidence about its political hegemony which caused them to oppose the advocates of independent labour representation with great vigour. Between 1890 and 1892 the class nature of the Liberal Party was fully exposed and credibility in its function as a popular movement destroyed; as Reynolds and Laybourn point out, 'support for Liberalism had been eroded among the most effectively politically motivated members of some of the most powerful craft unions.'[106] It was this that enabled the ILP to take control of the local labour movement and lead it towards independence, ousting from positions of influence the traditional Lib-Lab leadership.

In Manchester the same process was a far more protracted affair. There was never any point at which the ILP was able to act as the complete embodiment of labour interests: instead, the party had to settle for the role of a

105   Between 1906 and 1914 the Labour Party representation in Manchester City Council (including ILP members) was as follows: 1906 – 11; 1907 – 11; 1908 – 10; 1909 – 8; 1910 – 10; 1911 – 14; 1912 – 16; 1913 – 16; 1914 – 15. During the same period Conservative strength ranged from 38 to 57 and Liberal from 19 to 33. This information kindly supplied by the Local History Library, Manchester Public Library.

106   Reynolds and Laybourn, 'Emergence of the Independent Labour Party in Bradford', 336–7.

self-sufficient organization within the working-class movement. The internal contradictions of the Liberal-Labour relationship were resolved without any significant recourse to socialism, indeed the inability of the Liberals to make the most of their potential support – a failure compounded of social hauteur and lack of political insight – emerged as the crucial factor in this equation. Once the organised working-class movement had recognised that Lib-Labism was a blind alley, the ILP was able to make a distinctive contribution to the shaping of a third political force in Manchester and Salford. In the form of the Labour Party it sought to replace the ethic of individual improvement for the working man, which had been so characteristic of Liberalism, by the principle of improvement for the class as a whole.

Appendix I

Main Occupations South-East Lancashire, 1901				
Percentage of workforce employed in	*Manchester*	*Salford*	*Oldham*	*Bolton*
Textiles	8	14	42	38
Mining	0	1	1	3
Chemicals	1	0	0	0
Metal and engineering	9	8	18	12
Building	7	7	5	5
Transport	5	5	9	3
Food and drink	9	4	4	6
Commerce and professions	7	7	5	5
General trades and miscellaneous	53	54	17	27

Source: *Census of England and Wales, 1901* (Cd 1002)

Appendix II

Percentage of the Liberal Vote in Manchester Area, 1885–1900				
	1885	*1892*	*1895*	*1900*
Manchester				
East	45.0	48.0	46.1	36.6
North	43.2	51.8	52.8	50.1
North-East	40.0	49.3	48.4	45.5
North-West	46.7	47.4	41.4	35.2
South	54.8	51.1	49.6	42.9
South-West	46.1	51.0	46.7	37.4
Salford				
North	48.7	52.0	49.9	44.5
South	50.3	49.7	49.9	41.5
West	51.9	49.7	49.4	44.1
Gorton	60.5	51.1	42.1	47.3
Stretford	51.1	44.3	Uncontested by Liberals	39.4

Source: *Dod's Parliamentary Companion.*

CHAPTER FIVE

Lib-Labism, Socialism and Labour in Burnley, c. 1890–1918

In the general election of December 1918 the Labour Party won the parliamentary seat of Burnley for the first time. Those people who had gathered in the Co-op Rooms to celebrate the victory were told by James Eastham, the President of the local Trades Council: '… a working-class constituency like Burnley ought to have been in their present position years ago. (Hear, hear)'.[1] Eastham's audience was well aware of Burnley's anomalous place in Lancashire politics. Though one of the main centres of cotton weaving, with a well-organised trade unionism, Burnley had not figured in the landmark event of early Labour politics: the general election of 1906, when twenty-nine Labour Representation Committee (LRC) candidates were returned to Parliament, thirteen of them from constituencies in the North-West of England.[2] In the region that formed the new Labour Party's stronghold, Burnley went against the grain by returning a Lib-Lab who had been run close by a Conservative and a Socialist. In terms of the 'forward march of labour', therefore, Burnley seemed unpromising territory. This partly explains its neglect by historians of the pre-1914

1   *Burnley News*, 1 January 1919.
2   The most striking comparison with Burnley is that of nearby Nelson in the Clitheroe parliamentary division, which had returned the first Labour MP in this part of England in 1902, when the Liberals withdrew to allow David Shackleton an unopposed election. The Independent Labour Party (ILP) was active in Nelson, combining with trade unions in a 'labour alliance' which produced a brief Labour control of the town council from 1905 until 1907. On Nelson see: Frank Bealey, 'The Northern Weavers, Independent Labour Representation and Clitheroe, 1902', *Manchester School* (1957), 26–60; Jeffrey Hill, *Nelson: Politics, Economy, Community* (Keele: Keele University Press, 1997), esp. ch. 4.

Labour movement. Moreover, the active role played in Burnley by the Social-Democratic Federation (SDF), a body often regarded as inimical to Labour development and marginal in working-class politics, has further acted as a deterrent to the study of Burnley by 'orthodox' labour historians.[3]

The present essay seeks to reassess Burnley politics in the thirty or so years before 1918. It argues that political action was possible in a number of forms ('capacities') and that various political movements – in particular the SDF and the Liberal Party – were able to respond to them. The article is informed by approaches and insights drawn from two recent and highly original studies: Duncan Tanner's analysis of national political changes in the early years of the twentieth century, and Michael Savage's investigation of working-class politics in Preston between 1880 and 1940.[4] Tanner, in contrast to accounts that have averred the decline of Liberalism in the decade before 1914, asserts its continued vitality and relevance in a complex fabric of local and regional political loyalties. He refuses to see creeds such as 'old' Liberalism or Lib-Labism as dying or anachronistic, and seeks to rescue them from the oblivion to which many labour historians would consign them. Savage, more explicitly theoretical in approach, offers a novel understanding of the mainsprings of working-class politics in local

---

3   On the development of the Social-Democratic Federation, in both Lancashire and other areas, see the excellent history by Martin Crick, *The History of the Social-Democratic Federation* (Keele: Keele University Press, 1994). On general developments in labour history see: P.F. Clarke, *Lancashire and the New Liberalism* (Cambridge: Cambridge University Press, 1971); Ross McKibbin, *The Evolution of the Labour Party, 1910–1924* (Oxford: Oxford University Press, 1974). See also Martin Pugh, review in *History*, 77 (1992), 156–7; Bill Lancaster, review in *Labour History Review*, 57 (1992), 97–100; John K. Walton, review in *Society for the Study of Labour History*, Bulletin, 53 (1988), 78–9; Keith Laybourn, 'The Rise of Labour and the Decline of Liberalism: the state of the debate', *History*, 80 (1995), 207–26.

4   Michael Savage, *The Dynamics of Working-Class Politics: the Labour Movement in Preston, 1880–1940* (Cambridge: Cambridge University Press, 1987); Mike Savage and Andrew Miles, *The Remaking of the British Working Class. 1840–1940* (London: Routledge, 1994); Duncan Tanner, *Political Change and the Labour Party, 1900–1918* (Cambridge: Cambridge University Press, 1990).

communities. He invites us to consider the 'capacities' (as he describes them) for action in terms of three types. Each is related to opportunities available in local economies and labour markets for workers to confront a fundamental issue: the reducing of the insecurity of their material existence. The three types of action are: *mutualism* – action based on the independent provision of jobs and services through organizations such as co-operative and friendly societies, or individual self-help activity; secondly, *economism*, based upon attempts to control the labour market and 'de-commodify' labour, largely through trade union pressure; and thirdly, *statism*, or the search for the provision of jobs and services through the intervention of the local or national state.[5]

In a number of ways the work of these two historians has re-defined the agenda of labour history. Although it has confirmed the continuing relevance of local study in exploring this field, and stressed the diversity of politics at this time, it has also drawn us, if not as far as the idea of the primacy of politics, then at least away from the notion that politics is a simple by-product which can be 'read off' from prior economic and social change. Says Savage: 'There is no one "natural" way by which working-class interests manifest themselves in political action. The under-determination of political practice by social interests must be recognised'.[6]

II

The nature of Burnley's economic development created various opportunities for political action. In contrast with many other cotton towns the economy had undergone a late industrialization. Though factory-based spinning was present in Burnley by the 1830s, a second industrialization took place with the switch to cotton weaving by power-looms in the 1860s

5   Savage, *Dynamics*, 20.
6   Savage, *Dynamics*, 20.

and 1870s.[7] By the turn of the century almost three-quarters of the town's population were employed in the two industries of cotton weaving and coal-mining, though the latter accounted for little more than ten per cent of the workforce.[8] Although the growth of the two industries was closely interrelated, the pits providing fuel for the mills and for the homes of weavers, the industries exhibited quite different patterns of ownership and industrial relations.

In coal-mining there were thirteen collieries in operation by 1900 employing some 2,000 miners. They were owned by only three companies, one of which – the Executors of Colonel John Hargreaves (known locally as 'the Exors') – controlled seven of the pits and effectively dominated the local industry.[9] The firm was in the hands of the Thursby family (the 'Exors'). They were Tory landowners who also ran one of the local newspapers, the *Burnley Express*. Their mines were for the most part small scale affairs selling coal in a competitive market where there was much pressure on owners to keep labour costs at a minimum. As may be imagined the coal companies had a reputation for hostility towards trade unionism. They successfully prevented the formation of any permanent miners' trade-union lodge until the late 1880s, when a branch of the Lancashire Miners' Federation was established.[10] But even after this date, although the branch (Prosperity Lodge) maintained a continuous existence, it was constantly beset by employer intransigence. As a result, Burnley became a byword for industrial problems in the Lancashire Miners' Federation,

7   Waiter Bennett, *The History of Burnley*, 4 vols (Burnley: Burnley Corporation, 1951), III, 167–4; *Census of England and Wales*, 1891, 1901 and 1911.
8   *Census of England and Wales*, 1901.
9   Bennett, *Burnley*, IV, 109; K. Parker, 'Miners' Strike at Cheapside, 1900–1901' (MS article, Burnley Public Library, n.d.); *Barrett's Directory of Burnley and District* (Preston: P. Barret, 1899), 236, 238–9; G.N. Trodd, 'Political Change and the Working Class in Blackburn and Burnley, 1880 to 1914' (unpublished PhD thesis, Lancaster University, 1978).
10   Lancashire and Cheshire Miners' Federation (LCMF), Minute Books and Reports, 22 December 1888 (National Union of Mineworkers, Lancashire Area Office, Leigh); Raymond Challinor, *The Lancashire and Cheshire Miners* (Newcastle: Frank Graham, 1972), 207, 210, 266–7; Bennett, *Burnley*, IV, 130–3.

its members (led by their secretary John Sparling) almost as frequently in conflict with the Federation officials as with their own employers.[11] For the Burnley collier, industrial capitalism represented an oppressive and, what is more, a closed system. The ranks of the local colliery owning oligarchy offered no prospects of entry to the enterprising working man. In terms of Savage's 'capacities', the situation was very limited for self-help mutualism, though there were a few cases of co-operative ventures in mining. Nor was the economistic experience of controlling the labour market through trade unionism all that encouraging. A recourse to statism – pursuing improvement through municipal and parliamentary activity – seemed a likely option for miners. Though a volatile political force, capable of giving succour on occasions to Toryism, the Burnley miners did give early backing to the Socialist cause and pioneered, through the work of John Leeming, an independent labour position in municipal politics in the early 1890s. In contrast to miners in other regions, they were not strong supporters of Lib-Labism.[12]

The cotton industry presented, on the surface at least, a sharply contrasting picture. The expansion of weaving (accompanied as it was by a drastic reduction in Burnley's earlier emphasis on spinning) was achieved on the basis of a multiplicity of small firms. There were well over sixty separate weaving concerns by the close of the 1890s, and in addition a further twenty or so firms which combined weaving with some spinning processes.[13] The existence of so many small undertakings is explained largely by the

11 Challinor, *Lancashire and Cheshire Miners*, 266–7; on Sparling see: *Burnley Express and News*, 22 May 1940. See also R.P. Cook, 'Political Elites and Electoral Politics in late Nineteenth-Century Burnley' (unpublished MA thesis, Lancaster University, 1974), 52.

12 'Burnley and District Trades Council: Historical Notes' (MS notes and recollections covering the history of the Trades Council, 1880–1910, made in 1949 by R.B. Watson, Secretary of the Trades Council, 1906 to 1912; Burnley Public Library. Hereafter cited as RBWat); *Burnley Gazette*, 20 February, 2 November 1892; biographical details in *Burnley Express*, 7 November 1931; See also Jeffrey Hill, 'Social Democracy and the Labour Movement: the Social-Democratic Federation in Lancashire', North West Labour History Society, *Bulletin*, 8 (1982), 44–55.

13 Bennett, *Burnley*, IV, 95–8; *Barrett's Directory*, 1899, 238–9.

minimal overheads required to set up in cloth manufacturing. Rates were low and it was relatively easy for ambitious entrepreneurs to rent 'room and power': that is, floor space and looms provided by mill companies. Thus, in contrast with nearby Blackburn where weaving was conducted by a small elite of large manufacturers,[14] Burnley's cotton industry had an exceedingly widespread ownership structure. The many small enterprises were, naturally enough, very vulnerable to fluctuations in a highly competitive export market, and it is not surprising that the history of weaving in Burnley was sprinkled with bankruptcies during this period.[15]

In an endeavour to keep unit costs low, small producers maintained a variety of pressures on their workforce. The chief ones were short-time working in periods of bad trade, under-payment on the nominally agreed Standard List of piecework prices for the district, and a harsh industrial discipline enforced by mill overlookers, which routinely involved fining workers by deductions from wages for lateness or poor work.[16]

Resistance to pressures of this kind was the main business of the weavers' trade union, the Burnley Weavers' Association (BWA). It was in continuous existence from 1870 and enjoyed a steady increase in membership right through the period, making it one of the largest weavers' unions in the county-wide Amalgamated Weavers' Association (AWA).[17] Its fortunes were mixed, however. The fragmented nature of ownership meant that employers were less able to mount the kind of concerted front against trade unionism that occurred in mining, and this helped the BWA in consolidating its position. But the existence of so many small firms made the policing of the innumerable cases of victimization over finings and underpayment a very difficult task. Many of these cases made a mockery of the BWA's greatest official achievement – the negotiation in 1873 of

---

14   Trodd, thesis, 383–4.
15   Bennett, *Burnley*, IV, 98.
16   *Cotton Factory Times*, 21, 28 June, 12 July 1901. The problem reached a peak in the summer of 1901.
17   Amalgamated Weavers' Association, *Annual Report*, 1914 (Modern Records Centre, University of Warwick. MSS.192).

a Standard List for wage calculation – by circumventing its terms in one form or another.

Furthermore, though the BWA's membership figures looked impressive, they masked a significant chink in the union's armour. Taking the 1911 Census returns as a guide, it is clear that somewhere in the region of 34,000 people were employed in the various branches of weaving in Burnley in the years just before the First World War. The BWA's membership enjoyed a sharp increase between 1906 and 1914, during which time its numbers more than doubled to a recorded (but probably inflated) figure of 28,000. On the basis of these figures it seems that the union's coverage of the workforce in weaving was very extensive. It is doubtful, however, whether its real strength was as solid as the figures suggest. The workforce in weaving was unequally divided between the sexes. Women were in the majority, the 18,000 women weavers making up 60 per cent of all workers in the trade, though the supervisory role of loom mechanic ('tackler') was exclusively male. Moreover, although weaving was a significant form of employment for men, accounting for approximately one third of all male jobs in the town, it was not the only source of work; jobs were available in mining and, to a lesser extent, in engineering. Among women, on the other hand, weaving was by a long way the main employment. Thus, although weaving was not exclusively women's work (as it was, for example, in Preston) it was far more closely associated with them than with men. Furthermore, of the women who worked as weavers almost half (7,000) were between the ages twenty and thirty-five. This age group no doubt constituted a large proportion of the 11,865 female textile workers recorded in the 1911 census as unmarried.[18] These workers were particularly susceptible to factory pressures, which might have included sexual harassment from male tacklers.[19] They were a difficult section of the labour force for the BWA to recruit and retain because their problems were not easily resolvable by the trade union. They formed an important target in a membership drive

18 *Census of England and Wales*, 1911.
19 See Jan Lambertz, 'Sexual Harassment in the Nineteenth Century English Cotton Industry', *History Workshop Journal*, 19 (1985), 29–62.

of 1911 by the AWA which also attempted, ineffectively as it turned out, to enforce a closed shop in weaving.[20] The women's commitment to trade unionism as a form of working-class action must be doubted. The limited effectiveness of the BWA, and its all male leadership, in handling the specific industrial problems experienced by women probably caused many to place their faith in other forms of action.

In general then, weaving might be characterised as a trade that was prospering in the three decades before the First World War, albeit periodically disrupted by crises that stemmed from the small-scale business foundations upon which it rested. For weavers there were some prospects (because there were precedents) of making the transition from employee to master, and this provided an economic context that legitimated mutualism. But equally there was cause for discontent in the many trade practices that the BWA had only partially succeeded in curbing. Economism, therefore, did not appear a wholly satisfactory strategy, and there was potential for exploring alternatives to trade union struggle as a means of safeguarding workers' material interests.

The political life of Burnley nevertheless revealed extensive involvement in a brand of Liberalism that attached itself to both mutualist and economistic forms of action. The town possessed a radical tradition – it was, as one Tory observer despairingly put it, a 'Radical hole'[21] – and presented a picture of the classic Victorian alliance of small owners and workers against the forces of Privilege. Since attaining its status as a parliamentary borough in 1867, Burnley had returned with only occasional Conservative interludes, a succession of Liberal M.P.s of a mostly progressive stamp. Peter Rylands (notwithstanding his defection in 1886 to the Unionists) and Philip Stanhope were counted among the more 'advanced' wing of the party. The Burnley Liberal Association itself did not always mirror this progressive outlook, but nonetheless maintained a strongly populist and anti-Establishment posture, aiming for the 'Government of

---

20   See Joseph L. White, *The Limits of Trade Union Militancy: the Lancashire Textile Workers, 1910–1914* (Westport, Conn. USA: Greenwood Press, 1978), 141.
21   *Burnley Radical*, 8 January 1887.

the People in the School, Church, Town and Nation'. It also seems to have had an authentic working-class core of activists: the Liberal *Burnley News* claimed in 1894 that '... of the 400 composing the Executive, at least 300 are working men'.[22] This political culture was invigorated by immigration from outlying districts, where love of chapel and hatred of the squirearchy was deeply ingrained. Much of the labour force in Burnley's rapid economic expansion in the late nineteenth century originated in the villages of the Lancashire-Yorkshire border. In the early years of the next century roughly 15 per cent of the population had been born in other parts of the two counties. Their presence reinforced rather than fragmented existing political and religious communities. 'Their (the immigrants') political views are not only of the Liberal type', noted the *Burnley Radical* in 1887, 'but what may be regarded as considerably advanced'.[23]

Generally speaking, then, Burnley was reckoned a stronghold of Liberalism. Its strength derived from a number of social and cultural organizations in which the traditions of mutualism were firmly embedded. In certain situations (nineteenth-century France provided some examples of this) mutualism can produce an 'alternative' mentality, where voluntary and self-help organizations become a challenge to existing state or capitalist agencies. In Burnley, as in post-Owenite Britain generally, such an orientation did not develop. Mutualism was either a supplement to existing provision (in education for example) or a means of providing a service where no other existed (as in house purchase). Thus, prominent among the mutualist institutions were some half-dozen friendly societies providing

22   *Burnley Radical*, 8 January 1887; *Preston Guardian*, 7 November 1885; *Burnley Gazette*, 31 October 1885; 1 September 1894; *Preston Guardian*, 12, 26 June 1886; *Burnley Mid-Weekly Gazette*, 16, 23 February 1887; H.M. Hyndman, *Further Reminiscences* (London: Macmillan, 1912), 65–6. See also M.C. Hurst, *Joseph Chamberlain and the Liberal Re-Union: the Round Table Conference of 1887* (London: Kegan Paul, 1967), 313, 346–7.

23   Bennett, *Burnley*, III, 229; *Burnley Radical*, 1 January 1887; Census of England and Wales, 1911; *Burnley Mid-Weekly Gazette*, 16, 23 February 1887; *Burnley Express*, 10 December 1890; John Denvir, *The Irish in Britain: from the earliest times to the fall and death of Parnell* (London: Kegan, Paul, Trench, Trubner, 1892), 325, 328.

sickness and welfare services for their members, and a smaller number of building societies. Alongside them was the Co-operative movement, which had been active since the 1850s in both production and retailing, and in the pursuit of a vigorous culture of educational self-improvement that comprised a lively Women's Guild.[24] It was from voluntary associations of this kind that some of the most important of Burnley's social and health services sprang and remained important for many years. They included the town's main hospital and the infant and maternity welfare provision of the League of Social Service, established in 1912 and the precursor of the town's Maternity Home set up just after the First World War.[25] An important influence on mutualism was an extensive and varied community of Nonconformists, dominated by the Wesleyans with over a dozen chapels, together with schools, temperance clubs, benevolent and sick clubs, and sports teams.[26] The participation in all these cultural associations of both sexes was a further factor, in addition to the opportunities in the labour market, ensuring that women were not confined to a domestic role in the social life of the town. As in some other Lancashire cotton towns, notably Nelson, this had its effect on the nature of local politics, strengthening the appeal to both sexes of mutualist and statist politics. Though women were unenfranchised in parliamentary and, for the most part, local elections, their involvement in economic and social activities, and therefore the relative absence of a 'domestic sphere' synonymous with women, was an influence in causing men to consider statist solutions to domestic matters. Health and child care, for example, together with municipal provision of such services as bakeries and laundries, which in other places might have been left to the women's domestic sphere, could in Burnley logically be included as part of politics.

24   See D. Rotherham 'Chartism in Burnley', *Retrospect: the Journal of the Burnley and District Historical Society*, I (1980), 3–8; Bennett, *Burnley*, III, 289–94; IV, 99–100, 211–15.

25   See *Burnley News*, 27 February, 10 April 1915; I July 1916.

26   Bennett, Burnley, IV, ch. XI; *Nonconformist and Independent*, 2 February 1882; *Burnley Mid-Weekly Gazette*, 16 February 1887.

The Liberal ethos also found room for economism, largely through trade unionism. Like so many other unions in the Lancashire cotton industry, the BWA sought to avoid official liaisons with political parties and remained neutral politically. This meant that the virtual merging of trade union and political party into 'Lib-Labism', so common in the coalfields of the North-East of England where miner voters dominated the electorate, was not found in Burnley. The BWA, with its many unenfranchised women members, could not in any case have exercised the same electoral influence. However, very close individual ties existed between the Weavers and the Liberal Party. There is no doubt, for example, that soon after its formation in 1870 the BWA passed firmly under the control of a Lib-Lab leadership and remained so until the First World War. This brand of working-class Liberalism was most clearly personified in David Holmes, the President of the BWA from 1872 until his death in 1906. As a trade unionist Holmes was deeply committed to building and preserving industrial strength, and hostile to the introduction of a party political strategy into industrial relations. He would support the resort to legislation as a secondary tactic in the trade union struggle, as practised by the United Textile Factory Workers' Association (UTFWA) on behalf of the Lancashire cotton unions; but only when necessary, and only in a non-partisan form. He came bitterly to resent the local and national involvement of socialists in industrial matters during the 1890s, when they attempted to align socialism and trade unionism against the established political parties and to convert trade union branches into bases for political action. Holmes's attitude reflected years of personal commitment and self-denial in the cause of trade unionism, often aided by the services and companionship to be found in mutualist societies. In the course of time his position brought him status, respect and an accompanying political influence. He achieved regional prominence as an official of the AWA, and was nationally known as a member of the Trades Union Congress's Parliamentary Committee. In the political life of Burnley he sat as a Liberal on the Town Council for many years as the representative of Daneshouse Ward, and he was a long-serving member of both the School Board and the Board of Guardians.[27] His philosophy was

27 Biographical details from: *Cotton Factory Times*, 4 January 1895; 19 January 1906; Bennett, Burnley, IV, 128.

clearly expressed in an interview he gave in 1894 to the *Burnley Gazette*, shortly after returning from a lively meeting of the International Textile Workers' Federation in Manchester. Asked by his interviewer to describe the chief features of continental trade unionism, Holmes replied:

> Chiefly the ballot box and working on socialistic lines. They have been doing this for years and they have failed. We in England have relied on organisation and kept politics out of our societies ... and we have succeeded. Our socialist friends are now asking us to abandon the course which has been so successful and to adopt the measures which have proved such an utter failure abroad and left those workers today in a pitiable condition compared with those of this country.[28]

Such attitudes were perpetuated and reinforced through a second generation of Liberal leaders in the persons of Fred Thomas, James Hindle and Robert Pollard, who carried on Holmes's philosophy after his death in 1906. Up to that point, and especially in the crucial period early in the twentieth century that saw the formation of Labour Representation Committees (LRCs) locally and nationally, Holmes aligned the BWA firmly with Lib-Labism. But the industrial strategy of the BWA had not been so crowned with success as to leave no room for alternative approaches. The economistic approach, important though it was, never became the overriding moral force in Burnley working-class politics. As interpreted in Lib-Labism, it rested on a sense of class collaboration which was particularly evident in the cotton unions' close co-operation with employers on problems such as Indian tariffs and bimetallism. Beatrice Webb described the relationship as 'a union of all the producers against the outside world'.[29] The implication in this of an essential harmony between the social classes was something the socialists sought to expose as fallacious.

28   *Burnley Gazette*, 1 August 1894.
29   Beatrice and Sidney Webb, *Our Partnership* (London: Longmans, Green, 1948), 24.

III

For fifty years, from 1891 until its demise in 1940, the SDF exercised an influential role in the politics of organised labour in Burnley. Its local influence was far greater than the national reputation of the party might have suggested. The Burnley branch of the SDF was one of the most vigorous in the Federation, often rivalling in energy and initiative the branches in London.[30] The SDF branch in Burnley could usually command the active support of around 1,000 members, more in times of political ferment. 'They were of an excellent type', recalled one socialist agitator, 'mill foremen, loom tuners, craftsmen, with an unusual proportion of clerks and book-keepers'.[31] Although probably less coterminous with the labour aristocracy than this statement suggests, the SDF nevertheless embraced a wide range of workers in both main industries, with a capable group of leaders in Lawrence Rippon, John Tempest, J.H. Thornton. J.R. Widdup and the full-time secretary, Dan Irving. They ran an effective, disciplined organization with its own independent press, and sustained a solid basis of support over many years. The promise of electoral success was enough to tempt the Federation's leading figure, H.M. Hyndman, to stand for Parliament in Burnley on four occasions between 1895 and 1910, and to poll respectably on each.

The history of the SDF in Burnley is principally interesting for the challenge the party presented to other forms of working-class action, in particular to the philosophy and methods of Lib-Labism. What stood crucially at issue between them was the part to be played in working-class life and politics by trade unions. The official position of the SDF on trade unionism was less than charitable. The Federation had emerged essentially

30   See Hill, 'Social Democracy and the Labour Movement'; Crick, *History of the SDF*, ch. IX.
31   James Leatham, 'Sixty Years of World-Mending. Recollections and the More or Less Pertinent Reflections', *The Gateway: Journal of Life and Literature*, 29–30 (1942), 9–17; *Justice*, 10 December 1892 estimated the branch membership at 925, of which 600 were 'financial' (i.e. paid-up) members.

as a London organization in the early 1880s. Its policy reflected the outlook of London socialists, who saw trade unions as only a small and elitist part of the metropolitan working class. Consequently, trade unionism seemed an inappropriate basis from which to launch a mass socialist movement. This outlook was summed up in an editorial of 1891 in *Justice*, the SDF newspaper, written by its editor Harry Quelch:

> the business of the social democrats as trade unionists is to permeate their trade unions with social democracy and on no account whatever to sacrifice to *mere trade organisations* (author's italics) that energy and enthusiasm which ought to be devoted to the spread of social democracy and social democracy alone. Look at it how we will, trade unionism, old or new, can never re-organise society ... every social democrat ought to belong to the trade union of his particular trade just as every sensible man in the middle class insures against death and disablement for the sake of his family. But trade unions tend to degenerate into benefit societies and mere wage raising organisations. Therefore, every social democrat's first and paramount duty is to strengthen the only social democrat organisation in Britain – the SDF – and to work vigorously for the overthrow of capitalism.[32]

The Burnley social democrats generally tended to respect these stern injunctions. This was partly because they were reminded of them through frequent visits by members of the national leadership, but also because Dan Irving, the branch secretary, gave them consistent backing. Irving spoke a somewhat embittered and intransigent form of socialism which sprang in part from his background in Bristol, where an accident in his work as an engine driver had resulted in the amputation of one of his legs.[33] As the full-time organiser of the Burnley branch he brought to the SDF the same hostile attitude on trade unions that characterised Quelch's thinking.

---

32   *Justice*, 29 August 1891; *Socialist and North East Lancashire Labour News* (hereafter cited as *Socialist*), 14 October 1893.

33   Details from *Burnley News*, 1 January 1919; *Social Democrat*, III, 1899; H.W. Lee and E. Archbold, *Social-Democracy in Britain: Fifty Years of the Socialist Movement* (London: Twentieth Century Press, 1935), 92; Laurence Thompson, *The Enthusiasts: a Biography of John and Katharine Bruce Glasier* (London: Gollancz, 1971), pp. 70–3.

Irving's stance was never more clearly in evidence than during the lock-out that affected Lancashire cotton weaving in 1911–1912.[34] He used the situation to illustrate his view on the limitations of the industrial weapon. He clung to an idea originally advanced by the German socialist Lassalle, and still commonly held among SDF leaders, of the 'iron law of wages'. It posited that no amount of bargaining by trade unions could effectively raise working-class living standards under capitalism. During the lock-out Irving missed no opportunity of reminding workers of the reality of the 'iron law':

> Raise wages, just a little; stave off a reduction a little longer than otherwise would be the case; enforce some small improvement in trade regulations and workshop environment – yes. These very necessary things [trade unionism] can and does do. But the mere raising of nominal wages amounts to little. So long as the ownership of the means of life for all continues to be vested in the hands of a few, real wages cannot rise much above subsistence level.[35]

He was prepared to allow that 'the trade union is a necessity', but he insisted also that 'on its present lines, trade union organisation cannot bring us to social salvation'.[36]

Such views were consistent with those of the Burnley SDF branch in its pre-Irving days. Soon after its formation, for example, it launched into an attack on trade unionism over the issue of the Eight Hour Day. The establishment of the branch had occurred at a time of considerable discontent among rank-and-file trade unionists. In cotton, a downswing in the trade cycle had produced calls from employers for wage cuts as a way of reducing costs in the face of falling demand. To many weavers, however, a surer remedy for the industry's problems was thought to lie in restricting the length of the working day. That, it was argued, would have the effect of reducing output, thus relieving overstocked markets and restoring trade

34 See White, *Limits of Trade Union Militancy*, 126–45.
35 *Justice*, 6 January 1912.
36 *Pioneer: the Organ of the Labour and Socialist Movement in Burnley* (hereafter cited as *Pioneer*), September 1914.

equilibrium.[37] What particularly rankled with weavers was the fact that their leadership, unlike that of the miners, would countenance no such notion. Virtually all the regional cotton union leaders, in spinning as well as in weaving, opposed the principle of the limited working day.[38] Their reasoning was shaped by considerations of Lancashire's role as an exporter. As the *Cotton Factory Times*, the semi-official voice of the unions, had put it in 1887: 'if all the workers in the world were united in one grand union the business could be settled at once'.[39] David Holmes, speaking at Colne in 1890 during a leadership campaign to dampen rank-and-file enthusiasm for Eight Hours, spelt out the argument against a reduction of hours even more plainly.

> [Eight Hours] might be a good thing in matters pertaining to home industry ... but ... it was very unsafe for those engaged in the textile trades to support such a bill, at least until they could see a change taking place on the Continent and in the colonies and India and places where they were likely to meet with competition.[40]

Such attitudes set rank-and-file at odds with their leaders. To make matters worse, the stance of the latter was identical with that of the employers. This provided the SDF with an opportunity to counterpose a statist alternative to the managerial alliance. During its first few months of agitation in Burnley the SDF deployed the idea of a statutory restriction of hours, calling upon trade unionists to 'join the general movement to obtain a legal Eight Hours working day'.[41] By the summer of 1892 resolutions in support of Eight Hours had been passed by the Weavers' Associations in both Burnley and Nelson, and soon afterwards a large majority in favour was secured in the UTFWA – the body representing cotton workers for purposes of parliamentary lobbying.[42]

---

37   *Cotton Factory Times*, 26 September 1890; also 5 February 1886; 4 March, 2 December 1887; 14 November 15 December 1890; 11, 20, 27 May 1892.
38   *Cotton Factory Times*, 26 September 1890.
39   28 October 1887.
40   *Nelson Chronicle*, 14 October 1890.
41   *Justice*, 6 February 1892.
42   Burnley Weavers' Association, Minute Book, 11 May, 24 September 1892 (Lancashire Record Office, DDX 1274). Cotton Factory Times, 24 June 1892.

Moreover, by championing what was demonstrably a popular measure the SDF was able to make inroads into the union leadership itself. The election of SDF member John Markham to the post of Vice President of the BWA was an event of some significance, since it meant that Holmes's principal lieutenant, Robert Pollard, was displaced.[43] It inevitably aroused the hostility of the Lib-Labs, but it equally encouraged the SDF to bid for a more complete capture of the weavers' trade union structure.

Such a tactic accorded well with national SDF thinking. Control over trade unions was always preferable to accommodation with them. It meant, of course, an attempt to remove the Lib-Lab leadership, an objective made plain by socialist manoeuvres during the first two years of the SDF's existence. Socialist policy was aimed at converting the BWA into a political base for independent labour representation and, ultimately, socialism. But committing the weavers to this kind of strategy was a very different matter from agitating for an already established principle like Eight Hours. The BWA had twice refused to entertain the question of sponsoring labour candidates.[44] Resistance to such pressure was led by the Lib-Lab old guard, who in 1894 orchestrated an impressive anti-socialist campaign which demonstrated the residual support still available to them. It came after the SDF, by assiduous packing of weavers' meetings, had managed to secure the passage of two important resolutions, one removing from the Executive Committee the right to nominate BWA delegates to the TUC, the other committing the BWA to bringing out and funding labour candidates at municipal elections.[45] This, claimed Robert Pollard and his ally Robert Riddiough, was using the union 'to enact affairs emanating from St James's Hall' (the SDF headquarters). Taking a leaf from the SDF's book the Lib-Labs likewise summoned their full support for subsequent meetings of the union and succeeded in nullifying most of the gains made by the socialists.[46] By early 1895 the SDF threat to Lib-Lab control of the BWA had been repelled, and remained so for the next twenty years.

43   *Workman's Times*, 8 July 1893; *Burnley Gazette*, 4 August 1894.
44   Burnley Weavers, Minute Book, 18 May; 1 September 1892.
45   Burnley Weavers, Minute Book, 1, 10 August 1894; *Burnley Gazette*, 4 August 1894.
46   *Burnley Gazette*, 4 August 1894.

This early period of confrontation is revealing in two ways. First, it showed the true extent of SDF influence. Clearly there was a significant basis of support for socialist statism, but not enough to tip the scales decisively against trade union methods. In fact, by the end of 1894 J.R. Widdup, editor of the local SDF newspaper, was reporting to *Justice* that social democratic influence in Burnley seemed to be on the wane compared with two years earlier. The recognition of this brought about some interesting tensions inside the SDF itself which resulted, by the turn of the century, in a more 'gradualist' strategy towards local labour organizations.[47] Secondly, the conflict served to establish a pattern of politics within the working class for the whole of the period up to the First World War. The disunity in the local labour movement during these years had much to do with the battles of 1892–1894, which harboured long and deep personal and philosophical animosities. But they also set in opposition two contrasting and competing capacities of working-class action, both of which had relevance to the local labour market.

IV

For an explanation of the absence of a sustained labour alliance in Burnley during the early years of the new century, when LRCs were appearing and prospering in other Lancashire towns, we need to consider the position of the BWA. Without its defence of the old ways the town's politics might

---

47   *Justice*, 10 November 1894. See also *Burnley Gazette*, 2 November 1892; *Workman's Times*, 11 November 1893. Disputes in the SDF during the later 1890s turned on the relationship of the branch with trade unions, and resulted in John Spading's leaving the SDF to join the ILP and the setting up of a socialist-inspired trade union, the Textile Operatives, in which SDF member Lawrence Rippon was a leading figure. See *Justice*, 14, 28 November 1896; LCMF Minutes and Reports, 2 February, 4 March, 19 September 1899; 22 March 1900; White, *Limits of Trade Union Militancy*, ch. 8; *Burnley News*, 11 November 1933.

have been different. The SDF, so long as it sought co-operation rather than domination, had not found it difficult to reach accord with the societies represented in the Trades Council. In 1905, for example, socialists and trade unions had jointly formed an LRC which intervened with limited effect in municipal elections over the next three years.[48] Labour representation was an umbrella which could include both the statist politics of the SDF and the economistic methods of non-socialist trade unions, to the advantage of both. It was for this reason that the Burnley SDF became a leading advocate in the national SDF of the party's continued membership of the national LRC.[49] At the local level in Burnley, however, it was the refusal of the BWA to participate in such an alliance that accounted for the absence of a Labour candidate in the 1906 general election. The BWA committed itself only very briefly – and largely because of the adverse industrial situation of the time – to the local LRC.[50] But antagonism quickly developed over a number of issues, especially the SDF's attempts to include the principle of secular education in the LRC's municipal programme. It naturally provoked reaction from not only the Nonconformist camp but from the Roman Catholics as well, and led to renewed complaints of the SDF 'dominating' and 'monopolising' the labour movement.[51] In February 1906, only months after joining the body, the Lib-Labs in the Weavers' Association secured the passage of a vote to withdraw. It was taken after a membership ballot of over 12,000, though secured a majority of only 1,083.[52] Although the *Burnley Gazette* presented this as clear proof that most weavers wanted to withdraw from the LRC, a large minority clearly did not subscribe to the

48 *Burnley Gazette,* 22 October 1902. Details from: *Justice,* 9 April 1904; 11 November 1905; *Burnley Gazette,* 21 October 1905; 3 November 1906; *Burnley Express,* 4 November 1908; *Burnley Gazette,* 22 October 1902.

49 See Hill, 'Social Democracy and the Labour Movement', 51–3.

50 See Jeffrey Hill, 'Working Class Politics in Lancashire, 1885–1906; A Study in the Regional Origins of the Labour Party' (unpublished PhD thesis, Keele University, 1969), 343–52. Burnley Weavers, Minute Book, 6 June 1905; Burnley Textile Trades Federation, Minute Book, 6, 21 February 1905 (Lancashire Record Office, DDX 1274).

51 Burnley Textile Trades Federation, Minute Book, 6, 21 February 1905; *Burnley Gazette,* 21 October 1905; *Cotton Factory Times,* 9, 16 February 1906.

52 *Burnley Gazette,* 17 February 1906.

anti-socialist line of the leadership and would probably have been prepared to give the labour alliance a longer period of trial.

The outcome represented an assertion of self-confidence on the part of the Lib-Labs about their continuing viability as a political force. Considering the margin of their victory this confidence might have seemed misplaced, but parliamentary politics had provided their actions with some justification. The decision to withdraw from the LRC was taken immediately after the result of the general election, which had demonstrated more plainly than ever the deep divisions in Burnley's political culture. The contest had resulted in the victory of the Lib-Lab Fred Maddison over G.A. Arbuthnot, a Conservative Free Trader, and H.M. Hyndman, whom the SDF had put forward as early as 1903 in the hope of capitalising on the recently established co-operation between local labour forces. Probably because of BWA threats to disaffiliate if it were given, the Trades Council drew back from endorsing Hyndman, though he seems to have received moral backing from some elements in it.[53] Maddison, on the other hand, received little encouragement from the Trades Council (not persuaded by his 'labour' credentials) and still less from Prosperity Lodge. His programme, mainly a defence of freedom in trade and education, displayed a wide appreciation of social and industrial problems and of the legislative reforms needed to tackle them. The contest was close, and much rested on the ability of one of the three candidates to secure a marginal advantage. For a while it seemed that Hyndman might be the one to achieve it, especially after a wholehearted appeal on his behalf from the Irish Nationalist leader, Michael Davitt. But Burnley's Irish League eventually decided to cast its sizeable vote for the Liberals on the Home Rule issue. In a turn-out of 95 per cent only 350 votes separated the candidates. Hyndman finished last but polled 30 per cent of the vote and was only thirty-three behind the second-placed Conservative.[54]

53   RBWat; H.M. Hyndman Letters, letter to W.M. Thompson, 25 December 1905 (Burnley Public Library).

54   *Burnley Gazette*, 12 September 1903; *Justice*, 26 September 1903; 18 December 1905. The voting figures were: Maddison (Lib.), 5288; Arbuthnot (Con.), 4965; Hyndman (Socialist), 4932.

This result sealed the divisions in the working class for the next ten years. Burnley Liberal Association felt little compulsion to shed what Tanner describes as its 'conservative' outlook in order to accommodate labour, either by moving towards the 'New Liberal' position hinted at in Maddison's campaign, or by negotiating an electoral pact with the LRC of the kind applied in other towns.[55] Thus, while other parts of industrial Lancashire were witnessing important structural changes in their political alignments, Burnley appeared to be stuck in the past. It was not until well into the First World War that Burnley saw a united Labour Party, merging socialist and trade union elements in the manner of the earlier and short-lived LRC. It was strong enough to give Dan Irving three parliamentary successes for Labour between 1918 and 1924. Two developments help to explain this change of circumstances.

The first, and more important, was the crisis of confidence suffered by the Lib-Lab leadership of the BWA during the Weavers' lock-out of 1911–12. This event, more than anything else, provided the decisive rupture with the past. In Burnley, the situation was aggravated by the fact that Fred Thomas had assumed a leading regional role in the AWA's initiation of the dispute. Blame for the dispute therefore attached largely to him, and he became the chief target of attack. The circumstances that developed in the town were not dissimilar to those of 1892 when the SDF had led opposition to the leadership over Eight Hours. In 1912, the abject defeat of the AWA, following a month's cessation of work over Christmas which had brought severe hardship to striking weavers, emphasised the ill-conceived nature of the action; it served to remind weavers that many had counselled against the strategy, notably Dan Irving in the pages of *Justice* and in the SDF's local monthly, *The Pioneer*. In the aftermath of the lock-out local weavers censured the BWA leadership for its actions and forced the resignation of

55 Burnley had not been considered in the secret electoral pact between the Liberal and Labour parties in 1903. See, Viscount Gladstone Papers, British Library Add. MSS, 46484, vol CXLV; other details from *Burnley Gazette*, 6, 10, 13, 17 January 1906; *Northern Daily Telegraph*, 4, 6, 15 January 1906.

Thomas.[56] With his departure, followed in 1914 by the death of Robert Pollard, the main links with the Lib-Lab past were severed and the way laid open for new political alignments.

A second development helped in hastening this outcome. In complete contrast to the ILP, many of whose members took up an anti-war stance, the declaration of war in 1914 brought out a latent patriotism in many social democrats, especially those influenced by the super-patriot Hyndman. Irving and a considerable number of the Burnley SDF (now British Socialist Party) assumed a loyal stance from the outset, with Irving especially working enthusiastically in an all-party recruitment campaign. In 1916, in opposition to an anti-war faction within the BSP, he led the Burnley Socialists out of their parent body and set up, with Hyndman, the National Socialist Party.[57] This event helped to bring local Socialists into the mainstream of politics in a way that had not been possible previously, and it went a long way towards removing the taint of extremism that had put a distance between them and other sections of the labour movement. The decision in 1916 to affiliate the National Socialist Party to the Labour Party, though prompted by current ideological discord within British socialism over the specific issue of the war, connected with more distant conflicts over the role to be played by social democracy in the labour alliance. By joining the Labour Party in 1916 the Burnley SDF finally achieved what it had argued for fifteen years earlier.[58]

56   For full details of the lock-out see White, *Limits of Trade Union Militancy*, ch. 8; SDF reactions are reported in *Justice*, 6 and 27 January 1912; see also *Burnley Gazette*, 31 January 1912 – the protest meeting of Burnley weavers was exceptionally held on a Sunday, and the abuse heaped upon Thomas for his explanation of the conclusion of the lock-out caused the *Gazette* to comment that 'such a scene on a Sunday afternoon was unparallelled in Burnley'.

57   See *Pioneer*, June 1916.

58   *Justice*, 5 April 1902; 4 November 1903; 29 April 1905; 21 April 1906.

V

Labour's supplanting of Liberalism in 1918 marked an important change in the fabric of Burnley politics. What had made the town anomalous by contrast with many of its neighbours was the richness and diversity of its political life. All three of the capacities highlighted in the work of Savage – economism, mutualism and statism – possessed a relevance in Burnley as forms of working-class action. What is more, the political parties were able to fashion policies that made practical sense of each capacity. This ensured that the town remained divided, as much over political strategies and ideologies as over party choices. In this divided culture Liberalism, reaching as it did deep into the associational life of many of Burnley's inhabitants, and buoyed by the support of town's largest trade union, could draw upon many strengths politically. Its essentially old-fashioned radicalism offered a relevant, if increasingly nostalgic, analysis of the pre-1914 world, where the idea of the small man making good through collective mutualist effort still possessed credibility. It offered few solutions, however, to the economic realities of the 1930s. By this time the Labour Party's programme of working class security through the actions of the state – local and national – had swung the advantage in its favour against Liberalism in Burnley. Labour's ability to reap the electoral benefits, especially after 1945, owed much to the existence in the town's political culture of a statist tradition that had been embedded through the SDP's early work. In keeping alive the notion of statism before the First World War, in shaping a municipal reform programme in opposition to the perceived weaknesses of economism,[59] and in articulating to its own radical heritage a language of class solidarity, the SDF had done much to lay the foundations of a labour culture that went beyond trade union economism. It was a culture that subsumed a mutualist tradition into municipal socialism. In this crucial sense, therefore, the holding of Labour's 1918 victory celebrations in the Co-op Rooms had more than rhetorical significance: it symbolised the fusion of two political capacities.

---

59   See *Socialist*, 14 October 1893; D. Irving, *The Municipality, From a Worker's Point of View* (London: Twentieth Century Press: n.d.[1906]), 15.

CHAPTER SIX

Politics, Gender, and 'New' Toryism: Lancashire in the 1920s

If we define modern democratic politics by the criterion of 'one person, one vote', Great Britain more or less arrived at that position in 1928. In that year some seven million female voters over the age of 21 were included in the electoral register.[1] They augmented the eight million women over the age of 30 who had been given the vote in 1918, along with some 13 million males over 21. Thus for the first time women occupied a significant place in the parliamentary voting system, and thereby became the subject of serious attention by political parties.

I

This chapter presents a case study of the Conservative Party's grass roots in Lancashire during the first decade of what Jon Lawrence has called 'the "feminised" franchise'.[2] Several historians have already turned their attention to this period. Their researches have illuminated a number of important new characteristics in Conservative Party activity: a general

1 Barring a few exceptions (people who had not satisfied the three months residence qualification) everyone over the age of 21 now had at least one vote. Until 1948, however, some had two, owing to the continuation of the business and university franchises, abolished in that year.
2 Jon Lawrence, 'Class and Gender in the Making of Urban Toryism, 1880–1914', *English Historical Review*, July, 1993, 652.

improvement in party organisation and propaganda, with particular emphasis on the training of professional agents and fund raising; a strong antipa-
thy towards Labour socialism, trades unionism, and Bolshevism – often
with little distinction made between the three; another excursion into
the cause of protectionism and a re-fashioning of the idea of Empire; and
a strenuous attempt to enrol women and young people into the party as
both voters and activists.[3] Through these means the Conservatives were
able to absorb many former Liberal supporters, while at the same time
attempting to position Labour as an 'outsider' party pursuing sectional
rather than national interests – an image frequently invoked by reference
to the industrial conflicts of 1921 and 1926. By contrast the Conservative
Party itself, which after the Irish Treaty of 1921 had cast off some of its old
Unionist pre-occupations, sought to occupy an inclusive middle ground
of large and small property owners of both sexes. The formation in many
areas, more often in local government elections, of anti-socialist coalitions
of Liberals and Conservatives gave added force to this trend.[4] It created, in
Ross McKibbin's view, a party persona that was above politics, representing simply 'the public'.[5] Thus, any suggestion of Toryism as a vehicle for

3   For example: Neal R. McCrillis, *The British Conservative Party in the Age of Universal
     Suffrage: Popular Conservatism 1918–1929* (Columbus OH: Ohio State University
     Press, 1998); John Ramsden, *The Age of Balfour and Baldwin 1902–1940* (London:
     Longman, 1978); Stuart Ball, 'The Conservative Dominance, 1918–1940', *Modern
     History Review*, 3 (1991), 25–8; Martin Pugh, 'Popular Conservatism in Britain:
     Continuity and Change, 1880–1987', *Journal of British Studies*, 27 (July 1988), 254–82;
     David Jarvis, 'British Conservatism and Class Politics in the 1920s', *English Historical
     Review*, 211 (1996), 59–84; Ross McKibbin, 'Class and Conventional Wisdom: The
     Conservative Party and the "Public" in Interwar Britain', in *The Ideologies of Class*
     (Oxford: Clarendon Press, 1990); J.W.B. Bates, 'The Conservative Party in the
     Constituencies, 1918–1939', unpublished DPhil thesis, University of Oxford, 1994.
4   Nelson, traditionally a nonconformist radical town which became a Labour strong-
     hold, was a case in point. Anti-socialist coalitions appeared even before the 1914–1918
     war, and were common in the interwar period. Jeffrey Hill, *Nelson: Politics, Economy,
     Community* (Edinburgh: Keele University Press, 1997), 65, 103–4.
5   Ross McKibbin, *Parties and People: England 1914–1951* (Oxford: Oxford University
     Press, 2010), ch. 3, esp. 93–5; *Classes and Cultures, England 1918–1951* (Oxford: Oxford
     University Press, 1998), 58–9; 'Class and Conventional Wisdom', 284.

purely social class interests was elided into one that emphasised *national* identity and unity.

Lancashire provides fertile ground for considering these matters. It was a pivotal electoral region of some 60 constituencies where any party seeking national office had to perform well. This being so, the region was usually in the vanguard insofar as new political ideas and methods were concerned. It is surprising, then, that attention to its interwar Tory politics has been comparatively slight, especially since Lancashire had been a noted stronghold of popular Toryism in the years before 1914.[6] Unusually for an industrial area, Tory strength waxed rather waned with each extension of the franchise. Following the Reform Act of 1884 the Conservative Party's share of the vote in the region was generally greater than that of its main rival, the Liberal Party. Not until 1906 were the Liberals, partly through an electoral pact with the newly formed Labour Representation Committee (LRC) and with favourable political circumstances brought about largely by Chamberlain's tariff reform platform (further aided by the issues of 'Chinese slavery', laws on picketing in trade disputes, and education), significantly able to outpoll the Tories.[7]

6   'Toryism' is used throughout this chapter as the popular designation of Conservative politics. The party of toryism was variously referred to as the 'Conservative', 'Unionist', 'Conservative and Unionist', or simply 'Tory' party. In the National Union rules of 1925 'Unionist' was relegated to second place in the name of the party, which formally became the Conservative and Unionist Party. See Ramsden, *Age of Balfour and Baldwin*, 261.

7   On the Labour Party see: Henry Pelling, *The Origins of the Labour Party 1880–1900* (London: Macmillan and Co., 1954); *Social Geography of British Elections 1885–1910* (London: Macmillan, 1967); *Popular Politics and Society in Late Victorian Britain* London: Macmillan, 1968). See also: F. Bealey and H. Pelling, *Labour and Politics, 1900–1906* (London: Macmillan, 1958); Keith Laybourn, *A Century of Labour* (Stroud: Sutton, 2000); *Philip Snowden: A Biography* (Aldershot: Temple Smith/Gower, 1988); 'The Rise of Labour and the Decline of Liberalism: The State of the Debate', *History*, 80 (1995), 207–26; Ross McKibbin, *The Evolution of the Labour Party 1910–1924* (Oxford: Oxford University Press, 1974); Duncan Tanner, *Political Change and the Labour Party, 1900–1918* (Cambridge: Cambridge University Press, 1990). On the Liberal Party: P.F. Clarke, *Lancashire and the New Liberalism* (Cambridge:

Before that point, it is true, national electoral issues had tended to work in the Conservatives' favour. But what principally explains the durability of their support was is not so much matters of policy as the particular social and cultural environment of politics. This was especially evident in the western parts of Lancashire. Religion was fundamental to it. In Lancashire's voting patterns a clear association can be seen between the areas of Irish Roman Catholic immigration and those where the most enduring commitment to Toryism was found.[8] To be a Tory in these areas, of which Liverpool was a paradigm case, meant expressing an opposition (often violent) to the Irish Catholic presence.[9] Before 1914 popular Toryism's distinctive characteristic was a deep commitment to the Protestant religion, expressed in its most national form, namely the Anglican Church.[10] Not, moreover, any kind of Anglicanism; only a low-Church, evangelical Protestantism, free of the taint of crypto-Catholicism, would fit the bill.[11] The Irish Catholic presence

Cambridge University Press, 1971); 'British Politics and Blackburn Politics, 1900–1910', *The Historical Journal*, XII, 2(1969), 302–27.

8   Although the vast majority of Lancashire's Catholics were immigrants from Ireland, there was also a sizeable group of English Catholics, particularly in and around Preston. On Merseyside there were northern Irish immigrants who were not Catholic. See John Denvir, *The Irish in Britain, from the earliest times to the fall and death of Parnell* (London: Kegan, Paul, Trench, Trubner and Co., 1892), 430; B. Nightingale, *Lancashire Nonconformity* (Manchester, J. Heywood, 6 vols, 1890–1893), vol 1, 36.

9   Denvir, *Irish in Britain*, 429–33. See also Steven Fielding, *Class and Ethnicity: Irish Catholics in England, 1880–1939* (Buckingham: Open University Press, 1993), ch. 2.

10   J.W. Diggle, *The Lancashire Life of Bishop Fraser* (London: Sampson, Low, Marston, Searle and Rivington, 1890), 166–7, 265; Thomas Hughes, *James Fraser, Second Bishop of Manchester* (London: Macmillan, 1888 ed.), 184, 195, 246–57; E.A. Knox, *Reminiscences of an Octogenarian 1847–1934* (London: Hutchinson, 1934), 239. Patrick Joyce, 'Popular Toryism in Lancashire 1860–1890' (unpublished DPhil thesis, University of Oxford, 1975) describes the Church of England as 'the Church of the People' (189); Nonconformist churches were often regarded by working people in South East Lancashire as being for the better-off sections of the community.

11   For example, the Conservative defeat in the Southport by-election of 1899 was put down to the party's 'ritualist' sympathies. The local Conservative paper complained 'the Bishops have lost us Southport.' (*Southport Visiter*, 1 June 1899; also 30 May 1899); Salvidge, *Salvidge of Liverpool*, 33–4.

was greatest in Liverpool, and there met its most hostile opposition: an Orange faction headed by a group of 'bigoted, virulent and eloquent Irish parsons' who were Toryism's keenest advocates.[12] It received strong backing from the Working Men's Conservative Association, founded in the 1860s, whose chairman from 1892 was the brewer Archibald Salvidge, for a long time a thorn in the side of Liverpool's Conservative elite until, eventually, he himself became the city's political boss.[13] It was in Liverpool too that Pastor George Wise was active in the years immediately before the Great War, organising anti-Catholic meetings at which sashes, fifes and drums, passionate support for King and country, tariff reform and the singing of the national anthem were the staple items of the agitational repertoire.[14] Waller's study of Liverpool brings to life this extraordinary politico-religious milieu, more akin to that of Belfast than other parts of mainland Britain.[15] At times, notably during Wise's campaigns of 1909, it generated street conflicts of extreme brutality.[16] This was the essence of Lancashire popular Toryism: not essentially class based, though with a strong working-class support; physical, with a masculine political style similar to that noted by Lawrence in his work on the West Midlands;[17] and vehemently Protestant.

This was not all. The pub was an important source[18] from which flowed another chief marker of the true Tory – 'sportsmanship'. It was expressed in

12   Denvir, *Irish in Britain*, p. 119.
13   Stanley Salvidge, *Salvidge of Liverpool: Behind the Political Scene 1890–1928* (London: Hodder and Stoughton, 1934); P.J. Waller, *Democracry and Sectarianism: A Political and Social History of Liverpool, 1868–1939* (Liverpool: Liverpool University Press, 1981). John Belchem ed., *Liverpool 800: Culture, Character and History* (Liverpool: Liverpool University Press, 2008).
14   For example, *Liverpool Daily Post and Mercury*, 9, 18 January; 25 October 1909.
15   Waller, *Democracy and Sectarianism*, esp. ch. 12. The Belfast comparison is questioned by Gareth Jenkins, '"Rowdyism versus Respectability": Liverpool and Belfast's experiences of Protestant street preaching during the Edwardian period', *North West Labour History*, 36 (2011–2012), 37–46.
16   Waller, *Democracy and Sectarianism*, 237–9.
17   Jon Lawrence, 'Class and Gender in the Making of Urban Toryism, 1880–1914', *English Historical Review*, July 1993, 629–52.
18   Lawrence, 'Class and Gender'.

myriad forms, perhaps most obviously in the local social leaders who were 'champions' of their communities. The mill owner W.H. Hornby, MP for Blackburn (brother of A.N. Hornby the Lancashire cricketer and England rugby player, memorialised in Francis Thompson's poem 'At Lord's'[19]) was the most noteworthy. W.H. Hornby was known to his many admirers as 'th'owd gam cock', a sobriquet with Dionysian implications that recalled an old-fashioned passion for hunting, gambling and drinking that was seen as the freeborn Englishman's natural leisure right. The local Member of Parliament was expected to support these pursuits morally and financially.[20] In a long parliamentary career Hornby did little at Westminster, but successfully enacted in his locality the kind of 'non-political' Toryism developed by Stanley Baldwin a generation later. Before the War it fused with support for the brewers' cause and a general male hostility to what was regarded as the primly sanctimonious mentality of the Nonconformist chapel. To be sure, the taste for this 'cakes and ale' Toryism was probably diminishing by the beginning of the twentieth century as new sports and commercial leisure opportunities became available, but its passing was long drawn out. Even in the more urbanised areas access to open spaces was still possible, enabling some of the old pastimes such as hare coursing, ratting, and knurr and spell to continue. Tory politicians like Hornby were canny enough to sustain the old traditions, while simultaneously latching on to the newer pursuits when necessary.[21]

19   'Oh my Hornby and my Barlow long ago'. See Anthony Bateman, *Cricket, Literature and Culture: Symbolising the Nation, Destabilising Empire* (Farnham: Ashgate, 2009), 61–2.
20   Clarke, *Lancashire and the New Liberalism*, 226–7; Derek Beattie, *Blackburn: The Development of a Lancashire Cotton Town* (Halifax: Ryburn Publishing, 1992), 41–4. The price to be paid came in the form of generous subscriptions to a host of local voluntary associations. See Clarke, *Lancashire and the New Liberalism*, 23, 221 for Max Aitken's donations as Conservative MP for Ashton-under-Lyne.
21   Football grounds provided a particularly useful recruiting place at election times. Tony Mason, *Association Football and English Society 1863–1915*, 118, 226–9; Matthew Taylor, *The Association Game: A History of British Football* (Harlow: Pearson Education, 2008), 94; Dave Russell, *Football and the English: A Social History of Association Football in England, 1863–1995* (Preston: Carnegie Publishing, 1997), 65, 74, 119.

With a male-only parliamentary franchise much of this political culture was to be expected. It was, however, moderated by an organisation whose activities helped to induct women into the Tory cause at a time when they were excluded from Party membership. This was the Primrose League, formed in 1883 in honour of Disraeli and at its height as a popular movement in the years before the 1914–1918 War. Martin Pugh's research has amply demonstrated the vigour and popularity of this body. By the turn of the century it had a strong coverage of England and Wales (less so in Scotland) with well over a million members, making it one of the largest political movements in the country (though its connection with the Conservative Party was not a formal one). Through its emphasis on respectable social activities, its populist character – clearly articulated, as Pugh shows, in working-class industrial districts like Bolton – and the strongly monarchical and imperial tone of its gatherings the League proved able to involve women in large numbers. It established important organisational and propaganda precedents upon which the post-1918 Conservative Party was able to build.[22]

II

It has generally been acknowledged that this traditional Toryism, founded as it was on religious sectarianism, was declining from the early years of the twentieth century. Peter Clarke's research demonstrated the thrust in Lancashire of a 'New Liberalism' that drew successfully on social class

---

WH Hornby gave support, along with other leading citizens, to Blackburn Rovers FC. (Beattie, *Blackburn*, 124). There is scope for more work on this topic.

22 Martin Pugh, *The Tories and the People, 1880–1935* (Oxford: Basil Blackwell, 1985). Matthew Hendley, 'Constructing the Citizen: The Primrose League and the Definition of Citizenship in the Age of Mass Democracy in Britain, 1918–1928', *Journal of the Canadian Historical Association/Revue de la Societe historique du Canada*, 7, 1 (1996), 125–51; G.E Maguire, *Conservative Women: A History of Women in the Conservative Party, 1874–1997* (Basingstoke: Macmillan, 1998), ch. 2.

loyalties, and its is not surprising that at the end of the War, notwithstanding profound splits in the Liberal Party, many leading Tories foresaw a bleak future for their party. Philip Williamson has noted how 'Baldwin's anxieties were shared by almost all Conservatives in the 1920s: that the emergence of independent working-class politics in a context of a "new electorate" might condemn their party to a permanent minority and its causes to effective extinction.'[23] In fact, of course, the future brought about the very opposite: a sustained period of Conservative electoral hegemony that came to an end only with the general election of 1945.[24] Such consistent success suggests not simply a paradigm shift in political loyalties and identity – the classic 'status' to 'class' process[25] – but an across-the-board adoption of fresh political strategies attuned to the new electoral sociology of the post-War years.

A close reading of the activities of four local constituency organisations for which records have survived in the North West – Waterloo, Fylde, Clitheroe and Bolton – offers a glimpse of these strategies from

23   Philip Williamson, *Stanley Baldwin: Conservative Leadership and National Values* (Cambridge: Cambridge University Press, 1999), 338.
24   A simple measure of the Conservatives' adaptability can be found in the party's parliamentary performances in Lancashire in the seven interwar general elections. At the redistribution of 1918 the number of constituencies in Lancashire was increased from the pre-War 53 (returning, with the 4 double-member seats which were retained in the redistribution, 57 MPs) to 62, returning 66 MPs. Of these seats 35 were won more often than not by the Conservatives, for whom 15 borough and seven county seats might be accounted 'safe'. Four of these were in Liverpool. Two (Bury and Fylde) were even held in the Labour landslide of 1945. By contrast the Labour Party might normally (i.e. 1931 apart) have expected to win seven borough seats and 4 county divisions. Only three constituencies – Wigan, Ince and Westhoughton, all mining areas – were retained by Labour at every election in the interwar period. There were only three seats where the Liberals could expect to do very well. In two of these, Mossley and Stretford, they campaigned as Independents, often on an anti-socialist platform with Conservative support. In the other, Heywood, the Liberal Party won five of the eight parliamentary contests in this period (which included a by-election in 1921 won by Labour), the victor in 1931 being a National Liberal.
25   See, for example, D. Butler and D. Stokes, *Political Change in Britain: Forces Shaping Electoral Choice* (New York: St Martin's Press, 1969).

the bottom up. The first three constituencies were safe Conservative seats. Waterloo was a suburban middle-class county division abutting Bootle that had been created in the 1917 re-distribution largely from the old county seat of Southport. Fylde and Clitheroe were more rural in nature, though unlike Waterloo had small pockets of industry: the fishing port of Fleetwood in Fylde, and in Clitheroe the town itself, which had cotton mills, partly explaining why it had been won by Labour in 1918.[26] Bolton, a double-member constituency of engineering and cotton spinning, was more thoroughly industrial and was the only seat of the four where Labour posed a serious challenge to the Conservatives.

In each of these areas female support to deal with the extension of the franchise in 1918 had been mobilised early on. A firmly held belief developed in the Conservative Party that women were 'natural' Tories and that it had been the votes of women in 1918 that had kept the threatened advance of Labour at bay.[27] In each constituency women's associations had been established. In the case of the suburban seat of Waterloo pre-1914 Primrose League groups were brought into a closer relationship with the Party itself, quickly resulting in women's organisations at both ward and constituency levels.[28] Membership hovered around 300 in the later 1920s, but by the 1930s the group was claiming to have in the region of a thousand women enrolled from various parts of the constituency.[29] At Clitheroe women's organisations were reported in 10 localities by the end of 1921, with progress being made by the mid-1920s in introducing girls

---

26   The Clitheroe constituency had been strongly Labour before 1918, having been won for the then Labour Representation Committee by David Shackleton in a famous by-election of 1902. In the redistribution, however, the town of Nelson was removed into the new seat of Nelson and Colne thus depriving Clitheroe of much of its Labour support. (*Clitheroe Advertiser and Times*, 7 December 1923.)

27   *Crosby Herald*, 22 March 1919, 12 December 1921.

28   Southport Division, Waterloo District Conservative Association, Minute Book 1901–1918 (DDX 806 1/1), 21 November, 5 December 1919; 18 November 1921. *Crosby Herald*, 15 February 1919. (Lancashire County Record Office (LCRO), Preston.)

29   LCRO, Waterloo Conservative Association, Minute Book 1918–1925 (DDX 806 2/1), Annual Report 1924–1925, 1930–1931; Women's Central Committee, Minute Book 1928–1953 (DDX 806 2/2), Annual Reports 1930–1931, 32–3, 34–5.

into the formerly male-only junior groups. By the end of 1925 the Women's Association was reporting a membership close on 4000. Following the further extension of the franchise in 1928 the Clitheroe women, through a vigorous round of 'cottage meetings', succeeded, it was claimed, in reaching out to a number of women who had not previously been political, thus contributing to a turn-out of over 90 per cent in the general election of 1929 and returning the sitting member William Brass with a good majority.[30] In Fylde a women's association was formed in October 1919, with an emphasis on educating women in 'the use of the vote'. By the mid 1920s it was an active element in the local Tory cause, with summer open-air meetings and the usual round of socials; an innovative feature of education was seen with the arrival of the Conservative Central Office cinema van to tour the district. Funds did not always meet aspirations, however and the women's secretary, Muriel Openshaw, had to make a stern appeal to the branches for more financial support. In 1934 the accounts showed a deficit for the first time, and in 1938 the big annual ball – usually a good fund-raising event – was described as 'disappointing'. Nonetheless, as in the other two constituencies the women's organisation survived until, on the outbreak of war in 1939, the records break off.[31]

III

From the outset the women's sections remained separate from those of the men. This was largely on the advice of Central Office. For the most part the staple fare of women's activities was conventionally gendered: the

30   LCRO, Clitheroe Conservative and Unionist Association, Minute Book 1909–1921 (DDX 800), 12 and 16 November 1921, Annual Report, 31 December 1921; Minute Book 1921–1934 (DDX 800), 18 June, 27 November 1923; Annual Reports 1921, 24, 25, 26, 27, 29.
31   LCRO, Fylde Division Women's Constitutional Association, Minute Book 1919–1952 (DDX 1202 1/2), Annual Report (31 December) 1920, 21, 26, 29, 34, 37.

organising of whist drives, at homes, musical evenings, summer fetes, annual balls, children's Christmas parties, and, since it was assumed that women were inclined to be politically less well-informed, educational lectures with visiting speakers.[32] It goes without saying that the preparation of refreshments for all such events fell to women members. Fund raising fulfilled a major function in each of these activities, with a portion of the proceeds sometimes being donated to local branches of voluntary bodies such as the Red Cross. The annual report of Waterloo's women's secretary for 1923–1924 provides a typical record of all this energy whilst also, amidst the details of monthly whist drives, giving a revealing insight into gender relations in politics. The sitting member, Col. Albert Buckley, had decided to stand down at the 1923 general election in disagreement with Baldwin's policy on tariffs. 'To say the least', the report notes, 'we women were disappointed – he [Buckley] had endeared himself to us and it was always a pleasure to work for him. However, the difficulty had to be faced – we must see our Party through – and when our new candidate Captain Malcolm Bullock was brought before us, the more we saw of him, the more we liked him ... we women just said 'he's got to go back to the House of Commons to represent our Constituency, for the Party's sake and for his own ...' The report then goes on to outline the considerable contribution made by the women of the area to Bullock's campaign.[33] Bullock was a young man (born 1890), a firm Baldwinite, with a good war record and a wife who was the daughter of the Earl of Derby, the region's *grand seigneur*. He did not lack the necessary social and political credentials for this constituency, and clearly had an appeal for women voters that seemed almost to have matched that of contemporary film stars.[34]

---

32   See, eg, LCRO, DDX 806 2/1, Annual Report 1924–1925, 30–1; DDX 806 2/2, 26 November 1928, Annual Report 1928–1929.

33   LCRO, Waterloo Women's Conservative and Unionist Association, Minute Book 1918–1925 (DDX 806 2/1), 25 March 1924 (report of activities Feb. 1923 to Mar. 1924). On Bullock see Andrew Lee-Hart, *General Election Results for What is Now South Sefton* (South Sefton Local History Unit, Crosby Library, 2001).

34   The fact that he was widowed in 1927 when his wife died in an accident probably earned him a sympathy vote.

The separation of women in the party's organisation was mirrored in its electioneering, where there was a marked tendency to construct 'women's issues'. Fylde offers such an example. The MP between 1922 and his death in 1938 was Lord Stanley, the eldest son of Lord Derby. His stance on women's involvement in party affairs was not a progressive one, and in the late 1920s, as deputy chair of the Conservative Party, he had clashed with the party chairman J.C.C. Davidson on this very issue.[35] In the constituency, on the other hand, Stanley targeted the perceived concerns of the female voter, frequently using his wife to make a woman-to-woman appeal. Unemployment, for example, was approached from the point of view of the 'hardships' it placed on women: 'Nobody realises better than the women, who have to keep the home going', wrote Lady Stanley in 1923, 'what unemployment means.'[36] In 1929 her husband made a specific address to all the new voters to remind them that, in addition to the Conservatives having *given* women over 21 the vote for the first time, it should be used 'seriously' on the 'grave issues that are at stake.'[37] In appealing in 1935 to women voters Lady Stanley said that 'Every woman at heart wants security – in her home – for her husband's job – for the future of her Children – and against the possibility of war' and urged them to support Stanley and the National Government.[38] When Florence Rollo of Waterloo first stood for the local Urban District Council in 1935 her platform was what would have been regarded as a specific women's one – health and sanitation, maternity and child welfare; interestingly, she offered it 'without distinction of creed or party politics.'[39]

35   Ramsden, *Age of Balfour and Baldwin*, 224–5.
36   LCRO, Papers of J.R. Almond, election material 1906–1951 (DDX 1202 1/6), election leaflet from Lady Stanley, 1923.
37   *Ibid.*, election letter from Lord Stanley to all new women voters, 1929.
38   Election pamphlet *The Fylde Elector*, 'Lady Stanley's Letter to Women Voters', 5 November 1935, (DDX 1202 1/23).
39   Crosby Library, Election Poster and Address, Waterloo with Seaforth UDC, 18 March 1935 (Florence Rollo Items, C920p). A similar 'non-party' stance was assumed by Eleanor Rathbone, a more 'progressive' politician than Rollo, in Liverpool's Granby Ward, which she represented as an Independent from 1909 until 1935. Susan Pedersen,

Florence Rollo eventually rose to prominence in her local Conservative Party, one of only a few examples of women exercising, or even seeking to exercise, an influence outside their designated sphere. Another occurred in the Fylde constituency following the sudden death in 1938 of Lord Stanley. His wife Sibyl seems to have aspired to take over the seat herself, if not immediately then at some point in the future. She fought hard against the local constituency party to secure the nomination of a candidate favourable to herself, eventually supporting the old-Etonian former Guards officer C.G. Lancaster as the 'Stanley candidate'. Though her father-in-law Lord Derby appears to have ruled out the idea that Sybil might become a candidate, he admitted to the party agent J.R. Almond that Sibyl was 'very angry' that the local party had proposed a 'complete stranger' (Lord Douglas Hamilton) to replace her husband. No doubt as a result of Lady Stanley's determination Lancaster was chosen, and won the by-election (retaining the seat even in 1945). His Labour opponent in 1938 however was a woman, Dr Mabel Tylecote, and a reminder of how limited the advance of women in the senior ranks of the Conservative Party had been.[40]

To a large extent women's separate position in the party determined both their political prospects and the nature of their politics. The 'education' of women was confined to domestic matters. This was especially so in the 1920s, where the scope of female interest remained as defined by Mrs Harrison of Waterloo in 1921 – 'all subjects on Women's affairs connected with Politics'[41] – though by the following decade there are indications of change. The economic problems that prompted the formation of the National Government together with the question of India were two topics that began to intrude into the agenda of women's meetings (alongside the perennial whist drives and bridge parties). Members were sent off to the Conservative college at Ashridge or, nearer to home, to courses held at

---

    Eleanor Rathbone and the Politics of Conscience (New Haven: Yale University Press, 2004), 92–3, 381.

40   LCRO, correspondence and other material on Fylde by-election (DDX 1202 1/6, 1/47) especially letters from Derby to Almond 26 October and 5 November 1938.

41   LCRO, Waterloo Conservative Association, Minute Book 1918–1925, 18 November 1921 (DDX 806).

the Smedley Hydro in Southport. One recurring theme in Tory propaganda in these years seems particularly to have influenced the women's sections of the party. This was the bitter hostility shown throughout the period, though especially before 1931, towards the Labour Party (usually referred to in one form or another by the term 'socialist'). It gave Conservatism a somewhat contradictory appearance: the characteristic 'non-political' stance, notably seen in Baldwin's public persona and given further substance in the many electoral agreements made with the Liberals at this time, was interspersed with venomous rhetoric about Labour. In the years immediately after the war fears about the threat of Labour were strong, and to an extent had prompted the formation of Lloyd George's Coalition. In 1921 the *Crosby Herald* supported the recruitment of women as a force against what it described somewhat cryptically as 'certain propaganda efforts which were receiving support' and which were not in the interests of the British Empire.[42] In 1925 the Women's Central Committee of the Waterloo Conservative Association noted that 'this Committee view (*sic*) with deep concern the activities of the Socialist Party in this Division and wish to ask the Central Committee – is there any Conservative propaganda of activities to hand, likely to combat the influence of our opponents which seems to be gaining ground?'[43] Concerns about the possibility of a Labour parliamentary majority in the late 1920s prompted a spate of talks by the Crosby Conservative group in Waterloo on the challenge of socialism; when one meeting drew only 40 people it was regarded as a mark of complacency: 'it was a pity more advantage was not taken of the opportunity to hear of the fallacies of socialism as put forward by the Labour Party, and the bedrock facts of Capitalism and Industry working together for the common good.'[44] The sense of a civil crisis in the early 1920s was particularly acute among the women Conservatives of the Fylde, who called upon all

42   *Crosby Herald*, 17 December 1921. The cryptic reference was to either the Labour Party or protectionists in the Conservative Party.
43   LCRO, Waterloo Conservative Association, Women's Central Committee, Mrs EL Degge to Mr BG Worthington, 24 June 1925 (DDX 806 3/3).
44   LCRO, Waterloo Conservative Association, Women's Central Committee, Minute Book 1928–1953, 7 December 1928 (DDX 806 2/2).

who loved the Constitution to unite against the 'Socialist Labour' Party's attempts 'to create civil strife in the Country' and 'to render the attacks upon the life of the community and the attempts at the introduction of the Bolshevik methods of government into this country futile.'[45] Their MP, Lord Stanley, pledged himself 'to resist to the utmost the Socialist theories which far from bringing increased liberty to the workers will bind them to complete servitude to the state.'[46] It was some years before this near hysterical reaction to Labour subsided. In 1926, following the General Strike and the miners' lock-out, which, Stanley noted with satisfaction, had been 'crushed' by the Conservative government, the Women's Conservative Association in his constituency joined him in congratulating Baldwin on his 'strong measures'. 'If this Socialist Revolutionary plot had succeeded, it must, undoubtedly, have meant the end of Constitutional Government in this Country. The long drawn out Coal dispute fomented by the extremists of the Labour Party and financed to a great extent by foreign Bolshevist Agencies … came to an ignoble end.'[47] If the hand of Conservative Central Office is detectable in much of these local missives there is no doubt that the message was firmly endorsed by sitting members, and eagerly consumed by constituents. William Brass, another old Etonian/Cambridge University serving officer in the 1914–1918 war was an especially aggressive exponent of anti-socialism. In 1923, in a three-cornered contest in Clitheroe only shortly after the seat had been held by Labour, he denounced that party as being 'unfit to rule'.[48] The 'red menace' was a favourite theme in his speeches. He was strongly critical of the Labour front bench for not

45   LCRO, Fylde Women's Constitutional Association, Minute Book 1919–1952, Annual
     Report 31 December 1920 (DDX 1202 1/2).
46   LCRO, Fylde Election Material, Lord Stanley address to electors, November 1923
     (DDX 1202 1/6).
47   LCRO, Fylde Women's Constitutional Association, Annual Report, 31 December
     1926 (DDX 1202 1/2); Stanley described the General Strike in his 1929 election cam-
     paign, when he was opposed for the first time by a Labour candidate, as 'a Socialist
     conspiracy to destroy democratic government', Election Material 1906–1951 (DDX
     1202 1/6).
48   *Burnley Express*, 21 November 1923. See also *Clitheroe Advertiser and Times*, 3
     November 1922.

standing up to its left wingers and the 'Glasgow faction', and at the time of the legislation that overturned the 1913 Trade Union Act the local party followed his lead noting that 'the events of the past year proved that the Trade Unions are controlled by extremists, and that every endeavour is being made by the Socialists ... to capture the Co-operative Societies for the purpose of exploitation.'[49] When, however, the question was raised of breaking off relations with the USSR (as some wanted) Brass advised caution, for fear that trade might be jeopardised to Great Britain's detriment.[50] In this he touched a sentiment that was embedded in the heart of many Conservatives and which, in the 1930s, became the party's guiding principle. It was presciently summed up by the Clitheroe party chairman when, in 1921, he had deplored the activities of the labour movement in the disputes of that year and called for a government based on the two non-socialist parties to keep labour costs down and end the restrictive practices that were, it was claimed, driving business abroad.[51]

IV

The Conservative experience in Bolton provides an interesting contrast.[52] Bolton possessed a strong labour movement, and this demanded that Conservatives maintain a degree of working class support. In this they

49   LCRO, Clitheroe Conservative and Unionist Association, Minute Book 1921–1943, Annual Report 1927 (DDX 800); *Clitheroe Advertiser and Times*, 18 March 1927.
50   Ibid.
51   LCRO, Clitheroe Conservative and Unionist Association, Minute Book 1909–1921, 16 November 1921 (DDX 800).
52   See Trevor Griffiths, *The Lancashire Working Classes c. 1880–1930* (Oxford: The Clarendon Press, 2001), esp. ch. 8. A strike in the local iron trade in 1887 had been an important factor in prompting labour representation in municipal politics. Robert Tootill of the Bolton Trades Council was an early advocate of an independent labour stance. (Jeffrey Hill, 'Working Class Politics in Lancashire, 1885–1906: A Regional

met with some success for, as Trevor Griffiths has shown, Labour's performance, especially in municipal politics, was less impressive than might have been expected in this industrial town.[53] Two aspects of Conservative politics might partly explain this. One was the attempt to recruit members of trade unions. Labour's independence in Bolton had in part been compromised before the war by the electoral alliance in both parliamentary and local politics with the Liberals, which carried on into the immediate post-war period. As in other areas of Lancashire there was sufficient sensitivity among Tory trade unionists about their organisation's money going into a political fund to support rivals to the Conservatives. Thus, the Trade Union Act of 1913, with its 'contracting out' provision, became a hotly contested issue, with many trade unionists calling for a change in the law.[54] The Central Labour Committee (CLC) of Bolton Conservative Association acted as a rallying point for this cause, which by the mid-1920s was augmented by dissatisfaction of a more general nature. The action of the TUC in supporting the miners by calling a General Strike in 1926 was roundly condemned by Tory trade unionists, who objected that members had not been balloted on the decision and demanded new legislation that would require a two thirds majority of members before a strike could be called. Further anger was provoked over the questions of the eight-hour day – which, the CLC claimed, should be made 'legal but optional' – and a subsidy to the mining industry.[55] In a similar vein a good deal of passion was aroused over the Co-operative movement's links with the Labour Party. Campaigns were organised to elect Conservative working men to the executive of the local Co-operative Society in an attempt to prevent its funds being voted for political (ie Labour) purposes.[56]

Study in the Origins of the Labour Party', unpublished PhD thesis, Keele University, 1969, 191–5.)

53   Griffiths, *Lancashire Working Classes*, 294–319.
54   This was achieved with the Trade Union Act of 1927 which instituted 'contracting in'.
55   Bolton Archives and Library Service (hereafter BALS), Central Labour Committee, Minute Book 1920–1928, 18 May 1920, 22 January 1923, 10 June 1926 (FDC 1/2/1).
56   Ibid., 13 July 1920.

Equally important in engrossing Conservative support and loyalty in the district was the Party's success among women voters. In many ways the Bolton Conservative Women's Association was the most vigorous element in the local party, if not in the town as a whole. Like most such bodies it was 'women only', but mightily impressive in the energy it expended and in what it achieved. Formed in 1919, by the early 1920s the Women's Association had established committees in 19 of the town's wards, a position from which it never retreated and often advanced in the interwar years. Activities had initially formed around low-level electoral tasks such as addressing envelopes, distributing literature and canvassing – 'our chief usefulness ... lies in our electoral work' was the modest admission of the 1921 annual report – but even at this stage more ambitious schemes were in train.[57] A keen interest was displayed in educational work and in particular the services of the Party's Philip Stott college, with the result that public speaking was opened up to women, with competitions and prizes awarded for outstanding ward activity. The Women's Unionist Organisation newspaper *Home and Politics* (later *Home and Empire*) was distributed with sales reported in 1926 by the ladies of West Ward as being 140 a month. Among the constant round of political schools, garden parties, teas, dances, whist drives, concerts and (for male guests) 'smoking' evenings, was an annual summer outing that revealed considerable logistical skill; in 1931, for example, 400 ladies were transported for the day to Blackpool, while similar trips to Southport, Belle Vue, and the Wirral, were all part of the annual itineraries. Many of these activities had an essentially fund-raising purpose, but they also created a sense of female sociability that helped to create a feeling that Bolton Toryism was not simply a vote chasing machine but, in some sense, a movement of like-minded women, indeed an imperial sisterhood: 'We are proud to belong to the Womanhood of a great Empire – let us go forward.'[58]

57   BALS, Bolton Women's Conservative Association (BCWA), Scrapbook and Copies of Annual Reports 1920–1947, Annual Report 1920 (FDC 1/3/9).
58   *Ibid.*, Annual Reports of 1920, 21, 22, 26, 29, 31.

V

How far forward women were able to go, however, remained limited. Only a few achieved even local influence. The career of Florence Rollo of Waterloo is an exception. By the time of her death in 1964 at the age of 84 Miss Rollo commanded great respect in the locality as the leading female Conservative grandee. She had been Mayor of Crosby in 1949–1950, and for many years previously a principal figure in the formation of the Conservative women's organisation in the Waterloo constituency. A such she was deeply involved in the grassroots political changes that largely explain the survival and subsequent prospering of the Conservative Party in the years following the Great War. Her career was entirely conducted in a very middle-class environment. The constituency of Waterloo had been created in the redistribution of 1917–1918 largely out of the former middle-class county division of Southport, and though adjoining the more working-class seat of Bootle Waterloo contained little of the militant religious energies that characterised inner Liverpool. Rollo served as a JP from 1933 but only in 1935, at the relatively late age of 56, did she gain political office, when she was elected to the Waterloo with Seaforth Urban District Council. By this time she had built up a considerable network of connections in local society. As befitted the eldest child of an influential family in the shipping business she had been nurtured in a female version of the upper middle-class Tory tradition. She spent much of her twenties studying music and painting, first at the Royal Academy and later in Paris and Rome. From her early years, though, she had become associated with numerous civic voluntary organisations in the Liverpool area, starting as a teenager with the Silver Thimble League, a local charity. During the 1914–1918 war Rollo worked with service personnel and POWs, and in the Second World War took a leading part in the organisation of the Women's Voluntary Service and the Soldiers, Sailors and Air Force Association. She became the first woman president of the Liverpool Literary and Philosophical Society, a governor of Merchant Taylors School in Crosby, as well as several other local schools, and over a long period was closely involved with societies such as Blundellsands Amateur Dramatics, the Soroptimists, and the Crosby Caledonian Society. Among the local groups represented at her funeral in 1964 were the Waterloo Excelsior Women's Bowling Club, the West Lancashire Territorial and Auxiliary Forces, the British Legion, the Red Cross, and the National Society for the Prevention of Cruelty to Children (to which she had been especially committed), in addition to the Conservative Association itself.[59] Reflecting in 1955 on her years of local service Florence Rollo observed: 'It has always been a pleasure to help the Conservatives. My sister and I were members of the Primrose League. We were brought up in the faith, and have never erred from the straight and narrow path. Of course, our people were Conservatives.'[60]

VI

The case studies that form the bulk of this chapter have employed constituency records to a great extent. They are, of course, not always very revealing of the day-to-day workings of constituency associations. Nonetheless, they are not without some value in essaying an answer to one major question: can we speak of a 'new' Toryism in this period?

The outstanding innovation of the 1920s is without doubt the entry of women into the Party's activities. Florence Rollo's progress is, to be sure, untypical, but even so the notion of a 'feminisation' of politics is worthy of consideration. If only in terms of the numbers involved and the energies expended it seems a valid notion. In Burnley, for example, it was claimed in 1924 that female Tory membership exceeded the combined total of men and boys by six to one.[61] What is inescapable in the archival material

---

59   *Crosby Herald*, 24 January 1964, 11 March 1999.
60   *Ibid.* 16 February 1955.
61   Derby Papers, (17) 17/5, Burnley Conservative and Unionist Association, Annual Report, 1925. (Liverpool Record Office.) The numbers recorded were men 29, juniors 306, women 2000.

consulted is the fact that women generated a great deal of the dynamism of party organisation, pitching into the basic work that was essential in keeping party activity buoyant. No political party can function without this input. Of course, women members usually found themselves consigned to a separate and subordinate category. There were, as David Jarvis has shown, various types of Tory female, and the shadow of the vacuous and subordinate 'Betty' of party propaganda seemed all too frequently to darken the perception of women's status.[62] But even more elevated women members could be marginalised. This is amply illustrated in the response to the time and effort invested in establishing a cadre of trained women organisers across the North West. In spite of all this the women were told they could not join the male agents' association[63]

This ambivalence about women co-existed with the survival of older sectarian and gender mentalities. Male-Anglicanism was never more evident than in Liverpool, an exceptional though sizeable (with 11 parliamentary seats) island of 'old' Toryism. Salvidge's Liverpool Working Men's Association had long ploughed an independent furrow, refusing to kowtow to national policies deemed injurious to local interests.[64] With his death in 1928 the distinctive coloration of Liverpool politics began to pale, though by comparison with other areas much of the pre-War political scene remained intact into the 1930s, and to some extent beyond. Labour did not control the city's council chamber until 1955.[65]

62　This was illustrated in the dismay expressed by the women organisers that their male counterparts rejected them as members of the (male) Agents' Association. (CPA, ACUWO, 13 September 1932.) See also McCrillis, *British Conservative Party*, p. 81; David Jarvis, 'Mrs Maggs and Betty: The Conservative Appeal to Women Voters in the 1930s', *Twentieth Century British History*, 5, 2 (1994), 129–52.

63　Conservative Party Archive, Bodleian Library, Oxford, Association of Conservative and Unionist Women's Organisers: Lancashire and Cheshire Minute Books (ACUWO), 1926–1936, (ARE 3/11/9), 16 February, 21 April 1926; 17 April 1928; 14 October 1930; 17 April 1931. Also Women's Advisory Committee (ARE 3/11/1), Annual Reports, 1933–1934. Maguire, *Conservative Women*, 76–7.

64　Salvidge, *Salvidge of Liverpool*, 205–21; *Morning Post*, 16 November 1921.

65　Clarke, *Lancashire and the New Liberalism*, 404: Waller, *Democracy and Sectarianism*, ch. 16; Belchem, *Liverpool 800*, 325–44; 448–57. Sam Davies has sought to moderate

Other entrenched attitudes could be difficult to shake off. The persistence of a 'cakes and ale' mentality was evident in the resistance to regional initiatives aimed at engaging Lancashire's many Conservative Clubs in more serious political activity. In the dozen or so years before the outbreak of war in 1939 there was a determined, though largely unsuccessful, effort by the Clubs Advisory Committee to turn Conservative clubs away from their preferred function as male drinking establishments towards a more serious form of political activity. Rishton Conservative Working Men's Club, which won the Committee's banner for its general efficiency in 1934, was held up as a paragon. It ran classes and advice sessions on old age pensions, unemployment insurance, health matters, and performing rights. But elsewhere it was different. In some places it might even be doubted whether sympathy for the Conservative cause was a requirement for club membership. It was noted in 1935 that some clubs were admitting members 'whose political views were in doubt'.[66] The comment seems to hint at a weary resignation with male foibles.

Sociability sometimes appeared in a fresher form in relation to younger men. In Lancashire and Cheshire the official Conservative youth organisation, the Junior Imperial League (JIL), was represented by a semi-autonomous body known as the Lancashire and Cheshire Federation of Junior Unionist Associations (the 'Junior Unionists'). Unlike the JIL, which remained a male-only body well into the 1920s, the Junior Unionists had

———

the traditional explanation of sectarianism as the cause of Tory strength in Liverpool by emphasising the adverse effects of the local electoral system on Labour votes; he shows that the difference in council seats between Labour and Conservative distorted the differential between the two parties in terms of votes. Sam Davies, *Liverpool Labour: Social and Political Influences on the Development of the Labour Party in Liverpool, 1900–1939* (Keele: Keele University Press, 1996), 87–95.

66   Clubs Advisory Committee, Minutes 1927–1938 (ARE 3/17/1), 1 June 1935; also 19 November 1927, 17 March, 20 October, 17 November, 15 December 1928, 21 June 1930. (Conservative Party Archive (CPA), Bodleian Library, Oxford.) At a meeting at Burnley Conservative Club in 1926 Lord Derby had spoken to a member who said he would 'rather live in Russia'. Derby noted in a letter to the local agent: '... you might find out [his name] as he might be rather a dangerous man to have in the Club.' Derby Papers 920 DER (17), 17/4, Derby to G.W. Sherstone, 20 October 1926 (Liverpool Record Office).

since 1915 allowed its branches to enrol women members, or to form separate female branches.[67] The Junior Unionists were very active in promoting various sporting and public speaking competitions. By the late 1920s there were 205 branches in the North West, with an estimated membership of some 12,000, among which the newspapers *The Imp* and *Torchbearer* circulated copiously, often with a special North West supplement.[68] An indication of the extent of junior activity is provided in a vigorous recruitment campaign begun in 1933 – employing posters, leaflets, window cards, decorated lorries, newspapers, meetings, lantern lectures, sandwich boards and dances – aimed at extending membership by another 5,000.[69] As a prime example Bolton Junior Unionists, formed in 1908, had by the early 1920s some 800 members, with many attending courses on political economy and local history at the party's training centre in Northamptonshire.

It may well be that many such young Tories were also potential recruits for another, and rather more select, branch of the movement: the Freemasons. Bearing in mind the semi-secret nature of the organisation it is not surprising that documentary evidence of Masonic activity is hard to come by. A few glimpses, little more, are provided in the papers of J.R. Almond, the Conservative agent for Fylde for some thirty years from the early 1920s. Included among the extensive information on Almond's work in political management are miscellaneous references to the Stanley of Preston Masonic Lodge, to which Almond was initiated in December 1926. It seems from fragments of information about others proposed for membership that Almond was a not untypical middle class entrant to the Masons at this time. He had started his political life at the age of 14 as a lowly clerk in the Conservative agent's office in Blackpool before becoming

---

67   CPA, Lancashire and Cheshire Federation of Junior Unionist Associations (LCFJUA), General Purposes Committee Minutes, 1912–1940 (ARE 3/16/2), 20 March 1915. Women were accepted as branch members with the same standing as men in 1925 (GPC Minutes, 6 March 1925).

68   CPA, LCFJUA, Executive Committee Minutes 1926–1939 (ARE 3/16/5), 12 November 1927, 16 January 1929, 17 February 1939.

69   CPA, LCFJUA, General Purposes Committee Minutes 1912–1940 (ARE 3/16/2), 22 March 1934; also 19 December 1932, 1 September 1933.

assistant agent for Rugby and then full agent at Consett, County Durham. His application for the Fylde post was supported by several leading figures in the Party, and as agent he worked closely with the Stanley family. From them he profited from various personal financial rewards, as well as gaining in status by association with county society. Other men working their way up the professional career ladder figure in the records of the Lodge as having been initiated in the 1920s: a county officer in the Sheriff's department, an engineer, an accountant, a clerk in holy orders, a cinema proprietor, a solicitor, a haulage contractor, an architect, a civil servant, and a chief superintendent in the Lancashire police force. The Stanley influence in the Lodge, as in the Fylde constituency itself, was very strong. The 17th Earl of Derby had been Worshipful Master at the beginning of the century, as had other Stanleys at various times before and after the Great War. The 17th Earl's assiduous attention to political matters in all the areas of Lancashire to which his authority and influence as a landlord extended, the Preston and Fylde area being especially prominent in this respect, make it hard to imagine the Preston Lodge admitting men who were not of the 'right sort'. Invitations to meetings at which 'dark morning dress … [and] white gloves will be worn' marked a person out a having entered the Stanley orbit.[70] For their part the aspiring members no doubt imagined that membership would be a powerful boost to their social and material ambitions.

These gendered activities certainly fused with class identity. In most of the areas under scrutiny there is a marked middle-class content to Toryism. And if Tory members were not always of the middle class themselves (as, perhaps, was the case with the Bolton women) they might at least be anti-Labour. Hostility to Labour and socialism in the 1920s was the outward manifestation of a *grande peur* that affected property owners large and small at this time. It provided a rallying cry to join the Conservatives. Women were important recruiting agents in this. All those garden parties and whist drives were no mere sideshows, but the means of forging bonds that brought like-minded people together. And which, furthermore, created

---

70   LCRO, J.R. Almond Papers (DDX 1202 4/3), Masonic Lodge Records (c. 1926–1930).

the links with extensive civic and voluntary organisations that were such a feature of British democracy in the interwar years.[71]

In these senses 'new' Toryism seems to have less of the explicit political content that had marked out New Liberalism in the Edwardian period. There is little in Tory politics to suggest, for instance, that the entry of new female members into the Party provoked any radical scrutiny of traditional gender relations.[72] In the periods between elections – which is to say, most of the time – the absence of any vibrant political discourse (the pervasive anti-socialism apart) is the striking feature of constituency activity. Social gatherings of various kinds made up much of the party's day-to-day business. A sociability that followed on from and embellished the pre-War work of the Primrose League is the keynote of 'new' Toryism. It was largely upon this grass roots basis that the Conservative Party forged one of its longest periods of electoral hegemony in the twentieth century.

71 McKibbin, *Parties and People*, 93–5; 'Class and Conventional Wisdom', 284; *Classes and Cultures*, 529–31; Helen McCarthy, 'Parties, Voluntary Associations, and Democratic Politics in Interwar Britain', *Historical Journal*, 50, 04 (December 2007), 891–912; 'Associational Voluntarism in interwar Britain', in M. Hilton and J. Mackay eds, *The Ages of Voluntarism: How We Got to the Big Society* (Oxford: The British Academy, 2011), 47–68; *The British People and the League of Nations: Democracy, Citizenship and Internationalism, c. 1918–1945* (Manchester: Manchester University Press, 2011).

72 McCrillis claims that Conservative women 'embraced motherhood, domesticity and womanliness' (*British Conservative Party*, 81). See also Bates, 'The Conservative Party in the Constituencies', ch. 7.

PART II

Cricket and the Imperial Connection: Overseas Players in Lancashire in the Interwar Years

The global migration of sports talent in first-class cricket is now commonplace. Since the late 1960s England, with the most developed form of professional cricket, has become a magnet for star players from the world's major cricket-playing countries. With the exception until recently of Yorkshire all the English county clubs have felt it necessary to include one or more such stars in their teams.[1] This process, however, has not been without its critics. The importation of overseas sports talent has frequently been held responsible for the apparent decline of English test teams in international competition, particularly in the 1980s.[2] Indeed, the problems of cricket have often become subsumed in the wider discourse of 'decline' that has been a characteristic feature of British national life in recent years. But what is often overlooked when such ideas are voiced is the fact that players from overseas – from various parts of the Commonwealth and, before that, the Empire – have long been a feature of the game in England. For example, a glance through the *Wisden Cricketers' Almanack* for the 1953 season reveals a total of 17 Commonwealth players employed by nine of the 17 county clubs, at least 10 of them occupying leading batting or bowling places.[3] Not, admittedly, as great a number as were to figure in more recent seasons but a significant proportion none the less.

---

1   K.A.P. Sandiford, 'The Professionalization of Modern Cricket', *British Journal of Sport History*, 2, 3 (1985), 270–89.

2   *The Guardian*, 8 and 15 February 1986.

3   N. Preston ed, *Wisden Cricketers' Almanack* (London: Sporting Handbooks, 1954), 325, 403, 423, 441, 480, 499, 540, 582, 602.

This imperial connection in English cricket has a long, if not always very conspicuous, history. It started with the migratory activities of W.E. Midwinter, who played for both England and Australia in the 1870s and 1880s.[4] It continued through W.L. Murdoch, A.E. Trott, Alan Marshall and E.A. McDonald – all Australians who exercised a powerful influence in county cricket before and just after the First World War. Following the Second World War the connection expanded to include such leading players as George Tribe, Colin McCool, Bruce Dooland and the West Indian Roy Marshall, as well as a range of less famous names. It reached its fullest extent in the period after the 'Packer revolution' of the 1970s, when county clubs were seeking to maximise income from television coverage of cricket and were trusting in overseas players to provide the necessary star quality to ensure the game's appeal. By the late 1970s, it has been suggested, the game had become 'unashamedly commercialised'.[5]

But alongside this developing network in county cricket there was another, and in some ways more significant, imperial connection in the English game. Until the influx of the 1970s and 1980s the most concentrated presence of overseas players in English cricket was to be found, not in county cricket, but in the league cricket of the north, in particular that of Lancashire.

The role of league clubs in recruiting Empire and Commonwealth cricketers was probably first brought to the attention of a wide public in 1952. It was then that the Lancashire League club Nelson signed the Australian fast bowler Ray Lindwall, one of the best-known players in world cricket at that time, to play for them for one season.[6] Far from being an isolated event, the signing of Lindwall was part of a continuing process that had started in the northern leagues back in the inter-war period. At that time there had developed a steady migration of star players, chiefly from Australia and the Caribbean. This process is an interesting one for its

4   Eric Midwinter, *W.G. Grace: His Life and Times* (London: George Allen and Unwin, 1981).
5   Sandiford, 'Professionalization', 276.
6   Ray Lindwall, *Flying Stumps* (London: Stanley Paul, 1954), 101–2.

consequences were not limited to the field of play. The players themselves, their clubs, the type of cricket played in the leagues and the communities whose champions the overseas stars became, all were affected in a variety of ways by the migration.

In this part of the country cricket had become one of the major pastimes of the inhabitants of the industrial towns and villages by the end of the nineteenth century. Saturday afternoon leagues, staging competitive and partisan matches, were firmly installed in the cultural life of these communities. 'Cricket in this district', reported an Australian observer of Nelson in the early 1920s, 'is a live force.'[7] In most places a hierarchy of skill had developed. In the lowest stratum was the rough-and-ready cricket of church, Sunday school or even street teams often playing on ill-prepared pitches, sometimes of concrete or cinders.[8] At the highest level of the local cricketing world was the team which usually bore the community's name, and with that a good deal of the pride and hopes of the local population. At this level the ethos of professionalism was strong, no doubt as a consequence of the remarkable playing success of the professional clubs of the Football League, several of which were to be found in the north-west of England. Some cricket clubs in the late nineteenth century were employing as many as three 'pros' to assist with coaching, ground maintenance and, of course, playing.[9] In 1900 the premier league in the region – the Lancashire League, a group of 14 clubs situated in the north east of the county – agreed to restrict the number of professionals to one per club, chiefly in order to control the spread of professionalism and to encourage amateur talent.[10] By the time of the First World War it had become customary for the club professional in the Lancashire League sides to be a figure of some standing

7   *Sydney Daily Telegraph*, 9 July 1921.
8   Jack Williams, 'Recreational Cricket in the Bolton Area Between the Wars' in Holt, R. ed, *Sport and the Working Class in Modern Britain* (Manchester: Manchester University Press), 101–20.
9   Jeffrey Hill, 'The Development of Professionalism in English League Cricket, c. 1900–1940' in Mangan J.A. and R.B. Small, *Sport, Culture, Society: International Sociological and Historical Perspectives* (London: Spon, 1986), 109–16.
10 W. Barlow, *Athletic News*, 10 April 1922.

nationally in the cricket world, usually as a result of having played county cricket. Willis Cuttell, who played several seasons for Nelson, is a good example. Cuttell had served both Lancashire and Yorkshire with distinction and even played for England on a couple of occasions in the 1890s, but became disillusioned with county cricket following a disappointing benefit from Lancashire in 1906.[11]

Very occasionally overseas players would make an appearance in the leagues, though always through the same channel of county cricket. The South African C.B. Llewellyn played just before the war, and again in the 1920s, though he was in effect an English county professional by virtue of a dozen seasons with Hampshire from the turn of the century. Similarly the Australian bowler Alex Kermode played in the League after a spell with Lancashire.[12] But at this time the most celebrated, successful and notorious of all the professionals in league cricket, first in Lancashire and then in north Staffordshire, was undoubtedly the Englishman S.F. Barnes, most of whose 27 test match appearances occurred while he was engaged as a league professional.[13]

This pattern changed in the Lancashire League in the 1920s with the gradual acquisition of an overseas cadre of professionals. The change was triggered by Nelson Cricket Club, who signed the Australian fast-bowling star E.A. 'Ted' McDonald for the 1922 season.[14] McDonald stayed at Nelson for three seasons, before becoming the subject of an early cricket 'transfer deal' between Nelson and the Lancashire county club. He was replaced by another Empire player, the South African J.M. Blanckenberg, an experienced international who, like McDonald, had recently appeared with success in test matches in England. But at this time few other clubs in the Lancashire League saw reason to depart from their traditional practice of hiring English players. Indeed, strong doubts about both the financial and

11   Willis Cuttell, interview in *Nelson Leader*, 23 May 1924.
12   *Cricket*, 2 August 1913.
13   Leslie Duckworth, *S.F. Barnes – Master Bowler* (London: The Cricketer/Hutchinson, 1967).
14   Jeffrey Hill, 'League Cricket in the North and Midlands' in Holt, *Sport and the Working Class*, 121–41.

sporting validity of Nelson's strategy were raised in the local and national press.

Apart from the immense financial costs involved in hiring overseas stars – McDonald cost Nelson almost twice the wages paid to their previous professionals[15] – one of the chief complaints registered against the practice was that it would denude the colonies of scarce sporting talent. League clubs were accused of exploiting the rest of the world as a nursery for the development of star players whilst at the same time preventing local players from maturing. Criticisms of this kind continued well into the 1930s, even though by this time the practice being objected to was very firmly entrenched.[16] What, as much as anything, served to dispel many of these doubts and to gain more general acceptance for the idea of overseas players was the remarkable success of Nelson's third such professional, the Trinidadian Learie Constantine. Under Constantine's influence Nelson won the Lancashire League championship seven times and came second twice in the years from 1929 to 1937. It was largely in order to be in a position to compete on reasonably equal terms against this dynamic cricketer that other league clubs were drawn into a scramble to sign star players. With the contemporary English big names usually tied to the county and test circuit the attention of league committees was turned firmly in an overseas direction. During the 1930s a clutch of Empire cricketers was drafted into the Lancashire League: from Australia Arthur Richardson, Bill Hunt, Alan Fairfax, Syd Hird and, after retiring from county cricket, Ted McDonald once more; from New Zealand Bill Merritt, who later played in the Birmingham League; from India Amar Singh and Lala Amarnath: and from the Caribbean Manny Martindale, George Headley, Ellis Achong, Edwin St Hill and Constantine himself. There continued to be a sprinkling of well-known English players: Fred Root, for example, who had recently retired from county cricket; Nobby Clarke, the Northants fast bowler, who

15   Nelson Cricket and Bowling Club, *Annual Report and Balance Sheet*, 1920–1924 (Nelson Cricket Club).

16   G.A. Brooking, 'Northern Notes', *The Cricketer Winter Annual* (London: *The Cricketer*, 1921–1922), 124; *The Cricketer*, 19 May, 2 June 1934; *Nelson Leader*, 17 March 1922.

played in the League in the early 1930s following a disagreement with his county, which he later rejoined; and the everlasting Barnes, who continued to play (and to be unplayable) until well into his fifties. But the chief subject of attention was the overseas star.[17]

Underlying the immediate need to compete with Nelson under Constantine there was a deeper reason for the scramble for overseas talent. Unlike club cricket in the south of England, that of the northern leagues had always possessed a strong spectator appeal. Although, of course, the length of a cricket match, and its susceptibility to bad weather, prevented its having football's potential as a mass spectacle, there were nevertheless several occasions on which league cricket matches drew large crowds. Given the passion for cricket in these small communities, there was an inbuilt incentive for clubs to provide an attractive game and to pursue the quest for cups, league titles and the all-conquering professionals who might make what was frequently termed 'big cricket' possible. Club treasurers usually found themselves in an upward financial spiral as they signed the players who would produce success and then sought to recoup their costs through increased gate and membership receipts.

All this is exemplified in Nelson's going after Ted McDonald in 1921. The club had become accustomed to success as one of the League's leading teams before the Great War, but had failed to reproduce this position in the seasons immediately after. Support from both club members and the general public was proving difficult to sustain, and the idea of persuading a leading personality to come and play for Nelson was a compelling one. The club's chairman, T.E. Morgan, freely admitted in an article written some years later that the current professional, George Geary of Leicestershire, was 'a most competent cricketer, but he did not attract the crowds'.[18] The signing of McDonald, who was one of the stars of the all-conquering Australian touring team of 1921, was astutely timed to achieve maximum publicity, and had an instantaneous effect. Membership subscriptions revived, particularly among women; so, subsequently, did gate receipts for both home and

17   *The Cricketer Spring Annual* (London: *The Cricketer*, 1937), 105.
18   T.E. Morgan, interview in *Nelson Leader*, 23 July 1937.

away matches,[19] McDonald's presence had a stimulating effect throughout the League. So that the Nelson secretary could report with a mixture of satisfaction and regret in 1925, when the player left for Old Trafford:

> McDonald's departure is not only a loss to Nelson, but to the whole of the Lancashire League. Every club in the League has benefitted [sic] as a result of our enterprise in signing McDonald, and he brought new interest and enthusiasm into the League when there was a tendency for it to be weakening.[20]

In spite of all this, however, Nelson did not win the Lancashire League with McDonald, nor with his successor, which explains the club's determination to secure Constantine in 1929. The decision was amply rewarded.

As for the professionals themselves, the attractions of employment in the leagues were strong. In no part of the Empire was professional cricket strongly established and it was impossible even for players of high repute to earn their living by cricket alone. Don Bradman himself needed a patron, which explains his move from New South Wales to South Australia in 1935. Whether or not he was tempted to accept a reportedly generous offer from Accrington in 1934[21] is difficult to assess, but if even Bradman felt the lure of the Lancashire League it is hardly surprising that others succumbed. In Australia cricketers were technically amateurs and unless very famous were unlikely to make much money from the game. Players' attempts to secure a better deal had failed. As recently as 1912 the Board of Control in Australian cricket successfully rebuffed an attempt by leading players to control the profits from lucrative tours to England. Henceforward their touring fees were to be strictly regulated by the Board in the manner already well established for English touring teams.[22] One of the factors prompting McDonald to sign for Nelson was his inability to command regular earnings in Australia, and this was also the reason for Syd Hird's long association

19   G.A. Brooking, 'Northern Notes', *The Cricketer Annual* (London: *The Cricketer*, 1922–1923), 94–6.
20   E. Ashton, Nelson Cricket and Bowling Club, *Balance Sheet*, 1924 (Nelson CC).
21   Ric Sissons, *The Players: A Social History of the Professional Cricketer* (London: Kingswood Press, 1988), 238.
22   Sissons, *The Players*, 119–20.

with Ramsbottom (and, in fact, his later migration to South Africa). As punishment for his decision to leave Australia, McDonald was subjected to a test-match ban by the Board of Control, although he had doubtless estimated that at the age of 30 his time as an Australian test player was in any event limited. As it worked out, McDonald probably made the correct decision in migrating to England. The move served to extend his playing career and enabled him to make business contacts which secured reasonably comfortable post-playing prospects as a publican in Blackpool, though a road accident brought about his untimely death in 1937.[23]

For cricketers from the West Indies the attractions of league cricket were stronger still. Professional openings in the Caribbean were severely limited for black players, who suffered also the odious discriminations of the colour bar. West Indies cricket was rigidly stratified on both colour and class lines in all the islands, but especially in Barbados. It was impossible for black people (and some whites) to join the elite clubs – Queen's Park in Trinidad, Georgetown in British Guyana or Wanderers in Barbados. Most of the black cricketers who represented the islands in inter-colonial matches were drawn from clubs like Shannon (Constantine's club) in Trinidad or the rather higher-status Spartan or Empire clubs in Barbados, which drew socially from the black western educated elite. Employment opportunities were circumscribed too, especially for men who wanted time off to play cricket.[24] Learie Constantine, for example, was favoured by the patronage of H.B.G. Austin, the captain of the West Indies team at the time, in terms of his cricket career. But he was unable to secure similar patronage in his search for regular employment. It was not until an oil company manager (ironically a South African) offered him a job that Constantine was able to get time off to play. His acceptance of the professional's post

23   *The Cricketer*, 31 July 1937.
24   L.N. Constantine, 'Cricket in the Sun' in Constantine, L.N. and D. Batchelor, *The Changing Face of Cricket* (London: Eyre and Spottiswoode), 69–140; C.L.R. James, *Beyond a Boundary* (London: Stanley Paul, 1969 edn); Brian Stoddart, 'Cricket and Colonialism in the English-speaking Caribbean to 1914: Towards a Cultural Analysis' in Mangan J.A. ed, *Pleasure, Profit and Proselytism: British Culture and Sport at Home and Abroad* (London: Frank Cass, 1988), 231–57.

at Nelson in 1929, following a successful tour of England with the West Indies in 1928, has to be seen against this background of racial discrimination in the Caribbean. It was not simply a career move, as in the case of the Australians. It was a revolt, in C.L.R. James' memorable phrase, against 'the revolting contrast between his first-class status as a cricketer, and his third-class status as a man'[25].

Nevertheless, earnings were an important element in the overseas players' decisions to join the League and it would be misleading to underestimate this factor. Uniquely, Constantine was receiving upwards of £1,000 a season from Nelson as his basic wage in the early 1930s, a greater sum, no doubt, than any paid to contemporary British footballers.[26] McDonald's wages ten years earlier had been around £700 a season. Even relatively modest performers in some of the lesser leagues could earn weekly wages well in excess of those of most working men. In the Durham Senior League, for example, former English county players of no particular distinction were receiving around £5 a week in the 1920s.[27] In addition to the basic wage there were, of course, other sources of income. 'Collections' for outstanding performances (when a collection box would be sent around the ground) could increase the earnings of a good professional significantly. Bill Alley, the Australian who played for Colne in the immediate post-Second World War period estimated that a professional could earn between £30 and £50 from collections in a local derby match.[28] S.G. Barnes, another Australian, who played for Burnley at about the same time, also did very well out of collections, though it was typical of his truculent nature that he complained of having to carry home a heavy bag of copper coins after matches.[29] For truly outstanding, long-serving professionals there might be benefit matches arranged. Constantine was the beneficiary of such an

25 James, *Beyond a Boundary*, 110.
26 Gerald Howat, *Learie Constantine* (London: George Allen and Unwin, 1975), 87.
27 Jeffrey Hill, '"First Class" Cricket and the Leagues: Some Notes on the Development of English Cricket, 1900–1940', *International Journal of the History of Sport*, 4, 1 (1987), 68–81.
28 W.E. Alley, *My Incredible Innings* (London: Pelham Books, 1969), 37.
29 S.G. Barnes, *It Isn't Cricket* (London: William Kimber, 1953), 108–9.

event in 1936, when all the clubs in the League donated money for the staging of the match in recognition of his value throughout the League as a crowd-puller.[30] He took home around £500 from the proceeds of this event. For a skilful performer league cricket could offer handsome rewards. S.F. Barnes, a rational calculator in most things, spent only three seasons in county cricket in the whole of his long career. He had estimated that in the leagues, playing at most on only a couple of occasions each week, the lesser physical demands would allow him to play longer and thus increase his overall earnings.[31] The descriptions of Constantine's lifestyle in Nelson by both C.L.R. James (who knew him well) and Howat make it clear that the league professional could expect substantial material benefits.[32]

In addition to financial privileges, playing cricket in the leagues bestowed a respect, accorded by employers and public alike, that it would have been difficult to find in other walks of life, or even in other forms of sport. In the inter-war period professional sport was a subordinated form of labour. The inferior status of the paid sportsman as worker was no more clearly illustrated than in the notorious retain-and-transfer system of the Football League clubs.[33] Yet in first-class cricket the position of the paid player was, if anything, yet more lowly. It was subtly inscribed through a variety of forms in the very fabric of the game – from matters of pay and discipline to the separation of amateurs from professionals in changing-rooms and hotels, and even in the use of surnames only for professionals on scorecards.

In the leagues, on the other hand, the 'pro' was a far more liberated figure. He was valued for his intrinsic skills on the field, where he was a specific focus of attention for players and spectators alike ('the players in his team instinctively look to him when in difficulty', according to Constantine[34]). And he was respected as a man who somehow carried

30   *Nelson Leader*, 14 May 1937.
31   Duckworth, *Barnes*, 167.
32   James, *Beyond a Boundary*, 127–8; Howat, *Learie Constantine*, 79–80.
33   Tony Mason, *Association Football and English Society, 1863–1915* (Brighton: Harvester, 1981), 111–15.
34   L.N. Constantine, *Cricket and I* (London: Philip Allen, 1933), 139.

the reputation of the local community on his shoulders, much as Stanley Matthews in the 1930s was the embodiment of Stoke-on-Trent.[35] In fact, the identification of the league professional with his adopted community made him a local celebrity in a way that first-class cricketers were probably unable to emulate. Their community – the county – was a far more artificial one than that of the small, tightly knit and sometimes rather isolated industrial towns in which league cricket was played. Famous county and test players like Jack Hobbs were, to be sure, national figures by this time, especially as a result of the growth of advertising,[36] but they were unlikely any longer to have close sporting contacts with a specific community. It was the special relationship that existed between player and town that was so evident in the case of league professionals. It particularly impressed a visitor from New Zealand who attended a match at Nelson in 1937 when the League title was won for yet another time:

> I shall never forget the scene on that famous ground when the last wicket fell. Everyone went mad, hats, sticks and caps were thrown high in the air and 'Connie' (Constantine) was hoisted shoulder high and carried off the field ... His personality is tremendous, wonderful ... to say that he has been a 'godsend' to Nelson is to put it mildly. He has, to all people, both living in and out of Nelson, been Nelson itself.[37]

For black cricketers like Constantine, Headley, Martindale and the others, to receive the adulation of the local white population in this way was a stunning contrast to the prejudice they had experienced in their native land. In spite of the prevailing ideologies of 'white superiority' in British society at this time, there seems to have been remarkably little racial hostility displayed towards these men. Alan Tomlinson has recorded a former Colne player as saying: 'a black chap, it didn't matter ... 'e were an attraction as a cricketer if 'e were a good 'un.'[38]

35   Tony Mason, 'Stanley Matthews' in Holt, *Sport and the Working Class*, 159–78.
36   Sissons, *The Players*, 211–12.
37   *Nelson Leader*, 10 September 1937.
38   Alan Tomlinson, 'Good Times, Bad Times, and the Politics of Leisure: Working-Class Culture in the 1930s in a Small Northern England Working-Class Community' in Gruneau, R.S., *Leisure, Sport and Working-Class Cultures: Theory and Practice*.

Of course it is significant to note that, in contrast to the present-day population patterns of east Lancashire, there was no black immigrant community in the 1930s. When C.L.R. James went to Nelson in 1932 he claimed that, 'apart from someone who went around collecting refuse in an old pushcart, Learie and I were the only coloured men in Nelson.'[39] Such ethnic hostility as had existed in east Lancashire was directed at the Irish, though this had moderated considerably since the nineteenth century, and in any case had never been as marked in the small Pennine towns as in larger industrial centres of mid – and west Lancashire, particularly Liverpool.[40] On one occasion Constantine admitted that he had been the victim of some 'shots' (snubs) because of his colour,[41] but even after leaving the Nelson club to play for Rochdale in 1938 he continued to live in the town, and did so until 1949. The environment was obviously congenial. There was, it is true, a certain degree of benevolent racial patronising to be endured, of a kind that would be frowned upon in a later age, but nothing of the outright discrimination encountered by Constantine in London during the war, when the Imperial Hotel cut short his stay there in an attempt to appease the sensibilities of white American guests.[42]

Ironically, the most prejudiced attitudes seem to have been present in professional cricket circles. In the mid-1930s, when it was being rumoured that Constantine might join the Lancashire county club (as McDonald had done before him) the idea was seemingly not warmly received by the county players. Len Hopwood, a Lancashire professional of the time, later recalled:

> In those days, the thought of a coloured chap playing for Lancashire was ludicrous. We Lancastrians were clannish in those less enlightened days. We wanted none of Constantine ... We would refuse to play. In all fairness I must say we had nothing against Learie Constantine personally. He was, in fact, very popular with us. There

---

Working Papers in the Sociological Study of Sports and Leisure Studies (Kingston, Ontario: Queen's University, 1984), 78.

39   James, *Beyond a Boundary*, 127.
40   Colin Holmes, *John Bull's Island: Immigration and British Society 1871–1971* (London: Macmillan, 1988), 59–60.
41   *Nelson Leader*, 27 August 1937.
42   Holmes, *John Bull's Island*, 202–3.

was no personal vendetta. But the thought of a black man taking the place of a white man in our side was anathema. It was as simple as that.[43]

This, it is worth noting, was at a time when one of the leading boxers in the country was prevented from competing for the British title because he was a black man.[44]

In complete contrast to this the admirers of league cricket usually prided themselves on their tolerance, even though this sometimes came across in a fashion which smacked of the 'honorary white man': 'Constantine has proved that a man need not necessarily be possessed of white parents to claim the title of gentleman.'[45] 'I could not help but notice, when the League officials presented the Cup to Nelson on the balcony after the match, and made their speeches, what a pleasant change it was to hear Constantine's beautiful English compared to all the Presidents, past and present, with their broad Lancashire accent.'[46] But the sense of pride was justified. As one correspondent to the local press claimed, Constantine, Headley and the others were being given a chance by league clubs that might never have come their way in the counties, on account of their colour.[47] Bearing in mind Hopwood's recollections, this was a fair point.

Does all this have any significance in a broader social context? Sport as an agent of imperial bonding is not to be underestimated, as recent work by both Brian Stoddart and Richard Holt has revealed.[48] Sporting activity probably was an important means through which the idea of Empire was articulated, though imperial influences did not flow in an unproblematic,

43   Brian Bearshaw, *From the Stretford End: The Official History of Lancashire County Cricket Club* (London: Partridge Press, 1990), 271; Len Hopwood, interviewed in *Manchester Evening News*, 9 July 1975.

44   Ellis Cashmore, *Black Sportsmen* (London: Routledge and Kegan Paul, 1982), ch. 2.

45   *Nelson Leader*, 20 August 1937.

46   *Nelson Leader*, 10 September 1937.

47   *Nelson Leader*, 16 September 1938.

48   Richard Holt, *Sport and the British: A Modern History* (Oxford: Oxford University Press, 1990); Brian Stoddart, 'Sport, Cultural Imperialism and Colonial Response in the British Empire: A Framework for Analysis', *Proceedings of Fourth Annual Conference* (British Society of Sport Historians, July 1986), 1–28.

top-downwards fashion from elite to masses. Sport, and Empire, possessed different meanings for different people. The presence of so many Empire cricketers as local sporting champions in industrial Lancashire may well have served as confirmation for local people of a united British Empire. For the players themselves, however, sport was probably seen differently –as a route out of an ordinary life and an opportunity to secure a better future. Ric Sissons' phrase 'upwardly mobile professionals'[49] aptly describes the careers of many overseas players in the leagues. For black cricketers sport meant something more: a chance to assert their worth as men in a way that was never possible in the Caribbean. If (and it seems very likely) there was a link between the success of West Indies cricketers and the development of black nationalism in the Caribbean, then it might be suggested that this process was first launched in the 1930s by the activities of Constantine and his fellow professionals in Lancashire.

As far as the communities themselves are concerned, there is a sense in which the sporting star might be seen as fulfilling, not so much an idea of Empire, as a collective need for local identity. Some of these towns were of relatively recent origin. Nelson, for example, had only been incorporated as a borough in 1890 after a mushroom growth from virtually nothing in the 1860s.[50] Most inhabitants were therefore from one or another variety of immigrant stock, usually from not too far away but still looking for something to give their lives a focus. Sometimes it was the local football team that supplied this.[51] But the communities under discussion here were usually too small to sustain successful teams. Of the towns with clubs in the Lancashire League only Blackburn (East Lancashire CC) and Burnley could point to real soccer success, though not in the 1930s. The Burnley club, for example, was in the second division at this time and unable to hold

---

49   Sissons, *The Players*, 254.
50   Walter Bennett, *The History of Marsden and Nelson* (Nelson: Nelson Corporation, 1957), 175ff.
51   Richard Holt, 'Working-Class Football and the City: The Problem of Continuity', *British Journal of Sports History*, 4 (May 1986), 5–18.

on to its rising star Tommy Lawton in the face of big club competition.[52] And so the cricket club served as one of the chief institutions of cultural identity. Its deeds encapsulated the worth of the community and were the subject of avid attention and speculation. Perhaps more is revealed about the community of Nelson through the local paper's full-page spread of 12 April 1929, heralding with 'testimonials' from leading figures in the cricket world the arrival of Constantine, than in anything else reported in that particular edition.[53] It was as if the whole prestige of the community rested on the shoulders of this new messiah.

Yet the sporting champion also helped to give these small communities a place in a bigger firmament. When Ted McDonald went to Nelson in 1922, the town became for a time the centre of attention in the cricket world; a world which, to all intents and purposes, was the Empire, for cricket was not seriously played outside it. The Empire as an idea was constantly promoted in everyday life; from ubiquitous press reports of speeches which evoked the British Empire as a cricket team playing the game, through the flag-waving celebrations of Empire Day each May, the prominence in political debates of issues such as imperial tariffs and the future of India, and not least to the posters on the walls of the local Co-op proclaiming imperial trade.[54] But cricket did not simply connect these communities to the Empire. It made of them a leading partner in the imperial enterprise, capable of attracting the Empire's foremost sportsmen.

And is it stretching credulity too far if we align this sporting migration with certain other aspects of the region's popular culture? There was in the popular culture of the north a peculiar sense of modernity. League cricket was sometimes accused by the traditionalists of having a 'circus' mentality towards the sport.[55] There was some truth in this. Popularity and novelty were important considerations in the presentation of the game. The

---

52   Tommy Lawton, *Football Is My Business* (London: Sporting Handbooks, 1946), ch. 4.

53   *Nelson Leader*, 12 April 1929.

54   Stephen Constantine, *Buy and Build: The Advertising Posters of the Empire Marketing Board* (London: HMSO, 1986).

55   Fred Root, *A Cricket Pro's Lot* (London: Edward Arnold, 1937), 185.

cultivation of an image of Constantine as a dazzling virtuoso was entirely consistent with the 'star' fixation of that other manifestation of northern pleasure – Blackpool, the favourite holiday destination of many of those people whose other summer pastime was watching league cricket. Tony Bennett, in an intriguing discussion of 'Blackpoolness', has argued that the place represented a self-consciously northern culture, which cocked a snook at metropolitan pretentiousness and constantly refreshed itself with up-to-the-minute American style. To southerners, who rarely visited, it was synonymous with vulgarity. But to the northern working class it was the last word in modern pleasure – beach, ballrooms, theatres, sideshows and 'the lights'.[56]

It is no coincidence that the word most frequently used to describe Constantine was 'electric'. He too was a symbol of this New World modernity, a 'turn' come to thrill the people of the north with eccentric skills, in his case on the sports field rather than recorded music or cinema. Through him, and the other 'pros', the community was not merely on the map – it was there in neon lights. There is more to sporting migration than simply play. It can form an important part of a society's identity.

---

56   Tony Bennett, 'Hegemony, Ideology, Pleasure: Blackpool' in Bennett, T., C. Mercer and J. Wollacott eds, *Popular Culture and Social Relations* (Milton Keynes: Open University Press, 1986), 135–54.

CHAPTER EIGHT

A Hero in the Text: Race, Class and Gender Narratives in the Life of Learie Constantine

The Trinidadian cricketer Learie Constantine started out as a national hero in the diverse and fragmented society of the colonial West Indies in the 1920s. In the 1930s he acquired hero status in Nelson, Lancashire. After the Second World War, when his career as a player had ended, he became a representative figure for an idea of racial harmony and integration that was closely associated with the new Commonwealth and the move towards independence in the colonies. After a brief spell in politics in Trinidad in the 1950s he returned to England in 1962 as his country's High Commissioner, an appointment which served as the prelude to a succession of public honours bestowed on him during the course of the decade. It culminated in the award of a life peerage in 1969, a couple of years before his death.[1] By this time Constantine had, over some forty years, bridged several worlds: colonial and metropolitan, local and national, working class and middle

---

1   Constantine's life is covered in Gerald Howat, *Learie Constantine* (London: George Allen and Unwin, 1975), a study rightly described by Brian Stoddart as an 'excellent biography'. (See Hilary McD. Beckles and Brian Stoddart, *Liberation Cricket: West Indies Cricket Culture* (Manchester: Manchester University Press, 1995), 253, f.n. 21, a book which itself provides many valuable insights into Constantine and his colonial context. The case of Arthur Wharton, the first black sportsman to achieve some fame in English football and cricket, makes an interesting comparison. Wharton, who came from the Gold Coast (Ghana), played in goal for Preston North End and was a professional cricketer in the northern leagues at the turn of the century. He represents the antithesis of Constantine's success. He died in penury after working as a coalminer once his sporting days were over. He was buried in an unmarked grave. See Phil Vasili, *The First Black Footballer: Arthur Wharton 1865–1930: An Absence of Memory* (London: Frank Cass, 1998).

class, black and white. In contrast to most black people of his era, many of them well-loved sportsmen, Constantine's success in a climate of racial prejudice and hostility, seems both exceptional and praiseworthy. How might it be explained?

I

'The movements of Constantine in the field are strange, almost primitive, in their pouncing voracity and unconscious beauty, a dynamic beauty, not one of smooth curves and relaxations.'[2] It was Neville Cardus, a writer ever alert to the mythic dimension of sport, who created of Constantine the 'representative' West Indian cricketer. His superbly athletic, apparently spontaneous play expressed, claimed Cardus, the West Indian temperament:

> When we see Constantine bat, bowl or field we know at once that he is not an English player ... we know that his cuts and drives, his whirling fast balls, his leapings and clutching and dartings in the slips, are racial; we know they are the consequences of impulses born in the blood, heated by sun, and influenced by an environment and a way of life much more natural than ours – impulses not common to the psychology of the over-civilised quarters of the world.[3]

When this was originally written, in the 1930s, Cardus was celebrating Constantine's uninhibited style of cricket, perhaps even wishing that such a life-force could be injected into the English game. But beneath the Laurentian hints of western decadence there was something more prosaic here: a language fashioned from an ideology of race which still passed for 'common sense' in the Britain of the inter-war years. It saw in black people a capacity for spontaneous energy that stemmed from their assumed closeness to nature. Their very underdevelopment – in contrast to the 'over-civilised'

2   Neville Cardus, *Good Days* (London: Rupert Hart-Davis, 1948 edn), 33.
3   Cardus, *Good Days*, 33.

nature of Europeans – meant an absence of artifice, an ability to dispense with reason and science, and a predisposition to capture the joyous 'essence' of humankind. To Cardus, Constantine's play was simply an expression of himself: 'to say that he plays cricket ... is to say that a fish goes swimming'.

Though much of the press reporting of West Indian cricket in this period did not indulge in such image-making, the idea of Constantine as an *enfant sauvage* was nevertheless a popular one that remained with him during the whole of his playing career. The 'thick set rather slow boy' encountered by fellow Trinidadian C.L.R. James aged 11[4] had developed into a loose-limbed athlete who toured England with H.B.G. Austin's team of 1923 and astonished everyone by his speed and brilliance at cover point. Fascination with his predatory presence in the field was established at this time and never waned, from the day 'Cricketer' (Cardus again) watched him at Old Trafford in 1928 and wrote in the *Manchester Guardian* of his animal-like power:

> his action as he hurled the ball at the stumps was thrilling because of its vehemence and poise. Constantine is a graceful cricketer: his aggressiveness – nay ferocity – is expressed in beautiful curves. Strength comes out of his body so easily and swiftly that coarseness is expelled by manhood's own rhythm.[5]

Fielding is the least contrived of cricket's arts, and Constantine was one of the first cricketers to raise the art of fielding to a high plane. Its unrestrained physicality fitted perfectly the idea of the uninhibited negro. Throughout his life it was something always associated with him. Though he could bat and bowl in whirlwind fashion when needed (just as he could also play a restrained calculating game) the popular memory of Constantine was often not one of runs compiled and wickets captured but of arcane moments when a catch was seized or a ball swooped upon to produce an unconsidered run out. The moment is then embellished in memory. Thus an opponent from Colne recalled some thirty years later one such galvanising experience:

4   C.L.R. James, *Beyond a Boundary* (London: Stanley Paul, 1969 edn), 107.
5   Quoted in *Nelson Leader*, 6 July 1928.

Connie was fielding in the gully. I slammed the ball hard and low and expected four runs, but I turned round to find that Connie had caught the ball and put it in his pocket almost as everybody else on the field was looking for it at the boundary. It could not have been more than a few inches off the ground and Connie was only about four yards from the bat end. It was an unbelievable catch.[6]

Constantine's suppleness and speed of movement underlined the idea of the natural rhythm of the black man. John Arlott described him as being 'so joyously fluid and ... acrobatic, that he might have been made of springs and rubber'.[7] He was, indeed, jocularly known as 'electric heels', and 'electric' – with all its connotations of modernity – was the adjective most frequently employed to describe his play. 'There are no bones in his body' wrote Cardus, 'only great charges and flows of energy.'[8] His presence on the cricket field was sufficient in itself to draw the crowds, and during his time at Nelson he so boosted attendances in local matches that in 1935 all the clubs in the league joined together to stage a testimonial match for him.[9] There was no doubting his appeal. As one speaker observed at the dinner in Nelson to mark Constantine's election as a Freeman of the Borough in 1963, he was a 'variety act'.[10]

This idea of Constantine worked on a contemporary perception of the racial difference between black and white. Constantine represented 'otherness', something that defined white European-ness by being categorically not white or European. It further produced an ambivalence of meaning:

6   *Nelson Leader*, 26 April 1963. A letter in the BBC Archive written in 1950 by an anonymous well-wisher from Southampton praises Constantine on a recent broadcast. The writer adds: 'It was watching you in the field that amazed me. I have never seen anything quite like it.' (BBC Written Archives Centre (hereafter BBC Arch.), Caversham Park, Reading; Constantine File, Talks 1, 30 June 1950.) Sir Leonard Hutton, in an obituary for Constantine, recalled: '[H]e was by far the best [fielder] I had seen ... He ran as though his feet did not touch the ground'. *Observer*, 3 July 1971.
7   Benny Green ed., *The Wisden Book of Cricketers' Lives* (London: MacDonald Queen Anne Press, 1986), 178.
8   Cardus, *Good Days*, 33–4.
9   *Nelson Leader*, 14 May 1937.
10   *Nelson Leader*, 19 April 1963.

Constantine was both a source of wonder, but he was also a member of an inferior race. The qualities the image emphasised were physical ones, those of the senses and youth, rather than rational or 'constructive' ones. They belonged to the same ideology of race that had generated the environmental determinist idea of tropical riches, from which it was inferred that black people were naturally lazy, lacked a work ethic, and were therefore 'underdeveloped'. It was an ideology that continued to inform some aspects of colonial policy, especially in settler colonies, in the early years of the century, and it was responsible for much of the discrimination experienced by black people in Britain.[11] Black sportsmen, boxers in particular, were notable examples. Admired at the height of their athletic powers, they often suffered neglect in later life when unable to reproduce their physical prowess. A sad decline followed, usually more intense than that experienced by white heroes.[12] For their part white, usually working-class, figures were equally dependent on their athletic skill for their fame, and merged back into their communities as 'ordinary' people once their playing days were finished. They were remembered with affection, but this brought them no special material status.[13] Constantine particularly had reason to be aware of the contrast between sporting renown and social degradation. It was intensified by racial inequality, nowhere more than in the colonial Caribbean where he faced, in C.L.R. James's memorable

11   See Colin Holmes, *John Bull's Island: Immigration and British Society, 1871–1971* (Basingstoke: Macmillan, 1988), 152–60; Stuart Hall, 'The Spectacle of the "Other"' in S. Hall ed., *Representation: Cultural Representations and Signifying Practices* (London: Sage Publications, 1997), ch. 4.

12   On other black sportsmen from this era see E. Cashmore, *Black Sportsmen* (London: Routledge and Kegan Paul, 1982), ch. 2.

13   The case of the famous pre-1914 footballer Steve Bloomer is aptly illustrated in a photograph taken in the 1930s at the Derby County football ground. Bloomer is the object of an admiring group of youthful players but, significantly, he is wearing the overalls of the aged workman he had become, employed as a 'jack of all trades' at the club. (Bryon Butler, *The Official History of the Football League*, London: Blitz Editions, 1993 edn), 13.

phrase, 'the revolting contrast between his first-class status as a cricketer and his third-class status as a man.'[14]

The remarkable feature of Constantine's career is that he did not experience the customary decline in fortune. Instead of becoming the victim of a racial image, his race was turned into an advantage which enabled him to move onwards and upwards, into a life beyond sport. To an extent he was fortunate in that significant changes in imperial relationships were taking place at the point when Constantine's cricket career was coming to an end. But to be able to take advantage of this situation, which brought many West Indian workers to Britain during the Second World War, Constantine needed to demonstrate an aptitude and good sense that marked him out as an educated black man who had moved beyond the conventional racial image. There needed to be a different persona through which he could be identified, a white mask over the black skin. A significant contribution to this process of re-invention came from Constantine's time in Nelson.

II

Nelson in Lancashire was, and still is, a smallish town of some 40,000 people. It once specialised in cotton manufacture. Brought into being during the last phase of industrialisation in cotton that centred on northeast Lancashire in the final quarter of the nineteenth century, Nelson became the most specialised of the weaving towns. Some 70 per cent of its male and female labour force were engaged in weaving. But, in spite of its late development, Nelson possessed none of the economic advantages often enjoyed by latecomers. The town's growth was founded upon traditional forms of capitalisation, business organisation, and technology. To be sure, in comparison with the larger weaving centres of Burnley and Blackburn its cloth was of a finer quality and sold in dearer markets at home

14   James, *Beyond a Boundary*, 110.

and overseas. It was thus spared some of the harsher effects of the interwar depression, and its exposure to foreign competition delayed. But it soon followed the rest of the Lancashire cotton trade in succumbing to foreign competition after the Second World War. In many respects therefore the 1920s and 1930s represented the high peak of Nelson's achievement as a town, before the local economy went into decline.[15]

This was the time – a time of optimism fading into uncertainty – when Nelson received Learie Constantine from Trinidad. Two displays of exhilarating cricket, performed during the West Indies tour of England in 1928, had taken him there. Against Northamptonshire Constantine had scored 107 out of 141 runs in only ninety minutes. In a subsequent and more important match against Middlesex at Lord's in June he underlined his all-round abilities by taking six wickets for 11 in an explosive second innings spell of very fast bowling, and scoring 86 and 102. It was during this latter innings, played in an hour, that, as John Arlott later recalled, he struck a ball so hard that it broke Jack Hearne's finger and he was unable to play for the remainder of the season.[16] This performance caught the eye of officials of the Nelson club, whose interest in a star player of this quality was keen, and related to a series of developments in the cricket of the local area that had begun in the late-nineteenth century.

As in many industrial working-class communities sport formed an important part of Nelson's social life. Sports clubs flourished in a town where mills, chapels, pubs and neighbourhoods provided the basis for a rich culture of voluntary association. Being relatively small in population Nelson lacked the resources to sustain a League football club,[17] the usual symbol of civic identity in larger communities, and it was cricket rather than football that proclaimed the town through its sporting achievements.

---

15   On Nelson see: Walter Bennett, *A History of Marsden and Nelson* (Nelson: Nelson Corporation, 1957); Jeffrey Hill, *Nelson: Politics, Economy, Community* (Edinburgh: Keele/Edinburgh University Press, 1997).

16   Green, *Wisden Cricketers' Lives*, 178.

17   For ten years from 1921 Nelson FC competed in the Third (and briefly the Second) Division of the Football League. (See Dave Twydell, *Rejected FC*, vol. 1 (Harefield, Middlesex: Yore Publications, 1988), 289–90.)

Fittingly, though, it was a form of cricket that bore some of the features of commercial football. The Lancashire League, an organization formed in 1891 out of 14 clubs in the district of north-east Lancashire, had cultivated a competitive form of league cricket played during the afternoon and early evening of Saturday. It was attuned to the needs of the local working populations in the towns and villages that made up the League, who left work around midday on Saturday. Local rivalry and keen spectator interest were the main features of matches played in this form. But in addition the cricketing prowess displayed by each club's professional player, usually a man of some national standing engaged as the local champion, contributed greatly to the excitement of the sport. Nelson, as one of the larger clubs in the League, had a history of success in these competitions, and immediately after the First World War had raised the stakes by taking the unprecedented step of employing as its professional the famous Australian player E.A. 'Ted' McDonald. It was a bold move, designed to secure Nelson's pre-eminence in the League, though it was not without its critics. The respected national sporting journal *Athletic News* judged it a risky venture,[18] and even the *Nelson Leader*, whose editor was the Chairman of the Nelson club, noted that 'the spirit of the game is made none the healthier by business transactions of this kind.'[19] It was, however, easy to see why Nelson wanted McDonald. In addition to being an sporting personality of international fame, McDonald was a dangerous yet graceful bowler whose art could be admired for both its aesthetic and its match-winning qualities.[20] Moreover, he was tall and lithe with dark good looks which gave him a film-star appearance. There was a hint of sexual allure about him and news of his signing produced a noteworthy increase in the number of female membership subscriptions at Nelson for

---

18   *Athletic News*, 27 March 1922.
19   *Nelson Leader*, 17 March 1922.
20   Green, *Wisden Cricketers' Lives*, 611; See also Neville Cardus, *The Summer Game: A Cricketer's Journal* (London: Rupert Hart-Davis, 1949), 172–86. 'Whence does McDonald draw his terrible strength and velocity? His run to the wicket is so easy, so silent ... A more beautiful action ... was never seen on a cricket field, or a more inimical.' (183).

the 1922 season.[21] The *Athletic News* had been right, however, to under-line the financial risks involved in signing such players. McDonald, who played for three seasons before moving on to the Lancashire county club, and his white South African successor J.M. Blanckenburg (1925 to 1928) were expensive. McDonald reputedly cost Nelson £700 for each of the three seasons he played.[22] But they were popular, and the gate receipts and increased membership they brought in went some way towards repaying the outlay on them.[23] But it was a precarious strategy. Spectators grew to expect such stars, and the clubs had to seek out professionals of the calibre needed to fulfil spectator expectations. Not all did. In Constantine Nelson saw exactly the kind of magnetic performer who would propel the club and the League farther along the distinctive path that had been embarked upon a few years earlier. Thus, following the match against Middlesex, Constantine was signed as Nelson's professional on a three-year contract to begin in 1929. It was little wonder that the local newspaper hailed him as a 'cricketer with a touch of genius', a 'super-player', and, most important of all, a 'spectator-bringer'.[24]

When he arrived Constantine knew little about Nelson. To a black Roman Catholic from multi-ethnic Trinidad it doubtless seemed a strange environment. There were few Catholics, and no black people. Nelson was a proletarian town with a radical political history and, in its religious life, a strong Nonconformist ethos. Although, as a new town, Nelson's inhabit-ants were in many cases themselves immigrants or the children of immi-grants (mostly from nearby handloom-weaving villages in the Yorkshire Dales) they had little else in common with Constantine. Initially, he was plagued with doubts. In later years he was given to reflecting on this time in a narrative which emphasised, ultimately, the theme of perseverance. The first season was difficult: the cricket was a great success, but socially he felt isolated. He experienced problems of acceptance among some locals

21   *Nelson Leader*, 13 April 1922.
22   Nelson Cricket Club, *Treasurer's Annual Accounts*, 1922–1924 (Nelson CC); *Cricketer Annual* (London: The Cricketer, 1922–1923), 95.
23   Nelson Cricket Club, *Balance Sheet for Season 1924* (Nelson CC).
24   *Nelson Leader*, 13 July 1928.

who were ignorant of the West Indies and who had imbibed white conventional wisdom about black people. Nelson, though generally a tolerant
community, had pockets of right-wing sentiment that fostered hostility to
those who were different. It was later claimed by the pro-Labour *Nelson
Gazette* that Constantine had been treated with scorn by a minority of
'snooty' people on his arrival in Nelson, just as the Labour M.P, Sydney
Silverman, had been the subject of anti-semitic remarks when he first stood
for Parliament for Nelson and Colne in 1935.[25]

Constantine admitted to having received 'shots' [snubs] from people
who objected to his colour.[26] He had thought of breaking his contract
and returning home. He would have done this, though he knew that the
Caribbean could offer him nothing. He was persuaded to see it through
by his wife.[27] Racial hostility, however, stayed with him throughout
his career. When, for example, it was rumoured in the mid-1930s that
Constantine might join the Lancashire club the county professionals
allegedly thought the idea 'ludicrous'. It was felt that Constantine and
other West Indians in the local leagues would never play for the county
'because of their colour'.[28] During the war, in an incident that made the
national press, Constantine was refused lodging at a hotel in London

25 *Nelson Gazette*, 7 September 1943. The typescript autobiography of a local worker,
    Nellie Driver, suggests a pocket of sympathisers in Nelson for Mosley's fascist move-
    ment, especially among the well-to-do Tory business class. Driver and her mother
    appear to have helped organise a local branch of the British Union of Fascists. (See
    Nellie Driver, 'From the Shadows of Exile', Nelson Public Library, G3 DRI). See also
    Nelson Leader, 27 August 1937. For a suggestion that racial taunts were to be heard
    well before the era of black footballers, see *Nelson Gazette*, 30 August 1938. (The
    most complete run of the *Nelson Gazette* is at the Working Class Movement Library,
    Salford.) Also *Lancashire Evening Telegraph*, 13 June, 11 July 1989; Don Haworth,
    Figures in a Landscape: A Lancashire Childhood (London, Methuen, 1987), pp. 28–30
    (I am grateful to Jack Williams for these two references).
26 *Nelson Leader*, 27 August 1937; *Nelson Gazette*, 24 Sept 1943.
27 BBC Arch., script for 'Tonight's talk', Home Service, 3 September 1943 (m/f T89).
28 Brian Bearshaw, *From the Stretford End: the Official History Lancashire County Cricket
    Club* (London: Partridge Press, 1990), 271; *Manchester Evening News*, 9 July 1975.

where American guests objected to his presence. The manager, it was said, described Constantine as a 'nigger'.[29]

This version of events is, to an extent, that of an older man looking back and probably simplifying what must have been a difficult and confusing time. But it was a story that converged with another narrative about Constantine, and which represented him in ways quite different from his early 'animalistic' image. In place of the child of nature was created the idea of the dedicated, domesticated, loyal and ambitious man. It was a narrative which removed much of the discourse of race and replaced it with that of class and home. Constantine emerged from this as a solid middle-class paterfamilias who could readily be admired by respectable provincial society. It was, moreover, a portrayal that had a dual relevance. It related Constantine to his public in Nelson as a man they could admire; and it revealed qualities that were appropriate to the colonial society from which Constantine had come. In spite of the many differences between these two worlds, the discourse managed to combine some of the similarities. It was a story of 'getting on': of ambition, hard work and dedication to goals. It involved the fashioning of a man from overseas to fit the mentalities of a provincial English town, a process in which the local press had an important part.

To introduce him to its readers the *Leader*, a Liberal newspaper, ran full-page features with a prominent photograph in both July 1928, at the time of his signing, and April 1929, just before his arrival.[30] Together they construct an interesting and influential story. It begins by describing the manner of Constantine's signing by the club, and provides extracts from several articles in the regional and national press as testimonials in praise of his abilities as a cricketer. The thoughts of two leading English players, Wally Hammond and Ernest Tyldesley, are quoted, to underwrite the fact that Constantine was a dynamic and exciting player, and to confirm the astuteness of the Nelson club in securing such a catch. Beyond this, however, the narrative contains stories that serve to bring out those aspects

29   *Nelson Gazette, Daily Herald*, 7 September 1943; BBC Arch., Constantine File, Talks 1, Director of Overseas Programme Services to A/AC (OS), 12 August 1944.
30   *Nelson Leader*, 6 July 1928, 12 April 1929.

of the man's personal qualities which had importance for local society. Constantine, it is noted, is a family man, married with a baby daughter (who, for the time being, would be staying with the family in Trinidad). He is shown to be respectful to his parents, who had brought up a large and talented family. The principal theme of an account of Constantine's early cricketing career is deference to elders; it tells of his willingness to learn, and to accept defeat by wiser and older men with good grace. It presents him as modest yet not self-effacing, and possessing confidence in his own abilities. Above all, he demonstrates a self-discipline that ensures attention to success and self-improvement: 'I might say that conscientious training, exercise with chest developers, a love of fresh air and long walks help me considerably in my batting and bowling'.[31]

All this prefigured what later became the dominant motif in the story of Learie Constantine: the aim, eventually fulfilled after long and hard toil, to make the transition from legal clerk to qualified advocate. Constantine, with his wife's encouragement, enrolled on correspondence courses and, just before the onset of war in 1939, was taken on by a firm of solicitors in Nelson with a view to becoming articled.[32] Though the war brought quite different opportunities, the story of Constantine was being transformed into a story of ambition, hard work and dedication to goals. It was being accommodated to a view of the world as seen by an English provincial bourgeoisie. Cricket, moreover, was not simply a game, but a means of achieving a life beyond sport. In being attributed with these aspirations Constantine shared the ambitions of many Nelsonians, who understood very well the idea of 'getting on'. In Constantine's experience they were also ambitions transplanted from a particular stratum of colonial society and they expressed a mentality shaped in the context of racial inequality.

Constantine's family background is relevant here. His father, Lebrun ('Old Cons'), a foreman on a cocoa estate, had been a leading cricketer in the Caribbean before the First World War. He had represented the West

31   Constantine, *Cricket in the Sun*, 11.
32   Howat, *Constantine*, 81.

Indies with some distinction and toured England in 1900 and 1906.[33]
The journal *Cricket* described him, in the language of the day, as 'a fine
stalwart specimen of black manhood'.[34] Both Lebrun and his son, who had
gone through elementary school (taught by the father of C.L.R. James)
and become a clerk, therefore had some social standing, derived in equal
measure from sporting fame and from occupying responsible jobs. They
were members of the lower ranks of that broad grouping to be found in all
colonial societies and from which so many later nationalist activists were
drawn – the western educated elite. In the hierarchical world of West Indian
cricket, however, the Constantines were excluded from the leading clubs
and played for Shannon, a Trinidad club of moderate status: 'the club of
the black lower-middle class'.[35] Constantine's social origins thus gave him
a point of contact, at least psychologically, with many Nelsonians. As a
member of an incipient colonial middle class he could share some of the
concerns about status and advancement of the small bourgeoisie of Nelson,
for whom the cricket club was a natural focus of social life.[36] To a degree,
moreover, he also possessed a link with Nelson's working class. Though
they could, as Richard Hoggart has claimed,[37] be clannish, and certainly
abhorred behaviour which seemed 'stuck up' from people who 'gave themselves airs and graces', working people nonetheless respected ambition, as
illustrated in the desire for sons and daughters to 'get on', to get 'letters
after their name'. Constantine could relate to this from his experience of
the burning ambition of the western educated elite to compensate for its
racial insubordination by acquiring professional qualifications, and thereby
independence. It was a goal he set himself, and the first step towards it came
with the offer of the job at Nelson.

To some extent this image of the man making his way in the world
helped to marginalise his racial 'otherness'. The Constantine character

---

33   Green, *Wisden's Cricketers' Lives*, 177.

34   *Cricket*, 15 February 1913.

35   James, *Beyond a Boundary*, 56.

36   Howat, *Constantine*, 75–80.

37   Richard Hoggart, *The Uses of Literacy: aspects of working-class life with special reference to publications and entertainments* (London: Pelican, 1958 edn), 80–3, 178, 294–7.

became invested with 'good', one might almost say 'white', attributes. The qualities fashioned were important in two respects to local people. They were, firstly, laudable in themselves, betokening sound character. But equally they signified an ability to discharge that character in a sociable manner; not as someone distant from his community. This was especially important in a radical town like Nelson. In chapel, factory and neighbourhood a rough-hewn egalitarianism prevailed. There was no tradition of paternalism or social deference. It was this that made it possible for the Labour-dominated town council to refuse, in 1935, the granting of public money for celebrations to mark the King's silver jubilee.[38] In Nelson heroes had to be 'of' the people. In much that was said about Constantine there was ample reference to his heroic deeds on the field of play, but these exploits were generally framed in an image of the homely man. The language of home, family and neighbourhood was used to describe him. It stressed the very ordinariness of the Constantine household, the people next door. C.L.R. James, who lodged with the Constantines during a visit to England in 1932, portrayed Learie and his wife Norma in this neighbourly way. One anecdote in particular sums it up:

> Early one morning a friend turns up, has a chat and a cup of tea and rises to leave. 'Norma, I am just going to do my shopping. If you haven't done yours I'll do it for you.' Later Constantine said to me, 'You noticed?' I hadn't noticed anything. 'Look outside. It is a nasty day. She came so that Norma will not have to go out into the cold.'[39]

In this incident, recalled many years later by James, there is inscribed in the rituals of daily life (cups of tea, shopping, nasty weather) a wish to honour someone who, though special, is also a neighbour whose door is open to visitors. James's story is not entirely a fanciful confection dreamed up in later years; it sums up very well the way Constantine was regarded in Nelson. He was invited to meetings and expected to participate in the life of the community. He was even president of the Mickey Mouse

38   Hill, *Nelson*, 96.
39   James, *Beyond a Boundary*, 127. See also *Nelson Leader*, 27 May 1932.

Club at the Regent cinema.[40] Nelson, it seemed, wanted to display him because it was proud of him. In such a simple matter as speech, for example, Constantine's 'beautiful English' was remarked upon, and compared to the 'broad Lancashire accent' of those around him.[41] He had brought esteem to the town, and in turn the town revealed its respect by honouring a man whose race would, in many places, have put him in an ambiguous position. Constantine responded appropriately, always ready to affirm Nelson as his home. For 20 years he kept on a permanent house in the town and remained a resident long after he had ceased to be a Nelson player. It was a terraced house of a rather 'superior' kind but not set apart, and not very different from the kind of dwelling in which most Nelsonians themselves lived. He returned to it after cricket tours, visits to his family in Trinidad, and, during the war, his work as a welfare officer in Liverpool. He only departed finally for London in the late 1940s, in the quest for a qualification in the law, once his daughter had completed her education at grammar school and university.[42] His departure from Nelson was consistent with the legend. He was leaving to 'get on'. But he could always return 'home'. In 1963, just prior to being given the Freedom of the Borough, he turned up, now High Commissioner for Trinidad and Tobago, to speak to the local branch of the Rotarians: '[he] came home again to Nelson on Tuesday' announced the *Leader*, in the course of a piece about renewing old friendships and visiting familiar places. It reminded readers that Constantine's route to fame had started in their midst, and it was thus as much a story about the town as about its hero.[43]

What made this relationship with his public all the more remarkable was the very great divide that separated Constantine from them financially.

40 *Nelson Leader*, 23 April 1937.
41 *Nelson Leader*, 10 September 1937.
42 BBC Arch., script for 'Fields of Work and Play', North of England Home Service, 17 March 1946 (m/f T89). Also script for 'Tonight's Talk', 3 September 1943 (m/f T89). Constantine admitted to feeling 'at home' in Nelson, which he did not want to leave to live where his wartime job was based in Liverpool.
43 *Nelson Leader*, 15 February 1963. He was by this time Sir Learie Constantine, M.B.E., High Commissioner for Trinidad and Tobago.

It is not possible to be exact about the amount of Constantine's earnings in the 1930s. Material benefits provided by the Club over and above the basic salary, together with the frequent 'collections' he received from spectators following outstanding performances in matches, do not show up in the formal treasurer's balance sheets. Accounts do reveal, however, that he earned in the region of £500 in his first season of 1929, rising to over £700 in the mid-1930s. Constantine was money conscious. He struck a hard bargain (for a relatively untried player) when he signed for Nelson, insisting on a three-year contract, and it has been suggested that the opportunity of increasing his earnings through large 'collections' was a powerful incentive in his going to the Lancashire League. These income levels were probably beyond those attained by leading professional footballers in the days of the maximum wage (though we know little about under-the-counter payments) and are in stark contrast to the average weekly earnings of the mill workers who constituted Constantine's fan base. In the early 1930s, with many mills on short-time, and individual wage of 30 shillings (£1.50) would have been a good weekly return. Constantine no doubt earned ten times that amount by playing cricket for five months in the year. But his affluence was not flaunted in conspicuous spending.[44] All that aside, people no doubt expected their sporting hero to be at least a little out-of-the-ordinary.

Constantine's willingness to adapt to his community and its beliefs had a political side. It is a difficult area to probe because Constantine himself was circumspect about his political leanings in Nelson.[45] In later years his stance as a fighter against racial prejudice was typified in his book *Colour Bar*, and he was associated with numerous progressive causes. In Trinidad

44 Information based on interview with Mr Ken Hartley, Nelson, 20 September 2000.
45 Looking back on his political experiences of the early 1930s in a radio broadcast of 1946 Constantine claimed that he had originally supported MacDonald, Snowden and the Labour Government because they championed the cause of the common man. But the formation of the National Government in 1931 had sparked off a deeper political interest. In Nelson, he recalled, 'I loved to talk to the older members of the socialist party'. (BBC Arch., 'Fields of Work and Play', North of England Home Service, 17 March 1946, m/f T89).

he joined the People's National Movement and served in Eric Williams's left-wing government when it came to power in 1956.[46] But in the 1930s his politics were muted, and perforce had to be. Though he might well have seen eye-to-eye with the governing Labour Party in the municipal council, it must also be remembered that he was an employee of the Nelson Cricket Club. In some senses the club, or more precisely its leading officials, was a forum for an anti-Labour current of opinion which was developing in local politics as a counterweight to the strength of the Labour Party. The pro-Labour *Nelson Gazette* was quick to point this out.[47] An indication was provided at the club's annual dinner of 1937, which was also a farewell tribute to Constantine; one of the guest speakers, the local Conservative industrialist Sir Amos Nelson, seized the opportunity to make some critical remarks against the Labour majority in the council.[48] Constantine's position was therefore a delicate one, but he was already attuned to the subtle distinctions of race, class and politics in West Indies club cricket, and this stood him in good stead. Though he was often present at politically sponsored public occasions, usually in the Labour Rooms, he avoided giving any hint of partisanship; it was more a case of the sporting hero consenting to appear before his 'public', a ritual which had to be honoured, usually with a speech about his early life or cricket: 'the big room was packed, and the audience were keenly interested in what he had to say'.[49] Though his own views were probably left-of-centre, as a symbol of the town he was aware of the need to remain above politics.

Nontheless, some episodes in Constantine's career at this time suggest a man prepared to harbour radical ideas, and even challenge the status quo. In C.L.R. James's account Constantine was the 'eminence grise' behind *The Case for West Indian Self Government*, James's early tract on colonial nationalism which was written and produced in Nelson with Constantine's help. According to James, working together on the book unleashed in

46   See Learie Constantine, *Colour Bar* (London: Stanley Paul, 1954); 'Knight at Old Trafford', *New Statesman*, 7 June 1963, 861.
47   *Nelson Gazette*, 9 April 1935.
48   *Nelson Leader*, 26 November 1937.
49   *Nelson Gazette*, 20 October 1936.

Constantine political enthusiasms previously hidden: 'within five months we were supplementing each other in a working partnership which had West Indian self-government as its goal'.[50] With James's tract completed, in the following year a London publisher brought out Constantine's own book, *Cricket and I*.[51] Though more restrained than some of his later writings, notably *Cricket in the Sun*, which had some harsh comments on the state of English cricket, his first book nevertheless represented a bold step in an age when professional sportsmen, unless they were very famous, did not publish books. Nor did they consort on occasions with young Marxists like Eric Williams who came up to Nelson from his studies in Oxford to drag Constantine off on pub crawls in search of his favourite German beer.[52] But for the most part Constantine's politics were expressed within the world of cricket. Just as amateurs held the leading positions in English cricket, so in the West Indies white men dominated the game, and continued to do so almost until Independence. West Indian cricket was therefore a racially and politically subordinating experience for a black man. Nor was there much chance of contesting the subordination except, as Constantine father and son had done, to maintain a dignified sense of independence. As his cricketing reputation grew Learie no doubt felt able to assert a more forceful presence. Exactly how this manifested itself we can only guess, but we might imagine that in a number of small ways he became as 'political' as it was possible to be in this deeply conservative game. He appears not to have seen eye-to-eye with his captain, R.K. Nunes, during the 1928 tour, and indeed he was generally critical of the principle of white men captaining the West Indies team. In *Cricket and I* he examined the reasons for the lack of success of the West Indies cricket team. His explanation dismissed charges that the black players were temperamentally unsound, advancing instead the suggestion that the team lacked solidarity because of its mixed-race composition. Issues of race and social class were never

50   James, *Beyond a Boundary*, 117–19. See also Anna Grimshaw, *The C.L.R. James Reader* (Oxford: Blackwell, 1992), ch. 4.
51   L.N. Constantine, *Cricket and I* (London: Philip Allen, 1933).
52   BBC Arch., 'Return to Trinidad', Light Programme, 29 March 1954.

far from his thoughts. We learn in a later book that he was also critical of Jack Hobbs for refusing to accept the (temporary) captaincy of England during a match in which the official captain had fallen ill – Constantine interpreted Hobbs's reticence as a slight on the status of the English professional. By the late 1930s he appears, if his later observations on this are valid, to have become critical of the way English cricket was organised.[53] And of course his very leaving of the West Indies to join Nelson was itself an act of defiance. It deprived the West Indies team of one of its leading players for many test matches in the 1930s.[54]

In many ways, therefore, Constantine had chosen in Nelson an appropriate place in which to play his cricket, though the choice was an accidental one. The admiration and affection that developed for him during the 1930s was revealed in full in 1937 when Constantine announced his decision to leave the club. At the match against Lowerhouse in June the Old Prize Band struck up 'Abide With Me'[55] and Constantine himself admitted to being 'amazed, and deeply touched, by the pressure that was brought to bear on me to stay. People whom I scarcely knew stopped me in the street and asked me to reconsider my decision.'[56] It was fitting that Constantine produced his greatest batting display for Nelson in one of his last games, a record-breaking 192 not out against East Lancs at Blackburn on August Bank Holiday Monday. An 'admirer' wrote an appreciation in the *Leader* shortly afterwards which surely summed up the feelings of many people about local sporting heroes: 'apart from his cricket, Constantine has led a life which makes Nelson people proud to welcome him amongst us'. He continued:

53   Constantine, *Cricket in the Sun*, 50–1, 81–2, 92–3, 125–8.
54   Constantine played in only 18 test matches for the West Indies during the years 1928 to 1939. James described him as a 'league cricketer who played test cricket.' (C.L.R. James, 'Sir Learie Constantine' in John Arlott ed., *The Great All Rounders*, London: Pelham Books, 1969, 77.)
55   *Nelson Leader*, 4 June 1937.
56   *Nelson Leader*, 27 August 1937.

the people who object to him on account of his colour are very few indeed. For that Constantine is very grateful. It would be idle to pretend, of course, that such an objection did not exist. It does, but Constantine has proved that a man need not necessarily be possessed of white parents to claim the title of gentleman.[57]

II

During much of the 1930s Constantine's commitment to Nelson prevented his playing cricket for the West Indies. However, he returned to the team for the 1939 tour of England and this marked an important step for his future career. It placed him firmly in the national limelight. At the age of 38 his performances in the test matches were good, and in the final match of the series at the Oval he was outstanding. He took five wickets in England's first innings, and then scored a rapid 79 which recalled the explosive days of his youth. 'He ... hit a six off Perks, who was bowling from the Vauxhall End, to what geographically was the farthest part of the Oval, a stroke of immense power ... he had so disturbed the field that we were granted the unusual spectacle of a fast bowler, Perks, bowling without a slip fieldsman of any description'.[58] The reporter from the *Sunday Times* noted that Constantine was still his 'electric self' when, off his own bowling, he ran out an English batsman from a stroke to cover point.[59] The influential journal *Wisden Cricketers' Almanack* acknowledged his achievement by selecting him as one of its 'five cricketers of the year'.[60]

57   *Nelson Leader*, 20 August 1937.
58   *The Times*, 23 August 1939.
59   *Sunday Times*, 20 August 1939.
60   *Wisden Cricketers' Almanack 1940* (London, J. Whitaker and Sons, 1940), 34–6. The editors once again resorted to the racial stereotype, adding now a dash of environmental determinism: 'To the passionate love for the game which inspires so many of his countrymen, and to the lissomness of limb, the rapidity of vision and the elasticity of muscle which the climate of those islands engenders, he adds qualities peculiarly his own ...' (p. 34).

After this he continued to play league cricket in the North of England and figured in teams representing the Dominions during the war, but the 1939 test series was his last appearance in big cricket. It provided a timely farewell. Though he was later called to the Bar, and became a well-known writer, it was in no single occupation that Constantine made his mark. He became instead a symbol of a particular idea of racial harmony which was developing in liberal circles during the 1950s. It was in this context – progressively as civil servant, broadcaster, writer, politician, diplomat and public figure – that Constantine made the transition from local hero to national celebrity.

Of great importance in this evolution was Constantine's relationship with the British Broadcasting Corporation (BBC). As the *Nelson Leader* had presented him to a local audience, so the BBC projected him nationally. It began in 1939, when he was asked to do some short radio talks about the West Indies cricket team. He seems immediately to have taken to the medium and was regarded at the BBC as a natural broadcaster.[61] The relationship was sealed by the war, which for Constantine was undoubtedly a 'good' one. After drifting through a series of minor local government jobs in Nelson during the first few months of the war, he was appointed in 1941 by the Ministry of Labour and National Service as a welfare officer for West Indian technicians working in factories on Merseyside. As Constantine himself admitted, this spared him the prospect of being called up for national service, 'bootslogging' as he put it.[62] His new job involved watching over the interests of West Indian workers, smoothing relations between them, their employers and the community. It was a novel position which added to Constantine's existing renown, and in which he acquitted himself capably. It was in recognition of this work that he received the MBE in the 1946 New Year's Honours List. His new position also marked him out as an obvious contributor to radio programmes such as 'Calling the West Indies' and 'Empire Brains Trust' which went out to the colonies. He was also involved in a number of domestic programmes,

61   BBC Arch., Constantine File 1939–1962, Talks 1, 20 July 1939.
62   BBC Arch., Constantine, North Region File, N18/412 PF.

where he was presented as a symbol of the wartime unity of the Empire and its peoples.[63] A case in point was his autobiographical contribution of September 1943 to the 'Tonight's Talk' series. It reveals interesting wartime developments, both at the BBC and in Constantine's own character. His original script, considered for the Sunday *Postscript* programme, was hard-hitting on racial problems and revealed a radicalism in Constantine that had previously been latent. His original script had been objected to as being 'too controversial'. It stressed racial tensions at a time when the programme was trying to promote unity. Constantine willingly re-wrote it, drawing from his own experience of racial prejudice to remind listeners that there was still intolerance in British society. In spite of the BBC's censorship, Constantine addressed the listener directly as 'you' (white) and thus identified an individual responsibility for racial prejudice. But he ended by acknowledging that things had improved, citing the example of the factory workers for whom he was responsible as a group of men who were on an equal footing at work, getting the rate for the job.[64] This essentially moderate, humanitarian approach to race relations, informed by the conviction that it was possible to achieve harmony, remained a constant feature of Constantine's thinking on the subject for the rest of his life.

In the early 1950s, and then following his return to England in the 1960s, he made numerous broadcasts. They covered a variety of subjects, including race, the problems of youth, and, of course, sport. He grew into a relaxed radio performer whom the BBC was always happy to engage.[65] His relationships with producers were always cordial and in Margaret

63   See BBC Arch., Constantine File, Talks 1, September 1942; Peter Bax to Constantine, 17 February, 27 April 1944.

64   BBC Arch., Constantine File, Talks 1, Director of Talks (G.R. Barnes) to Margaret Bucknall, 8 July 1943; script for 'Tonight's Talk', Home Service, 3 September 1943 (m/f T89).

65   BBC Arch., Constantine File, Talks 1, Arnold Watson to Margaret Bucknall, 18 April 1944: Watson, an official of the Ministry of Labour in Manchester, commented on Constantine's 'pleasant and distinctive voice at the microphone'. Some years later a Light programme producer noted '[W]e think him an excellent b[road]caster'. (Constantine File, Talks 1, H.R. Pelletier to D.F. Boyd, 7 August 1953.)

Bucknall and Jack Singleton he found two with whom he could work in particularly congenial ways. They presented him in talks and discussions as a beacon of quiet good sense and reasonableness. Typical of this was the discussion forum he chaired for the Third Programme in 1950 on the colour bar, the issue which was to form the subject of his first non-cricket book. The broadcast, which took as its focus the colonies and the prospects for change, articulated a liberal viewpoint. Constantine had the role of balancing the contrasting arguments expressed, on the one hand, by academics E.J. Dingwall and L.S. Penrose, and on the other by the writer Elspeth Huxley.[66] In *Colour Bar* which appeared in 1954 – the year in which he was called to the Bar – Constantine used an opening theme that was by now characteristic of his position on race: 'While I was writing this book, a white man and a coloured man together climbed the highest peak in the world. There are no heights to which we cannot rise ... together'.[67]

It was this stance which assured for Constantine, on his return to England after his period of political activity in Trinidad, a place as an august and respected public figure: one of 'the great and the good'. Within a few years at the end of his life a succession of state honours was bestowed on him. He was knighted in 1962, appointed to the Race Relations Board in 1966, made a Governor of the BBC and, in 1969, elevated to the House of Lords by the Labour government as a life peer: 'Baron Constantine, of Maraval in Trinidad and Tobago, and of Nelson in the County Palatine of Lancaster'. All this affirmed his position as a member of the 'establishment'. That he was still also a figure whose name was recognised by millions was illustrated by his being selected as the subject for the popular television programme 'This Is Your Life'.[68]

---

66   BBC Arch., Constantine File, Talks 1, Prudence Smith to Constantine, 5, 15, 16 May 1950; 'Why Are There Colour Bars Today?', Third Programme, 9 June 1950 (m/f T89).

67   Constantine, *Colour Bar, vi.*

68   The verdict of the *Nelson Leader* on the programme was 'disappointing'. It failed to give sufficient attention to Constantine's time in Nelson. (19 April 1963). For later life see the obituaries in *The Times* and *Guardian*, 2 July 1971; also *Evening Standard* (London), 25 March 1969.

III

Learie Constantine combined a number of virtues that the English expected of their sporting heroes. In his modest, respectable, family centred life he displayed that convergence of remarkable skill with a decent lifestyle that characterised many of the cricket heroes of the early to mid-twentieth century. Jack Hobbs, Herbert Sutcliffe and Len Hutton were the exemplars of this sporting persona, but Constantine could have joined them and not been out of place.[69] Because he played much of his cricket in a more local context than that of the county circuit he also acquired the close attachment to a community that professional cricketers rarely achieved. Even most league professionals did not have the enduring connection with a particular town that Constantine could claim. His predecessor at Nelson, McDonald, though he continued to play in Lancashire until the time of his death in 1937, was always a more peripatetic figure as he plied his trade from club to club and town to town. Constantine's nine years at Nelson made up an exceptional tenure of office, and placed him in the position occupied by many football heroes in the era before the abolition of the maximum wage. It was little wonder that an observer, seeing Constantine chaired off the field at Nelson in 1937 after his final match, could write:

> Connie was hoisted shoulder high and carried off the field ... His personality is tremendous, wonderful ... to say that he has been a 'godsend' to Nelson is to put it mildly. He has, to all people, both living in and out of Nelson, *been Nelson itself*.[70]

This valediction, printed in the local newspaper, reminded readers that affection for Constantine was not confined to his own town. His presence had boosted attendances on cricket fields wherever he played and ensured that the strategy Nelson had embarked upon in the early 1920s

---

69   See Richard Holt, 'Cricket and Englishness: The Batsman as Hero' in R. Holt, J.A. Mangan and P. Lanfranchi ed, *European Heroes: Myth, Identity, Sport* (London: Frank Cass, 1996), 48–70.

70   *Nelson Leader*, 10 September 1937.

had succeeded throughout the Lancashire League. His success blazed a trail for many others, notably fellow West Indians such as George Headley and Manny Martindale, who made their way to the League in the 1930s. If, as has been suggested, it was the brilliance of W.G. Grace that clinched the establishment of county cricket in the 1860s and 1870s,[71] it was certainly Learie Constantine who brought about the success enjoyed by the Lancashire League in a remarkable period that lasted for some 30 years from the late 1920s: 'one of the historic periods of English cricket'.[72]

In this sense Constantine's legacy was particularly important in the North of England. Richard Holt has written that northern sporting heroes embodied qualities and attitudes through sport which were seen to express an idea of the North.[73] Learie Constantine, whose fame was unquestionably established in this region, also came to represent some of these ideals. Sporting skill, loyalty to place, self-discipline, and gentlemanliness were all qualities expected of northern heroes and Constantine possessed them in full measure. Such men were what Chas Critcher, writing about football, has termed 'traditional/located' heroes, a type epitomised in the figure of Stanley Matthews who drew on 'the values of a traditional respectable working-class culture'.[74] Where Constantine departed from this was in making the transition to Critcher's other hero category of 'transitional/mobile'. In other words, he was able to exploit economic and cultural opportunities to 'seek and find acceptance into middle-class lifestyles'.[75] He did this by turning to advantage that which disadvantaged most other black people – his difference. Racial attitudes condemned ordinary black people to a life of prejudice and discrimination. Their difference threatened. Few, if

71   Simon Rae, *W.G. Grace: A Life* (London: Faber and Faber, 1998), 42.
72   James, 'Constantine' in Arlott ed., *Great All Rounders*, 77.
73   Richard Holt, 'Heroes of the North: sport and the shaping of regional identity' in J. Hill and J. Williams, *Sport and Identity in the North of England* (Keele: Keele University Press, 1996), 137–64.
74   Chas Critcher, 'Football Since the War' in J. Clarke, C. Critcher and R. Johnson, *Working Class Culture: Studies in History and Theory* (London: Hutchinson, 1979), 161–84.
75   Critcher, 'Football', 164.

any, black sportsmen of Constantine's era found it possible to achieve the same transition. In Constantine's case, however, the difference had been elided. When he became a national figure Learie Constantine was already the black cricketer reconstructed as the white hero who 'got on'. He had bridged not only the worlds of the West Indies and Britain, nor even just the social barrier between the classes, he had also made the most difficult transition of all: that between black and white. It was achieved by fulfilling the expectations of white society, and was thus a process of assimilation. Constantine had become an 'honorary white' whose understanding of race relations came eventually to be seen by some as a little naive. By the 1960s it was bringing accusations of 'Jim Crowism' from the more militant exponents of black consciousness. Constantine, though he launched a bitter attack on the British Conservative Party's immigration policy in 1968[76], did not persuade his black critics by his reiteration of the essentially humane position on race to which he had long been attached. Calls for 'an appreciation of each other's point of view', and statements such as, 'Once [black] people are here, they should behave like good guests'[77] did not convince his detractors that this man of the Establishment comprehended the problems in the same way as they did.

In the making of sporting heroes a number of influences converge. As Tony Mason has shown, the local environment exercises a critical role.[78] It might almost be the case that in provincial towns such as Swindon, Derby and the rather smaller Nelson there was a *need* for a successful figure who could bring prestige to a place not otherwise much heeded by those outside its boundaries. In this respect it helps if the hero figure is not only talented, but is also of good character. Though to an extent they also make themselves through their actions, heroes are also fashioned. Not all of their

---

76   *The Guardian*, 23 September 1968.
77   *Evening Standard*, 25 March 1969.
78   Tony Mason, '"Our Stephen" and "Our Harold": Edwardian Footballers as Local Heroes' in R. Holt, J.A. Mangan and P. Lanfranchi eds, *European Heroes: Myth, Identity, Sport* (London: Frank Cass, 1996), 71–85; 'Stanley Matthews' in R. Holt ed., *Sport and the Working Class in Modern Britain* (Manchester: Manchester University Press, 1990), 159–78.

admirers – perhaps not even a majority – have first-hand knowledge of the hero. Hero-worship thus depends to a great extent on what is *told* (and, equally, what is not told) about the hero to the worshipper. The means of communication are therefore another important influence in the making of the hero. In the variety of written, oral and visual stories that circulate about them people are offered images to which they then add their own nuances and embellishments. In the time and place under consideration here, the local press played a key part in the construction of heroes. What it chose to write (which was determined in part by what it thought its readers would want to hear) provided the principal 'language' for knowing and understanding the hero. Press reports and stories about sportsmen like Learie Constantine provide a fascinating narrative on hero figures, who exist as much on the page as on the field of play.

Acknowledgement

I would like to acknowledge the help of the late Mr Ken Hartley of Barrowford, a former Chairman of Nelson Cricket Club, who most generously gave of his time and hospitality to talk to me and share his vast knowledge of Learie Constantine and Lancashire cricket, during a visit to Barrowford in September 2000. I should like also to express my thanks to members of the North West Labour History Society, whose comments on my paper on Learie Constantine (Manchester, October 1998) helped me to finesse my thinking on the subject of this essay, and to my friend and fellow historian Jack Williams for providing me with thoughts and material on Constantine.

CHAPTER NINE

Rite of Spring: Cup Finals and Community in the North of England

Ideology, Althusser once remarked, is something that takes place 'behind our backs'. In other words, the social construction of meaning through the signs and symbols that represent our world to us is a process of which we are largely unaware. It is the very 'taken-for-grantedness' of the cultural artefacts – whether films, television programmes, newspapers, sporting events or simply everyday speech – which structure our thoughts and give meaning to our lives, that obscures their ideological significance.

For millions of (mostly male) followers of association or rugby football the Cup Final is just such a symbol. However measured, its appeal has been immense. Its hold on the male psyche is neatly summed up in the oft-quoted story of the former Prime Minister Harold Wilson who, it is said, carried in his wallet a photograph of the Huddersfield Town Cup-winning side of 1922. Moreover, at the slightest provocation, he would reel off their names. Wilson, of course (as the obituaries following his death in 1995 did not fail to point out) was a man of the people. His own social origins were sufficiently close to the working class for him to have assimilated a culture in which sport – and especially football – had a peculiarly strong place. The connection between working class, football and Cup is an intimate one. The historian Patrick Joyce has described the FA Cup Final, in fact, as 'that most distinctive of proletarian rituals'.[1]

It is this aspect of the Cup Final that makes its cultural meaning particularly difficult to penetrate. As with other facets of working-class life it was there to be enjoyed, or endured, not to be analysed. Although there

1   Patrick Joyce, *Visions of the People: Industrial England and the Question of Class* (Cambridge: Cambridge University Press, 1994 edn), 159.

has been a multitude of books and pamphlets commemorating the Cup
Final none has attempted to lay bare the meaning of the event to those
who held it dear.[2] It is extremely rare to encounter the kind of reflection
offered by the writer and academic Fred Inglis, who looked back on a visit
as a child to the Cup Final:

> The occasion took on for me the shape of an unrepeatable rite – a long train jour-
> ney, a night in a London hotel, the packed unprecedented ride to the stadium, and
> then the unbelievable numbers of people. After all this the football: the goals and
> the sacred cup were the operatic climax of two days of the most intense, purposeful
> living I had known.[3]

Such an attempt to record the personal experience and meaning of the
event is so rare as to make the analysing of Cup Finals by means of such
evidence impossible. There is, however, a more commonplace source,
from which an idea of the collective meaning of the Cup Final might
be gleaned.

Each year the newspaper press devoted ample space to reports of the
event. The national press, for the most part, confined its attention to the
match itself. But the local newspapers of the towns whose teams were competing in the Final offered a far less circumscribed coverage. Until well after
the Second World War the local press celebrated its team's appearance in
the Cup Final in numerous ways which reveal much about the ritual and
impact of a Cup Final on a local community.

Newspapers are, of course, extensively exploited sources for historians,
who tend often to treat them simply as repositories of information. But
one of the most intriguing features of newspaper coverage is its duality.
That is to say, the press not only provides, through its routine reporting,
a description of a community's activities; at the same time, in its choice of
stories and 'angle' and through the very language used, there is an element
of creativity about newspaper reporting. It creates legends about people

2   Of the many publications commemorating the 'magic' of the Cup Final one of the
     most interesting, and one that has been very helpful in preparing the present chapter,
     is Tony Pawson, *100 Years of the FA Cup* (London: Heinemann, 1971).
3   Fred Inglis, *The Name of the Game: Sport and Society* (London: Heinemann, 1977), 37.

and places. Approaching the newspaper text from this perspective there emerges from it a multiplicity of ideas about community, bringing into play a sense of the interrelated loyalties and identities of locality, region and nation. As such, the press is not simply a passive reflector of local life and thought but an active source in the creation of local feeling. And in reading press accounts of themselves and their community the people who buy the newspapers become accomplices in the perpetuation of these legends. To paraphrase a famous observation by Clifford Geertz, the local press is one of the principal agencies for 'telling ourselves stories about ourselves'.[4] The Cup Final was one of many subjects to figure in this process of storytelling and the formation of identity.

Because of the preponderance of Northern teams in the FA Cup Final until at least the 1960s – and because by its very nature the Rugby League Challenge Cup was always a Northern affair – legends of the Cup have a particular resonance in Northern industrial communities. In fact, alongside the working-class connotations of the Cup there has been a strong association in the popular mind between the Cup and the North – never better illustrated than in the Southerner's image of the Northerner in London 'Oop for the Coop'. Donald Read has stressed the 'football mania' which took root in the North in the late nineteenth century. He further argues that it was one of the chief causes of an 'inward-looking spirit' which developed in the North and which replaced the more nationally minded, political provincialism to be found in Chartist and early Labour movements.[5] But it should be remembered that, as the subject for a text in which a variety of identities were juxtaposed, the Cup Final was never an event of exclusively local significance. In the story of the Cup, people were being invited to identify themselves in a number of guises and with a variety of allegiances. Of these, membership of the nation was perhaps the most obvious.

4   Clifford Geertz, 'Deep play: notes on the Balinese cockfight', *Daedalus* 10, 1 (Winter 1972), 1–37.
5   Donald Read, *The English Provinces c. 1760–1960: A Study in Influence* (London: Edward Arnold, 1964), 231–2.

I

For all its local significance, it is the Cup Final's status as a national event that first and foremost establishes its claim to our attention. Its national prominence dates from the emergence of football itself as a mass spectator sport in the late-nineteenth century, and has much to do with the close association between the Cup Final and London. From its inception in 1872 the Final Tie of the Football Association Challenge Cup has been staged in London except for the three occasions in 1893, 1894 and 1915 when it moved to Manchester (1893 and 1915) and Liverpool.[6] When it settled at the Crystal Palace in 1895, where it was to remain until 1914, the first historians of football commented: 'It is good that the Cup Final is played in the great Metropolis again, for however much our cynical provincial friends may affect to despise Lunnun and Cockneyism, there is no denial that London is the place for a great sporting battle.'[7] The somewhat incongruous venue for the contest at this time was a Victorian pleasure-garden in the south London suburb of Sydenham, where a less than adequate pitch was overlooked by a variety of amusement attractions including the fearsome 'Switchback' and the famous glass structure of the Crystal Palace itself. Nevertheless, in these surroundings a popular festival was quickly established with attendances exceeding 100,000 on occasions. The Final was frequently played in fine, dry weather, which added to the holiday atmosphere of the event.

When the Final moved across London to the Empire Stadium at Wembley in 1923 its national mystique was not only continued but instantly amplified as a result of the particular circumstances of the first Wembley Final. For one thing the new stadium's size – 'a monument to sport so vast as to be unrivalled' as the *Bolton Evening News* loftily and inaccurately

6   The 1970 Final was replayed at Old Trafford, Manchester.
7   Alfred Gibson and William Pickford, *Association Football and the Men Who Made It*, 4 vols (London: Carton Publishing Co., 1905), IV, 4.

alleged (ignoring the larger Hampden Park in Glasgow)[8] – and its link with the Great Empire Exhibition of 1924 assured it of immediate attention from a clientele wider than that of the football enthusiast. But its place in the public memory was most clearly guaranteed by the near-disaster that accompanied its inaugural match – the Final of 1923 between Bolton Wanderers and West Ham United. The Football Association and the stadium management had underestimated the attraction of this fixture (neither club had a big reputation and attendances in the immediately preceding Finals – played at Stamford Bridge – had not been excessive) and allowed tickets for some parts of the ground to be purchased at the turnstiles. This encouraged speculative attendance which, along with thousands of 'gate-crashers', resulted in an excess of at least 50,000 spectators over and above the official capacity of the ground. But instead of tragedy – though there were more casualties than the subsequent legend allowed for – the first Wembley Cup Final produced a national epic. The myth of the solitary mounted policeman on his white horse methodically clearing the playing area, where many of the excess spectators had congregated, survived in the folklore of 1923 until well into the post-Second World War era. Equally compelling was the image of the calming and obedient atmosphere instilled by the arrival at the stadium of King George V, whose presence ensured that the innate orderliness, deference and good humour of the English public prevailed. The crowning achievement was the fact that, though delayed by 45 minutes, the match itself went ahead. And in a masterpiece of under-statement typical of the legend already being created, the victorious Bolton captain summed up: 'It was a good hard game, and I was delighted with the way our boys played.'[9] In this way the 1923 Final came to represent a certain kind of Englishness, a feeling which was no doubt responsible for T.S. Eliot's inclusion of the Cup Final – or, at least, 'a cup final' – in his constellation of rituals that defined the national culture.[10]

8   *Bolton Evening News*, 30 April 1923; other accounts from *The Times*, 27 and 30 April 1923.

9   *Bolton Evening News*, 30 April 1923.

10   T.S. Eliot, *Notes Towards the Definition of Culture* (London: Faber & Faber, 1948), 31.

Apart from the myths of 1923, a number of other features accounted for the Cup Final's continuing place as an icon of nationality. For one thing, the event was the culmination of a long and complex competition of national proportions organised by the Football Association, the governing body for football in England. The FA has itself been one of the keenest promoters of the national symbolism of the Final, being especially anxious to ensure its preservation as a national occasion rather than one which foregrounds the partisanship of the two clubs involved. This is exemplified in the philosophy which underpins the distribution of tickets, a longstanding source of grievance among local supporters.[11] Following the introduction of 'all-ticket' Finals after the problems of 1923, the FA took over control of ticket distribution and allocated less than half of the available tickets to the two clubs competing in the Final. The majority have gone in a strictly proportionate way to the various sections of the Association itself. The justification for marginalising local loyalties in this way has been that the Final is not simply a match between two professional clubs, but the conclusion of a competition in which several hundred clubs of varying abilities have participated during the course of the season and whose contributions, however brief, should be acknowledged, however nominally.[12] One consequence of this policy, of course, has been the FA's ability to control the composition of the Wembley crowd. Not only were the disorderly scenes of 1923 never repeated, but ticket allocation ensured a 'mixed' crowd at the Final. In spite of the tendency for the local press to emphasise the 'take-over' of London on Cup Final day by hordes of enthusiasts from the provinces, Wembley never was so dominated. Indeed, there was good reason to believe that the Cup Final crowd was a reasonable cross-section of the nation.

11   For example the Preston player Tom Finney described how, for weeks before the Final of 1954, he was plagued by requests from Preston North End supporters for tickets. 'The allocation to each competing club is pitifully inadequate', he claimed. Tom Finney, *Finney on Football* (London: Nicholas Kaye, 1958), 128.
12   Pawson, *100 Years of the FA Cup*, 203–4.

Moreover, the FA was always anxious to preserve the metropolitan location of the Final.[13] This has been reinforced by the increasing and since the 1960s exclusive use of Wembley as the venue for England's international football fixtures. In this way Wembley, though simply a privately owned sport and entertainment centre, has come to be seen as the 'national' stadium. Though scarcely an architectural masterpiece its outward appearance, dominated by two squat towers symmetrically framing the main entrance, has a memorable simplicity, and the 'twin towers' have passed into popular imagery as a visual signifier of England, similar to Big Ben and the Union Jack. This image has been reinforced in sporting literature, especially in the 'ghosted' autobiographies of leading footballers, where the twin towers are treated with totemistic reverence. 'Butterflies started at the beginning of Wembley Way', says the rugby player David Watkins, of his first visit to Wembley in a Rugby League Final. 'We had been scanning the horizon for the famous twin towers and suddenly there they were … Even the few brave souls who had been trying to break the tension by singing, lapsed into silence.'[14] This mystique is understandable when it is considered that to play in a Wembley Final was the goal of many professional players' careers, though many careers concluded without the twin towers corning into sight. Getting to Wembley was a 'rocky road', as Harry Johnston – the captain of Blackpool in the famous 'Matthews Final' of 1953 – put it in the title of his autobiography.[15]

Gary Whannel has pointed out that the FA Cup Final combines several 'messages' simultaneously. It is, he says, 'an event that manages to be a popular celebration, with strong working class roots, a shared national ritual and a constitutional link between royalty and popular culture.'[16] It was this last element – the link between royalty and popular culture – that most conclusively assured the Cup Final of national status. The link, however, was

13   Geoffrey Green, *The Official History of the FA Cup* (London: Naldrett Press, 1949), 60.

14   David Watkins and Brian Dobbs, *The David Watkins Story* (London: Pelham Books, 1971), 138.

15   Harry Johnston, *The Rocky Road to Wembley* (London: Museum Press, 1954).

16   Gary Whannel, *Fields in Vision: Television Sport and Cultural Transformation* (London: Routledge, 1992), 3.

always a restrained one. The Cup Final never became a 'royal' event in the same way as, for example, the Ascot race meeting,[17] nor was it ever made an occasion on which to stage a ritualised state pageant.[18] More so than most football grounds on match days, Wembley might be viewed as a symbolic representation of English society, with its hierarchically structured crowd, the singing of the national anthem before the kick-off and the prevailing presence of the monarchy in the Royal Box. But these were scarcely the predominant messages. For one thing, the Cup Final had established itself as a popular festival long before the monarchy became associated with it. In spite of the origins of the game in the public schools and the respectable social backgrounds of its legislators, football (and indeed ball games of all kinds) lay well outside the interests of the Royal Family. George V's sporting proclivities, for example, were essentially those of the aristocrat[19] and this distanced him socially from football which, by the time he came to the throne in 1910, had acquired a distinctly 'cloth cap' image. Neither Victoria nor Edward VII had attended football occasions, though the latter had accepted in 1892, as Prince of Wales, the role of Patron of the FA, having earlier declined the offer.[20]

The restrained nature of the royal involvement in the Cup Final was set by the very first visit made by a monarch when George V attended the Crystal Palace match of 1914. By this time there could be little doubt that the Final, which in its early years had been an event of limited social and geographical appeal, was now an occasion of countrywide significance which justified the King's presence. *The Times* celebrated this new

17   See Ilse Hayden, *Symbol and Privilege: The Ritual Context of British Royalty* (Tucson: University of Arizona Press, 1987), 27.

18   See David Cannadine, 'The context, performance and meaning of ritual: the British monarchy and the 'invention of tradition', c. 1829–1977', in Eric Hobsbawm and Terence Ranger eds, *The Invention of Tradition* (Cambridge: Cambridge University Press, 1984 edn), 101–64.

19   See J. Wentworth Day, *King George V as a Sportsman: An Informal Study of the First Country Gentleman in Europe* (London: Cassell, 1935).

20   Football Association, *The History of the Football Association* (London: Naldrett Press, 1953), 62, 262.

departure with an eccentric piece of reporting which (perhaps for the first and last time) placed emphasis on the royal aspects of the event. The anonymous reporter devoted much space to describing the King's mode of travel (motorcar) and the route to be taken to Sydenham, the flora to be enjoyed in the vicinity of the Crystal Palace, the ground improvements recently made, the likelihood of hearing a cuckoo, and the precautions being made against possible suffragette demonstrations. All this came before attention was turned to the match itself, on which the reporter gave what proved to be a remarkably prescient analysis. The chosen emphasis served to confirm the social status of the match to the readers of the newspaper. Though, in keeping with the unostentatious royal presence, the King's entourage was wearing only workaday clothes – 'bowler hats and short coats' – *The Times* nevertheless felt compelled to mark the event as having sealed a new social acceptability for the game:

> professional football of the best kind is no longer regarded as a spectacle only suitable for the proletariat ... the fact that the King himself has attended a Cup Tie [sic] and shown a keen interest in its vicissitudes ... will, let us hope, put an end to the old snobbish notion that true-blue sportsmen ought to ignore games played by those who cannot afford to play without being paid for their services.[21]

Association football's success in thus establishing a 'national' sport and a Final with strong resonances in popular consciousness is underlined when the contrasting experiences of rugby league are taken into account. This professional variant of the game of rugby, which had been developed in the North of England following the secession of several Northern clubs from the Rugby Union in the 1890s,[22] had played the final tie of its Challenge Cup competition at various Northern venues before the decision was made to stage it at Wembley in 1929. This decision is an interesting one in that it seems to reflect a conscious wish by the Rugby League authorities to take its game onto the same national stage

21   *The Times*, 27 April 1914.
22   See Robert Gate, *Rugby League: An Illustrated History* (London: Arthur Barker, 1989).

as that of its arch-rival the Rugby Football Union.[23] It is very doubtful, however, whether the attempt to shed the game's regional character was successful. Although the attendance of 41,000 at Wembley for the 1929 Final exceeded that for previous Rugby League Finals, the stadium was less than half full and the match itself – Wigan v. Dewsbury – was one-sided and rather dull.[24] As the *Yorkshire Post*, not a strong supporter of the league code, commented, the match was unlikely to have impressed 'the habituees of Twickenham, Richmond and Blackheath'.[25] Whether the Wembley venue, which was retained for all subsequent Finals,[26] justi-fied the cost of travelling to London for the relatively small contingents of Northern spectators who made the journey before the Second World War must be doubted. There was always a lobby of rugby league support-ers who campaigned for using one of the larger Northern grounds for the Final, and the immense attendance at Odsal Stadium, Bradford, for the replayed Final of 1954 added fuel to their arguments. According to one influential critic of Wembley, the 1954 match 'demonstrated to the rulers of the Rugby Football League in a clear and unmistakable manner that [people] desired the final of the game's major trophy to be played in their midst'.[27] Although attendances at Wembley Finals soared after the Second World War – especially following the first Final to be attended by the monarch in 1948[28] – it is interesting that the St Helens player Vince Karalius felt it worth observing in his autobiography that as late as 1953

23   Rugby Football League (RFL), Minute Book; Meeting of the Cup Committee, 24 October 1928 (consulted by kind permission of the Chief Executive, RFL, Leeds). Wembley was chosen in preference to the Crystal Palace, probably because it offered a better financial deal, though the minutes are unclear on this point.
24   *Sporting Chronicle*, 6 May 1929.
25   *Yorkshire Post*, 6 May 1929.
26   Except that of 1932, played at Wigan because Wembley was not available at the earlier date when the RFL wished to stage the Final. The replayed Final of 1954 was held at Bradford and that of 1982 at Leeds.
27   Stanley Chadwick, 'The will of the north', *Rugby League Review*, 13 May 1954. I am indebted to Robert Gate for drawing my attention to this article.
28   See Graham Morris and John Huxley, *Wembley Magic: A History of the Rugby League Challenge Cup* (London: Evans Brothers, 1983).

the Wembley programme notes still included an explanation of the scoring system in Rugby League.[29] There must remain some doubt over the impact made by the game outside the North before the BBC began to promote it vigorously on television in the late 1950s.

Even in this respect, there was an obvious difference in the representation of the sport by contrast with association football. The latter found its national status enhanced by the embrace extended to it by the broadcasting authorities. In spite of recurring fears – largely on the part of the Football League rather than the FA – about the effect of broadcasting on match attendances, the FA Cup Final has long been regarded as (in the BBC's own language) 'a must': an event in the sporting calendar that cannot be overlooked.[30] Radio commentaries have been continuous since 1930, television coverage since 1936 (with the exception of 1952). There can be little doubt that the link between the monarch and the Cup Final caused the Reithian BBC to treat the event seriously. Rugby league, on the other hand, was viewed warily 'a socially inferior, local sport', according to Briggs[31] – and even its biggest event was not regarded as a 'must' in the schedules. When attitudes changed in the 1950s and rugby league matches came to be televised nationally they were presented in a self-consciously 'Northern' style; the commentators – usually Alan Dixon or Eddie Waring – had Northern accents which distinguished them from the orthodox style set by the BBC's football commentators, from 'By Jove' Allison to Raymond Glendenning and Kenneth Wolstenholme.[32] Eddie Waring, through whom the BBC later sought to personify rugby league, became almost a caricature of Northernness, to the dismay of many of the game's followers.[33]

29 Vince Karalius, *Lucky 13* (London: Stanley Paul, 1964), 53.
30 See Asa Briggs, *The History of Broadcasting in the United Kingdom* (Oxford: Oxford University Press, 1979), IV, 854, 861; Football Association, *History of the FA*, 508–17.
31 Briggs, *History of Broadcasting*, IV, 854.
32 Although Wolstenholme came from Bolton, he never developed a 'Northern' persona as a BBC commentator.
33 See, for example, Geoffrey Moorhouse, *At the George: And Other Essays on Rugby League* (London: Sceptre, 1990), 44–5.

Until the image of the football crowd underwent a transformation in the 1970s with the onset of 'hooliganism', it had invariably been represented by press, radio and television in a comforting form, almost as a physical manifestation of a united English nation. This was particularly so of Cup Final crowds. The first Wembley Final, for example, was accounted by *The Times* an 'ugly day', retrieved by two things: the spirit of the people and the police, and the loyalty of the 'mixed congregation' to the King. Spectators responded enthusiastically to the arrival of the monarch, and sang 'God Save the King'. As to general behaviour, 'there seems to have been no hooliganism or wanton disorder'.[34] In the more structured space of Wembley (by comparison with the rather chaotic nature of the Crystal Palace), the Final acquired a more stage-managed appearance during the 1920s, with military bands, the presentation of teams to the royal party, and community singing. Perhaps the most striking feature of all this, and of almost ineffable significance in the meaning of Wembley, was the singing of the Victorian hymn 'Abide With Me'. It was introduced in 1927, apparently on the suggestion of the master of ceremonies (and possibly because it was a favourite hymn of the Queen). Despite (or, perhaps, because of) its dirge-like tones it provided, as one historian has put it, 'a moment of deep emotion that moved the great crowds'.[35] Only by the wildest stretch of the imagination could the words be thought have any connection with football and yet the hymn somehow aroused sentiments that could never have been provoked by the national anthem itself. The Scot Pat Crerand of Manchester United apparently found it a very calming experience just before his appearance in the Final of 1963,[36] and for many ordinary working-class spectators the singing of 'Abide With Me' was possibly the nearest they came to any formal spiritual experience. Its impact, both personal and collective, on a Wembley crowd almost defies analysis. No doubt in a general sense, because it was recognised as a hymn through its words and form, it was accorded respect, in the same way that

34   *The Times*, 30 April 1923.
35   Pawson, *100 Years of the FA Cup*, 215.
36   Noel Cantwell, *United We Stand* (London: Stanley Paul, 1965), 55.

clergymen are accorded respect even in a largely secular society. But the meaning of the song surely transcended religion. Patrick Joyce has suggested that it expressed feelings of home, fatherhood, rest and peace, which were deeply embedded in working-class culture.[37] Perhaps also, being sung in common in circumstances of extremely close physical contiguity, the, song evoked memories of adversity and loss, striking chords in the minds of people in much the same way as Armistice Day did in the inter-war years.[38] If, as Simon Inglis has suggested, there is an 'almost indefinable, inherent Englishness' about Wembley[39] then the singing of 'Abide With Me' at the FA Cup Final has surely been one of the chief ingredients of that national feeling.

II

Previewing the 1962 Cup Final, the association football correspondent of *The Times* echoed an idea expressed some thirty years earlier by the long-serving secretary of the FA, Frederick Wall. Wall had described the FA Cup as a 'national football festival' and whiggishly noted its steady development as such from the 1880s onwards.[40] The correspondent of *The Times* took up this theme in positively lyrical mood:

> This is the national stage of football at home ... here is an occasion that lives on in the hearts of those who follow the game in these islands. Beyond the company compressed within the rim of Wembley itself will be another army. Countless and unseen, they will have the setting brought to front parlours north, south, east and west by the eye of television. This is more than a football match. This is a festive day in the sporting calendar; a day out, a day for celebration, no matter how good

37   Joyce, *Visions*, 159.
38   See Bob Bushaway, 'Name upon name: the Great War and remembrance', in Roy Porter (ed.), *Myths of the English* (Cambridge: Polity Press, 1992), 136–67.
39   Simon Inglis, *The Football Grounds of Europe* (London: Willow Books, 1990), 99.
40   Sir Frederick Wall, *Fifty Years of Football* (London: Cassell, 1935), 167.

or how poor the game itself. And when north faces south, as it does this afternoon, a spice is added to the picnic.[41]

The writer here was highlighting something central to the Cup Final: 'a day out, a day for celebration'. But if Cup Final day was presented to us through various 'official' agencies – the FA, the Wembley stadium authorities, *The Times* newspaper – as a celebration in which we were invited to see ourselves as part of a nation at play, there were also other celebrations fusing with these national ones, coalescing the national with the local and inflecting the 'official' text of celebration with popular practices.

Although Frederick Wall was no doubt correct in seeing the Final as a national institution, the competition of which it formed the climax had, for much of its first fifty or so years, possessed strong regional characteristics. It had been dominated by Northern and Midlands clubs. As Keith Robbins has pointed out, early professional football introduced as much regional diversity into sporting competition as it did national integration.[42] The FA Challenge Cup perfectly exemplified the point, being virtually monopolised by the clubs of the Football League, a Midlands-North organization whose headquarters from 1902 until 1959 were in Preston and whose leading officials possessed a self-consciously 'northern' identity.[43] Between 1882, when the first northern club (Blackburn Rovers) appeared in a Cup Final, and the outbreak of the Second World War, there were only nine Finals in which a team from Lancashire, Yorkshire or the North East did not figure. Thirteen Finals during this period were exclusively northern affairs.

This northern presence in the Cup Final provoked, from an early stage in the competition, a remarkable display of local festivity which endured in a more or less unchanged form until well after the Second World War. The three main strands of this sustained celebration were: 1) the journey of spectators

41   *The Times*, 5 May 1962.
42   Keith Robbins, *Nineteenth-Century Britain: Integration and Diversity* (Oxford: Clarendon Press, 1988), 163, 168.
43   Alan Tomlinson, 'North and south: the rivalry of the Football League and the Football Association', in John Williams and Stephen Wagg eds, *British Football and Social Change: Getting into Europe* (Leicester: Leicester University Press, 1991), 25–47.

to London; 2) the enjoyment of the match itself, not only inside the stadium itself but vicariously by thousands of followers at home; and 3) the welcoming home of the team, usually on the Monday after the Final, with or without the trophy. The scenes associated with these various activities produced possibly the clearest illustration that urban areas were able to produce in the twentieth century of the nebulous concept of 'community'. It was the reporting of these events by the local press that served to foster the sense of community.

The dominant image of the Cup Final is of masses on the move:
INVASION OF LONDON
Great Trek to Wembley from the North
By Rail Road and Air
Big Bolton Crowds to Cheer the
Wanderers

Thus was the first visit to Wembley from the North proclaimed by the *Bolton Evening News*.[44] 'Contingents of the Northern Army', it went on, 'armed with megaphones, bells, rattles and bedecked with favours arrived by crowded trains, more travelled in motor coaches and others descended from aeroplanes today.'[45] Thirty years later 17 special trains left Newcastle for the 1952 Final, though an indication of the increasing use of motor travel was provided when local papers started printing maps of the road approaches to Wembley.[46] For the most part, however, it was the availability of relatively cheap rail travel that made the journey to London possible. By the early years of the century a cheap day excursion was obtainable for approximately one quarter of a working man's average weekly wage. For the 1914 Final, for example, the Lancashire and Yorkshire Railway advertised such trips for 12s. (60p) starting between late Friday night and the early hours of Saturday. Weekend excursions of between two and three days were

44 *Bolton Evening News*, 27 April 1923.
45 Unfortunately, because of the poor organisation of the event, many returned home without having seen the match, or having even got near the stadium because of the traffic congestion.
46 See e.g. *Northern Daily Telegraph*, 25 April 1947.

also offered and towards the end of April the advertisements of the railway companies in the local press were joined by those of London businesses offering overnight accommodation, refreshments and amusements, such as the Zoological Gardens and Madame Tussaud's. But most people no doubt minimised expenses by eliminating the overnight accommodation. For the 1914 Final the Burnley newspapers estimated that most travelling supporters would complete their excursion in one day, sleeping on the crowded trains or at the station on arrival, possibly having taken advantage of the packed meals of sandwiches and pies offered by local grocers for 'saloon parties'.[47]

The cost of all this for many working people could be steep, even in the so-called 'age of affluence' after the Second World War. In his autobiography Gus Risman, who was the player-manager of Workington Town at the time of their appearance in the Rugby League Final of 1952, tells a story (which had been current in the local press at the time) of Workington people mortgaging their radios and television sets to raise money for the journey.[48] The irony was that, as the *Workington Star* pointed out, 'only a fraction of the stadium crowd could have seen [the game] so well' as those who watched it on television.[49] In the early days there seems to have been recourse to mutualist efforts to meet the cost. Gibson and Pickford, in their comprehensive history of the early game, dwell at some length on what they term (in a subsequently much-overused phrase) 'cup fever'. In particular they explain the 'clubbing principle', which they date from the visit of the working-class team Blackburn Olympic, the first professional club to win the FA Cup, in 1883. These 'outing clubs' seem to have been especially well supported in the North. Supporters clubbed together their savings in order to make what was, for many, a unique visit to London, combining sporting enthusiasm with an atmosphere of holiday. 'Next to the annual holiday at Blackpool, there is no objective dearer to the provincial's heart than the "Coop" Final.'[50] The savings were not just for the price

47   See *Burnley Express*, 22, 29 April 1914.
48   Gus Risman, *Rugby Renegade* (London: Stanley Paul, 1958), 78.
49   *Workington Star*, 25 April 1952.
50   Gibson and Pickford, *Association Football*, IV, 41–2.

of ticket and travel, but also contributed to carnival. Eating and drinking were clearly important parts of the proceedings, though the experience of a Sheffield outing club, whose barrel of beer was too gargantuan to go through the railway carriage door, was perhaps exceptional. But excess was nevertheless expected. In spite of a tendency for some parties to be independently victualled – excursionists from Bury in 1903 laid up a stockpile of food and drink in two large parcel vans at Euston station for their return journey[51] – London business people generally welcomed spectators from the North and Midlands because (it was said), unlike Southerners they spent good money. 'The southern spectator', claimed the Crystal Palace company, 'only comes to see the football, and not to spend his money.'[52] Presumably they went straight home after the match.

Northern supporters stayed on, conspicuously. Over many years a fixed pattern of pleasures was indulged in. Prominent among them was sightseeing of national monuments: Buckingham Palace, St Paul's Cathedral, the Tower of London, Westminster Abbey and the Houses of Parliament were all on the itinerary. Visits to the Commons to meet the local MP were popular before the First World War. One man had written beforehand, accepting the invitation of Philip Morrell, MP for Burnley: 'I have reached the age of 77 years, and I am coming to London for the first time, bringing my five sons with me. Hoping we shall have a good time and win the Cup.'[53] After the Great War the Cenotaph was added to the list of places to visit, especially for official parties representing clubs, players and supporters' groups. 'Old Hand' of the *Dewsbury Reporter* noted the few moments of solemnity in 1929 when representatives of both teams playing in the first Rugby League Final at Wembley placed wreaths at the Cenotaph: 'it was at this period of the day that the fun and shouts of the partisans subsided, hats were removed, and except for the noise of the passing traffic, there were periods of impressive silence'.[54] After which, exuberance was restored.

51   *Bury Times*, 22 April 1903.
52   Gibson and Pickford, *Association Football*, IV, 41–2.
53   *Burnley Express*, 29 April 1914.
54   *Dewsbury Reporter*, 4 May 1929.

Club colours, favours, mascots, carnival costumes and chants were ostenta-
tiously exhibited. Huddersfield Town supporters took their mascot donkey
on the train for the 1922 Stamford Bridge Final, parading it down the
Strand and stopping the traffic.[55] In 1947 Burnley's supporters, in a now
well-rooted tradition, swept four-abreast through the West End, bedecked
with streamers and wearing skull caps or three foot-high top hats in claret
and blue.[56] The bizarre was, for many, the order of the day and few scaled
greater heights in the pursuit of the surreal than Blackpool's Atomic Boys,
the pinnacle of whose exploits in the 1940s and 1950s was their delivery
of Blackpool Rock to 10 Downing Street.[57] Alertness to style and respectability for those 'on show' in the metropolis was not forgotten, however.
The Elton Ironworks excursion party from Bury no doubt felt that they
had struck the right note for London fashion in 1900 when it was made
a condition of joining that members wore 'new clogs and slouched hats'
for any visit to London.[58] Behaviour was noisy and rowdy, but not usually violent. In 1923 some threats of physical violence seem to have been
exchanged between groups of the respective supporters, but it was treated
lightly by the press. In a portentous comment which nevertheless revealed
deep local pride the *Bolton Evening News* noted:

> Cockney sportsmen found their first taste of a dish of 'Trotters' very unpalatable, and
> far from being the wholesome feast as suggested by we Boltonians. It is whispered that
> some of them angrily tried in vain to find the young collier who paraded the Strand
> early on Saturday morning, draped in the Wanderers' blue and white colours, with a
> string of trotters dangling round the front and back of him in very curious fashion.[59]

The main physical danger in 1923, however, seems to have been confined
to the stadium itself, with around a thousand people treated for injuries,
many at the local hospital.[60]

55   *Huddersfield Examiner*, 6 May 1922.
56   *Northern Daily Telegraph*, 25 April 1947.
57   *West Lancashire Evening Gazette*, 2 May 1953.
58   *Bury Times*, 18 April 1900.
59   *Bolton Evening News*, 30 April 1923.
60   *Bolton Evening News*, 28, 30 April 1923.

For those who stayed at home there was a different atmosphere to be experienced. Before the arrival of mass radio and television, it was not uncommon for crowds of people to congregate in the central parts of the town in the hope of picking up news of the match. Elaborate arrangements had been made to relay the news by local shops in Blackburn for the 1885 Cup Final, and conflicting reports caused confusion among the throng of people massed in the town centre.[61] In Bolton in 1923 there was 'great pandemonium' in the middle of the town, as people gathered to hear latest scores. Rumour abounded to the effect that the match had been called off, but when the news came through that David Jack had scored the opening goal 'people were shaking hands with one another, slapping backs, being as familiar and hail-fellow-well-met as most other folk would be if their team was winning the English Cup; and David Jack was the hero of the piece'. At the news that Bolton had scored a second goal, traders in the Market Hall went wild in a spontaneous display of rough music: 'crockery dealers rattled plates ... hardware merchants banged out their joyous feelings with the aid of pans, toy-sellers blew trumpets, twirled rattles and rang bells, whilst those who had no noise-producing instruments handy joined the general public in a glad shout which echoed and re-echoed through the great glass-roofed building'.[62] Clubs competing in Finals at this time often played reserve team fixtures on the same day, and if these matches were at home the crowds would be swollen dramatically from their usual numbers; not only would messages constantly be issued about the state of play in the Final, but the camaraderie of the crowd provided a substitute for being in London. At such a match in Huddersfield in 1922, when the news was announced that Town had taken the lead over Preston North End with a penalty, 'Hats, caps and sticks were hurled wildly in the air, and the scared carrier pigeons which were released to carry the glad tidings to many outlying districts were fortunate to escape injury.'[63] As radio developed, but before many homes possessed receivers of their own, people gathered

61   *Blackburn Times*, 11 April 1885.
62   *Bolton Evening News*, 30 April 1923.
63   *Huddersfield Examiner*, 6 May 1922.

outside the premises of retailers to hear the commentary, or bought seats at local cinemas where enterprising managers had made an arrangement with electrical dealers for sets to be installed to provide a 'listening-in' service.[64]

In a later age of electronic media these surrogate Wembley crowds disappeared. Those who did not journey to London watched or listened to the Final in the more privatised settings of family or neighbourhood groups. The legend of the 'ghost town' was thus created. So quiet was Workington in 1952 (in contrast to the 'pandemonium' of Bolton in 1923) that shopkeepers complained of loss of business.[65] In St Helens in 1956 complaints intensified. It was estimated that a fifth of the town's population would actually make the trip to Wembley and many of the remainder would stay indoors rather than go out shopping. One local paper, whose headline proclaimed 'Wembley Match will make St Helens a Ghost Town', quoted local tradespeople concerned about business losses; one greengrocer was worried about leftover lettuces, potatoes and fruit; publicans reckoned that their beer takings would be down by £500. The Chamber of Trade put overall losses at something like £150,000. More darkly, the comments of the business community were directed disapprovingly at working-class hedonism and irrationality; rents would fall into arrears and hire-purchase instalments would be missed – 'and they won't be made up, you know', warned one furniture shop manager.[66]

Such pessimism did not, however, prevent a general air of festivity from prevailing. There was, as in carnival, a sense of the normal conventions and routines being temporarily suspended. In the days when the working week continued into Saturday a visit to the Cup Final represented a welcome break from work. For those who stayed behind the peak of enthusiasm was reached when the local football team returned from London to be greeted rapturously by thousands of its followers, many of whom had taken at least the afternoon off. The ritual followed a well-established protocol whose origins were in the 1880s. The welcome given to the victorious St Helens

64   E.g. *Dewsbury Reporter*, 1 May 1929.
65   *Workington Star*, 28 March, 25 April 1952.
66   *Prescot and District Newspaper and Advertiser*, 26 April 1956.

team in 1956 provides a typical example. The players detrained at Liverpool where, though the city was not a rugby league stronghold, ethnic and religious ties ensured them of a large reception. A coach ride to St Helens in pouring rain, the players covering themselves in blankets to keep dry as they sat atop the coach, brought out (it was estimated) 100,000 people along the processional route. It climaxed in an enthusiastic reception in St Helens itself, with some 30,000 'packed like sardines' into Victoria Square. Speeches and cheering followed, and the players went on to visit local hospitals to display the Cup they had won for the first time in 59 years, accompanied by the local industrial magnate Sir Harry Pilkington.[67]

This kind of scene differed little whether the team had won or lost. When Preston North End returned in 1937 following a defeat by Sunderland there was a throng of 8,000–10,000 people in a Market Square appropriately bedecked with bunting for Coronation Day. 'The reception could not have been more spontaneous,' claimed the *Preston Guardian*, 'if the club had brought the Cup with them.'[68] They actually did the following year, when the *Guardian* reported 'the greatest crowd ever to assemble' in the main square.[69] Nine years later the Burnley team, who had narrowly lost in the Final to Charlton Athletic, were similarly received as heroes. 'Watchman' of the *Northern Daily Telegraph*, under the headline 'ALL BURNLEY OUT TO GREET CUP LOSERS', reported that from Bury onwards the team's coach was cheered, and as it entered Burnley itself the crowds were so enthusiastic that the last mile of the journey took twenty minutes. The club chairman, Tom Clegg, announced: 'I have lived in Burnley 75 years and I have never felt as proud of the town and its people as I do tonight.' The captain, Alan Brown, greatly moved by the display of affection shown to his team, told the thousands assembled outside the Town Hall: 'We lost the Cup, but you have given us something Charlton cannot win from us.'[70] The scenes in Burnley were virtually identical to those of 1914 when

67   *Prescot and District Newspaper and Advertiser*, 3 May 1956.
68   *Preston Guardian*, 8 May 1937.
69   *Preston Guardian*, 7 May 1938.
70   *Northern Daily Telegraph*, 29 April 1947.

the club had returned with the Cup and the mills stopped on Monday to allow everyone to celebrate.[71]

Emotions such as these were a remarkably constant feature of Cup Final celebration. There was little, if any, variation, either over time or in relation to the size and sporting renown of the community involved. Thus, for example, it might be expected that Huddersfield, a medium-sized industrial town whose previous association football history was undistinguished, would go wild after the victory of its team in 1922. So overwhelming was the welcome for the returning players that the *Huddersfield Examiner* was moved to comment that it was 'probably the biggest demonstration ever known in Huddersfield'; its ecstatic nature was of a kind 'which could have been secured only by a monarch, or by the more famous kinema artists'.[72] Similar scenes were witnessed in the isolated West Cumbrian heavy industrial town of Workington in 1952. The professional Rugby League club, which had only been in existence since the end of the Second World War, quite suddenly shot into the limelight by winning the League Championship in 1951 and, in the following year, the Cup. 'What a return we had on the Monday', recalled Gus Risman, for whom the Cup victory was the fulfilment of a prediction he had made on becoming the club manager in 1946: 'We travelled North by train and then went across country by coach from Scotch Corner. And every village in Cumberland turned out to cheer us home. When we reached Workington you could hardly get near the Town Hall.'[73]

Very similar was the reception given to Newcastle United's FA Cup-winning team a week later. In Newcastle's case, however, it was a large regional centre with a long history of football success. 1952 was the club's ninth Cup Final appearance, and it had never lost at Wembley. But neither this tradition, nor the narrow margin of the victory over Arsenal – with an injury to one of their players resulting in much sympathy in the national and local press for the losers – prevented an estimated quarter of a million people coming into the centre of the city to give the players what the *Newcastle*

71   *Burnley Express*, 29 April 1914.
72   *Huddersfield Examiner*, 6 May 1922.
73   Risman, *Rugby Renegade*, 80.

Journal described as a 'delirious welcome'. 'When the team paraded around their stadium with the Cup, some 45,000 supporters "nearly took the roof off the stands", to the extent that some players looked overwhelmed, even after Wembley'.[74] Clearly, mass enthusiasm was not confined to small town parvenu teams, and the more recent examples of civic celebration following the Liverpool-Everton Finals of 1986 and 1989 confirm the continuing ability of the Cup Final to influence big city consciousness.

However, beneath the surface of these seemingly changeless celebrations of local achievement were concealed interesting developments in civic relationships. In short, the reception of the Cup Final team was gradually transformed from being a spontaneous celebration of club into a semi-official glorification of town. The reception was appropriated into civic ideology. The spontaneity of the occasion was typified in the very first mass reception for a Cup team in the North. This occurred at Blackburn in 1883 after Blackburn Olympic had defeated Old Etonians in the Final at Kennington Oval and thus become the first provincial and professional team to win the Cup. Olympic's victory provoked a torrent of eulogies from press and public figures, none more redolent of class consciousness and local patriotism than the one offered by the *Blackburn Times*:

> It is the meeting and vanquishing, in a most severe trial of athletic skill, of a club composed of the sons of some of the best families of the upper class of the Kingdom – of born and bred gentlemen who may be justly described as 'the glass of fashion and the mould of form' – as the Old Etonians club is, by a provincial Club composed entirely, we believe, of Lancashire Lads of the manual working class, sons of small tradesmen, artizans and operatives.[75]

It also provoked a demonstration of affection and enthusiasm from the people of Blackburn that far exceeded any expectations. As the train carrying the players approached the town it was cheered by supporters who had gathered along the line. In Blackburn the crowds were so large that the fifty or so policemen on duty were completely unable to enforce any

74   *Newcastle Journal*, 6 May 1952.
75   *Blackburn Times*, 7 April 1883.

kind of control. The procession of four wagonettes and three bands that headed off in the direction of the Cherry Tree Inn, the club's headquarters, was frequently dispersed and several times had to pause and reform. Celebrations and speeches were held at the Cherry Tree, and later in private houses, but there was no formal attempt to place a civic stamp upon the proceedings. Nor was there in the following year when the socially superior Blackburn Rovers won the Cup. This time the police were better prepared and at least cleared a space outside the station for the vehicles to assemble, but otherwise the scenes were identical, with the procession making for the White Bull on this occasion.

In 1885, when the Rovers won again, there was no reception at all when the team returned on the Sunday morning. Celebrations took place at the Rovers' ground after a scheduled match on the Monday evening.[76]

By the turn of the century official attitudes towards Cup teams had noticeably changed. Whereas the Cup Final in the 1880s was a relatively small-scale affair – still regarded by some as less important than the Lancashire Cup – by the 1890s its success at the Crystal Palace ensured national prominence for those taking part. This no doubt explains the increased attention paid to it by local corporations. By the time Bury appeared in two Finals (1900 and 1903, winning both by record margins), an attempt was being made to elevate the reception onto a semi-official footing. The team's arrival on Monday evening was to be greeted with a carefully laid plan which foregrounded the Mayor and his entourage: 'arrangements were made for keeping the railway platforms clear of persons who had no business there, and a few minutes before the train arrived there was no one on the platform but a few privileged persons'.

Nevertheless, 'unofficial' interlopers did break through on the first of these occasions, so that the Mayor's party was not alone when the train arrived. In 1903, however, the 'privileged' were kept apart from the masses. But thereafter the customary wagonette and band procession made off, accompanied by the Mayoral party, for the public house where the club normally met, rather than an official reception at the Town Hall.[77]

76   *Blackburn Times*, 7 April 1883; 5 April 1884; 11 April 1885.
77   *Bury Times*, 25 April 1900; 22 April 1903.

The Town Hall, however, was certainly the focus of the proceedings at Huddersfield in 1922, when the event was virtually an official celebration. The team was met at the station by a Mayor's party and conveyed through the streets in two Corporation buses to the Town Hall, where a reception and speeches were held before the Cup was displayed to the crowds from the balcony.[78] This became the usual pattern for Cup celebrations by the 1920s. At Sunderland in 1937 a moral element was introduced when the arrival of the team, originally scheduled for 3.30 pm, was delayed until the evening to avoid the temptation for men to stay away from work.[79] The stage-managing of the event probably reached its most carefully rehearsed proportions at Newcastle in 1952. Here, the linking of civic authority to football culture was achieved by having the Lord Mayor and the Town Clerk, who had been at Wembley, leave the team's train at Durham in order to arrive slightly earlier in Newcastle. There they changed into their official robes and, equipped with sword and mace, were ready to greet the team formally when its train arrived at the station.[80]

III

In the reporting of the rituals which made the Cup Final a popular festival, the press often stepped into the realm of myth-making. By offering comment and opinion on the events, or simply by selecting certain aspects for attention, newspaper editors and reporters played upon notions of identity which drew on and at the same time reinforced a sense of local distinctiveness.

Like Northern dialect literature, with which they have a close affinity, stories about the Cup Final hinged on ideas of the locality and its customs in

---

78   *Huddersfield Examiner*, 6 May 1922.
79   *Sunderland Echo*, 3 May 1937.
80   *Newcastle Journal*, 4 May 1952.

the face of the 'otherness' of the rest of the country, particularly London.[81] Part of the attraction of the Cup Final was the opportunity it afforded for small, comparatively unknown places to enjoy a brief moment in the limelight and to parade their locality on a national stage. '[N]othing has been produced in this district nor has there been an event to attract to it a spotlight of such brilliance', commented the *Workington Star* on the town's Wembley success of 1952.[82] Sometimes this opportunity was seen as a chance to put the community on the map with a view to reviving its economic fortunes; Burnley's Wembley appearance in 1962, for example, came at a time of absolute decline in the cotton industry and it was felt that it might attract new industries.[83] But often the story was about less material issues. It was about local pride, an opportunity simply to assert the local identity. This was what Dewsbury seemed to extract from their Cup defeat by Wigan in the 1929 Rugby League Final. 'We are very proud', said their captain, Joe Lyman, 'that our men come from within six miles of Dewsbury. That means a great deal. It means that if we win it will be a real Dewsbury victory, and also there will be a far greater team spirit than ever one could find in a side made up of players from all parts of the country. We know one another well, and we shall all work together.'[84] 'Old Hand' of the *Dewsbury Reporter* analysed the team's qualities as 'grit, staying power, team spirit, all-round soundness'.[85] the very stuff of Yorkshire. By contrast Wigan was a more cosmopolitan team which included Welsh, Scottish and New Zealand as well as English players, and ten of them were internationals.[86] The authentic Yorkshireness of Dewsbury consoled their supporters in defeat – 'it's nobbut t'League o' Nations that bet us': as if Dewsbury had been the victim of international forces beyond its control.[87]

81   See Martha Vicinus, *The Industrial Muse* (London: Croom Helm, 1974), 190
82   *Workington Star*, 4 April 1952.
83   *Burnley Express and News*, 2 May 1962.
84   *Sporting Chronicle*, 4 May 1929.
85   *Dewsbury Reporter*, 4 May 1929.
86   *Sporting Chronicle*, 4 May 1929.
87   *Dewsbury Reporter*, 11 May 1929.

The linking of football to local traditions and customs was usually a marked feature of press coverage. Dialect was a convenient mark of distinctiveness and identity. '"WOR CUP" COMES BACK TO THE GALLOWGATE ROAR' proclaimed the *Newcastle Journal* in 1952 and recorded the lusty singing of 'Blaydon Races' at the station, 'loud enough, it seemed, to reach Scotswood Road'. On this occasion there was a strong North East sentiment evident. Newcastle were seen to be carrying the pride of a distinctive region to London for their match against Arsenal, and local rivalries were suspended as the people of Sunderland, Hartlepool, Shields, 'the Northumberland farms and the Easington pits' all united behind Newcastle.[88] For the other North East club, Sunderland, the local paper made great play of the cries of 'Ha-way the lads' by their supporters in the Final of 1937.[89]

The dialect tradition also extended to features on local personalities. An interesting example was included in the *Northern Daily Telegraph*'s coverage of Burnley's appearance in the Final of 1947. 'Ma' Bray of Oswaldtwistle, the mother of one of Burnley's players, was interviewed. She was portrayed as the embodiment of locality and family. She stood stoically behind her two sons, both professional footballers, and kept firm to solid Northern values in the face of the 'magic' of Wembley and, one may suppose, the lure of the metropolis. She recalled how, when her elder son had returned home to Oswaldtwistle after taking part in Manchester City's Cup victory of 1934, the entire street had been decorated end-to-end. But such enthusiasm was for family and neighbourhood. The Final itself was put firmly in its place. 'I don't want to go ... I don't think I could face it. I've never been to London, and I've no desire to go.' The reporter summed up: 'She'll be proud tomorrow as she sits by the wireless, win or lose. And if it's "win" she won't swank. She's not that kind.'[90]

'Ma' Bray's reluctance to leave Oswaldtwistle was not, of course, shared by the thousands who relished the opportunity to make a rare, possibly

88   *Newcastle Journal*, 3, 6 May 1952.
89   *Sunderland Echo*, 4 May 1937.
90   *Northern Daily Telegraph*, 25 April 1947.

unique, visit to London. The mass excursion, and the various holiday activities associated with it, brought into play in press reporting a series of oppositions that would not have been present if the Final had been staged at a Northern venue. These essentially converged around the idea of London and the South as being not only different but also the seat of power, which was temporarily being 'occupied' by the North. 'Lancashire takes over as London is invaded – Atomic Boys at No. 10' declared the *Evening Gazette* on the day of the Blackpool–Bolton Final of 1953.

> The West End was Lancashire on the Thames today. They came in their thousands from Blackpool and Bolton. Hundreds were in town before a grey dawn which heralded a day of sunshine and gentle breezes. They went out on the streets, waking the sleeping city at four o'clock in the morning. Only the old and the weary huddled in Euston's waiting rooms till the early morning cafes opened. They made the traditional tour of the town. They went to Covent Garden, Buckingham Palace and a few made a pilgrimage to Whitehall, where they left posies of flowers tied with tangerine and white and black and white ribbons.[91]

This piece, utilising the idea of the 'Northern invasion', could have been written at any time during the previous sixty years. The images, even the language, had changed little.[92] London, in the days before motorways and high-speed trains, was still distant enough from the North for there to be a sense of expedition about the journey. The *Workington Star* reported a 'trickle of cars leaving Workington for the South' as early as Wednesday evening in 1952.[93] Advanced columns of Burnley's invading army in 1947 were greeted 'where Middlesex meets London' by the exhortation of an emigre Lancashire greengrocer, whose shop-window sign urged: 'Wap it Whoam, Burnley'.[94] It was, of course, a friendly invasion. 'London loved it all', claimed the *Northern Daily Telegraph*; compared to the reception of

91   *West Lancashire Evening Gazette*, 2 May 1953.
92   Compare the *Burnley Express* of 1914: 'Long before London itself woke up for business, the invaders had moved far afield. They took possession of the Strand, Piccadilly, Holborn and Regent Street before London had aroused itself.' (29 April 1914).
93   *Workington Star*, 18 April 1952.
94   *Northern Daily Telegraph*, 26 April 1947.

the Scottish supporters who had visited earlier for an international match, the liaisons between Londoners and Lancastrians were all waves and greetings.[95] Nevertheless, there was a sense in which London was to be placed in true proportions. Northerners were determined not to be seduced by the sophistication of the city. Here the tone of the press reports was often that of the seaside postcard, where the Northerner abroad implants authentic Northern values in an alien soil, but at the same time indulges in gentle self-mockery. At the Crystal Palace in 1914, for example, spectators had to pay a shilling (5p) admission to the pleasure grounds before gaining access, at additional cost, to the football stadium. This was naturally frowned upon at first, but having seen the famous glass edifice visitors generally reckoned it to have been worth the money. The grandiose was nonetheless placed in realistic perspective. 'By gum,' remarked a Burnleyite, 'aw wouldn't like to go and mend a brokken pane up theer.'[96] This was local humour, presenting a reassuring image of the Northerner to readers back home. But there was also a feeling that Londoners themselves could not fail to be amused by the jokes, songs and accents of this invading force. Boltonians arrived for their visit of 1923 apparently armed to the teeth with all kinds of street maps and directories. Their confused antics in the vicinity of the railway station became the scenario for much humour, some of it inevitably pitched at the mythical 'gormless' Northerner at large in the big city, asking directions to the pub called the 'Old Lady of Threadneedle Street', or declining the theatre after the match in favour of a visit to the circus at Piccadilly.[97] Boltonians could recognise and laugh at this, but so too should Londoners; according to the *Bolton Evening News*, 'The city that is too busy living to take much notice of life will surely spare a glance and a laugh here.'[98]

95 *Northern Daily Telegraph*, 26 April 1947.
96 *Burnley Express*, 19 April 1914.
97 The Northern simpleton had been the stock-in-trade of the music hall artist George Formby Snr, whose character 'John Willie' from Lancashire 'embodied the gormless, guileless Lancashire lad adrift in the wicked city'; Colin MacInnes, *Sweet Saturday Night* (London: Panther, 1969), 81–2.
98 *Bolton Evening News*, 27 April 1923.

The point at which the relationship between North and metropolis merged into a more general sense of national community is difficult to locate. But in none of the identities being created in this reporting was there any sense of the North being apart from the symbolic nation of the Cup Final. The 'taking' of the capital was simply a projecting of Northern local and regional identities on a national stage, an opportunity to exploit momentary renown. Local and national converged naturally. This was never more evident than in the Cup Final of 1914, when the presence of the King provided an opportunity to parade and glorify the North's place in the nation. 'It was,' proclaimed the *Burnley Express* with pride, 'a Royal Lancashire Day', noting that it had been Lord Derby, the Northern aristocrat, who had been instrumental in persuading the King to attend. Red roses, the symbol of Lancashire, were to be worn by the royal party, in celebration not only of the Lancashire origin of the two teams – Liverpool and Burnley – but because the King was also Duke of Lancaster, and it was this title that the press appropriated as a way of linking the monarchy with local sentiment.[99] At the time of another impending war, 'Townsman' of the *Preston Guardian*, reporting North End's reception after their Cup win of 1938, was moved to portray the English crowd as a bulwark of decency in the face of threats from abroad. He contrasted the essentially humane, English good-naturedness of the vast crowd in Preston with the 'large, disciplined gatherings' to be found in continental Europe. The difference was pointed up when a woman in the crowd, on the point of fainting, passed her child to a policeman for safe keeping. This commonplace incident, with its comforting stereotypes of mother, child and friendly bobby, somehow gave 'Townsman' an insight into his community that revealed it to be much more than mere locality: 'for all our bickerings we are all one big family on these great occasions'.[100]

99   *Burnley Express*, 29 April 1914.
100 *Preston Guardian*, 7 May 1938.

IV

Preston North End was the last of the clubs from medium-sized Northern industrial towns to appear in the FA Cup Final, in 1964. So much of the culture of the Final had been based on this type of community, and with its passing as a force in football during the 1960s and 1970s the meaning of the Final changed. With the increased frequency of appearances by big-city teams from London, Liverpool and Manchester, each with its clutch of internationally famous players rendered into 'personalities' by press, radio and television, the Final has lost some of its local flavour. Wembley, too, has changed. The segregation of spectators to minimise crowd disturbances has seemed to accentuate divisions at the expense of the unity the stadium symbolised in former times. Even 'Abide With Me' was removed from the programme for a time when fans either ignored or sought to subvert it. And 'God Save the Queen' became 'God Save Our Gracious Team' in the 1970s. It is perhaps to the Wembley Finals of the lesser trophies that have proliferated since the 1980s, and to the recently instituted 'play-off' system in the lower divisions of the Football League (where many of the former Cup-winning Northern clubs now reside), that we should look to recapture some of the old local fervour of Cup Final Day.

This occasion, in its broadest terms as both sporting and cultural event, has good claim to be seen as a cardinal element in northern popular culture. Of course, it is not uniquely northern: plenty of Midland and Southern clubs (an increasing number of the latter since the 1960s) have appeared in the Final, and their appearance has no doubt served to bind local identities in Wolverhampton, Watford, Islington and other places. But there is something peculiarly northern about the Cup. It probably derives from the frequency with which northern clubs have appeared in the Final and the way in which the festival aspect of Cup Final day has been embraced in northern communities. In this way it has become an important site for the myths by which people live their lives. John Walton is surely correct in seeing these as an important subject for the regional historian.[101] Through the cultural practices and the text of the Cup Final were created and reproduced for many years ideas about the people of the North and their communities, and the wider community of which they were a part.

Ideologically, one of the most intriguing themes in all this is that of the *unified* community. It is represented most clearly in the image of the crowd welcoming the local heroes on their return from London. This image, it might be suggested, sought a magical resolution of the many internal tensions and conflicts that in fact beset the communities. Though in many cases we are dealing with towns which possessed a dominant industry and therefore a marked uniformity of social class and occupation, frequently underpinned by the kind of solidarity produced through strong trades unionism, this had not invariably produced a sense of unified civic identity. In reality, divisions of gender, age, ethnic group, religion and status could provide powerful forces pulling against civic coherence. This was very clearly represented in the town of Burnley, for example, at the point when its football team won the Cup in 1914. Its politics manifested deep ideological and social divisions which had prevented the working-class uniformity of the town from being translated into a class-based political identity. Burnley, perhaps surprisingly, did not share in that emergence of Labour representation which was so noticeable in North West England in the few years before the First World War.[102] Similarly, perhaps in even more acute form, there were the religious tensions – Protestant and Catholic as well as intra-Protestant – that had afflicted these towns for at least three generations by the 1920s. The Irish and Catholic traditions of a town like St Helens were still marked after the Second World War, as was the quite different English Roman Catholic culture of Preston, in spite of the unifying leaven created in both towns through work and labour

---

101   John K. Walton, 'Professor Musgrove's North of England: a critique', *Journal of Regional and Local Studies*, 12 (1992), 25–31.
102   See, for example, Jeffrey Hill, 'Social democracy and the labour movement: the Social-Democratic Federation in Lancashire', *Bulletin of the North West Labour History Society*, 8 (1982–1983), 44–55.

movement.[103] Parallel with these sectarian loyalties was the fundamental division of gender, whose existence is emphasised by the focus of this very study: football. There were few other pastimes which served more to generate a feeling of male sociability and exclusiveness than football, whether in its participant or spectating forms. It reminds us that British social life, especially working-class life, reproduced a sexual division of leisure, just as the world of work had its sexual division of labour, for the whole of the period under consideration.

Running alongside these identities was a discourse which counterposed an alternative sense of a united community of people. It took many forms and the story of the Cup Final was but one of them. Its principal creator and perpetuator was the local press. And what is most remarkable about this story of the Cup Final is its unchangingness, both across time and place. It is as if there was a journalistic model to which reporters had recourse, a narrative form which structured the story. It represented an 'imaginary constitution of the social order', as Joyce has termed it.[104] What it sought to assert, in the face of division, was a civic and national unity of seamless communities. Its abiding image nationally was that of Wembley and all it connoted in terms of a united social hierarchy. Locally it was the image, reproduced in so many local press photographs, of the physical presence of the town assembled to greet and laud its heroes (many of them not local men, of course) on their return from the Final. There was, perhaps, an element of wish-fulfilment in this. In the same way that some historians of the British cinema have suggested that the images of unity, and narratives in which social contradictions are magically harmonised and resolved, might have masked an underlying fear about discord in society,[105] so the story of the Cup Final might be seen as offering an idealised vision of community. There is no doubt that people of all sorts did turn out to welcome their

103   See Michael Savage, *The Dynamics of Working Class Politics: The Labour Movement in Preston, 1880–1940* (Cambridge: Cambridge University Press, 1987).

104   Joyce, *Visions*, 213 and 336ff.

105   See, for example, Tony Bennett and James Donald, 'The historical development of popular culture in Britain' in *Popular Culture* (Milton Keynes: Open University Press, 1981), Block 2, 79–85.

teams home, but perhaps the wish to amplify this occasional event into a more generalised image of the authentic nature of community reveals an all-too-keen awareness of the actual disharmonies present in the everyday life of Northern towns. The image of the seamless community existed, perhaps, more readily in the imagination than in reality.

Howard Jacobson's *The Mighty Walzer* and Manchester

Manchester could scarcely be called a neglected city. On the contrary, it has been much-observed. Since its emergence in the nineteenth century as the place synonymous with industrialism it has been attended with close scrutiny by historians, sociologists, urban commentators and creative writers. Asa Briggs's comment has been frequently invoked: '[...] all roads led to Manchester in the 1840s [...] it was the shock city of the age'.[1] It is perhaps not surprising that, being so much in the forefront of 'history', Manchester became the focus, one might say the 'embodiment', of a discourse on modernity, and its citizens and their publicists quickly developed from this a sense that their city was unique. 'What Manchester does today, the rest of the world does tomorrow' was a popular maxim that summed up very well Manchester's idea of itself. The historian A.J.P. Taylor, in a memorable essay, noted that in its heyday the city's renowned newspaper the *Manchester Guardian* led with *local* news on its first page, before moving on to other domestic and international issues inside.[2] As if to underline its special position Manchester was one of only two provincial British cities (the other was Warrington) to erect a statue in honour of Oliver Cromwell.[3]

1   Asa Briggs, *Victorian Cities* (Harmondsworth: Pelican Books, 1968 edn), 96. Briggs comments on the range of observers of Manchester in the nineteenth century (see ch. 3).

2   A.J.P. Taylor, 'Manchester', in *Essays in English History* (Harmondsworth: Penguin Books, 1976), 307–25. This essay originally appeared in *Encounter*, 42, 1957.

3   Terry Wykes, *Public Sculpture of Greater Manchester* (Liverpool: Liverpool University Press, 2004).

I

Manchester, an old Lancashire town, became an industrial city in the early-nineteenth century. Then, as its mill economy declined in the third quarter of the century, it re-developed as a business centre dealing in the buying and selling of cotton and cotton goods. It had introduced to the world a new form of production and the new social relationships that went with it. That is why Frederick Engels, coming from western Germany in the late 1830s to manage Ermen and Engels's cotton-spinning factory in Manchester, was so fascinated by the place. Immigrants of all social classes were, like Engels, important to Manchester, though most were not fortunate enough to enjoy Engels's wealth, which enabled him in time to leave the city behind and live the life of a country squire in Cheshire. By the beginning of the twentieth century large parts of Manchester were given over to communities of people recently arrived from other parts of the world, many of them refugees from both poverty and persecution in Europe, taking advantage of Britain's economically buoyant and tolerant society.[4] The most familiar and largest of these groups was, however, from nearer to England. With some 30,000 Irish-*born* inhabitants (and a possible further 50,000 by extraction) Manchester was the third largest English host of the Irish diaspora after London and Liverpool.[5] The great majority of the Irish were Catholics, concentrated in some of the poorest parts of the city. By the later part of the nineteenth century these were mainly in the St Michael's ward to the north of the city centre.[6] The Irish possessed a distinctive cultural life evident in their occupations, trade unions, politics and, of course, their religious organisation.[7] The strong presence of Irish

4   N.J. Frangopulo, 'Foreign Communities in Victorian Manchester', *ManchesterReview*, 10: 1965, 189–206.
5   See John Denvir, *The Irish in Britain: from the earliest times to the fall and death of Parnell* (London: Kegan, Paul, Trench, Trubner and Co., 1892), 429–33.
6   *Manchester Guardian*, 16 November 1885, 16.
7   See Steven Fielding, *Class and Ethnicity: Irish Catholics in England, 1880–1939* (Buckingham: Open University Press, 1993), 27–31.

Catholics, not only in Manchester but in many of the western parts of Lancashire, had a profound impact on the region's political and social life until well into the twentieth century. It was arguably the cause of the social and cultural cleavages that characterised the north-west of England and which produced its distinctive political allegiances – notably an enduring form of working-class toryism. Because of this the emphasis given to the Irish presence by historians and others has tended to divert attention away from other, smaller immigrant groups in the region.[8]

Among these, and for many years a source of consensus rather than conflict, was an important Jewish community which had become established in the Cheetham Hill district of Manchester, also just to the north of the city centre. Manchester's Jewish community was not only the largest in provincial England but had its origins well before the familiar mass migration of Jews from Polish and Russian lands following the pogroms of the early 1880s.[9] It dated back to the eighteenth century.[10] As its historian Bill Williams has noted: 'Manchester Jewry grew with Manchester'.[11] In fact, Williams shows that immigration from eastern Europe had also begun in Manchester before the 1880s, so much so that by 1875 some half of the Manchester Jewish population was made up of migrants from Poland and Russia; 'in no sense', he says, 'can the Jewish community be regarded as "alien" to Manchester. It was not a late addition to an established pattern of urban life, but an integral part of the pattern itself.'[12] This state of affairs had given prominence to the middle-class Jewish community – initially some twenty families – which sought to take on the social leadership of Manchester Jewry and to impose on its poorer immigrant members the liberal values of the host community. In return it was favoured by a

8   See Panikos Panayi, *Immigration, Ethnicity and Racism in Britain 1815–1945* (Manchester: Manchester University Press, 1994).

9   Neville Laski, 'The Manchester and Salford Jewish Community 1912–1962', *Manchester Review*, 10, Spring 1964, 97–108.

10   Frangopulo, 'Foreign Communities'.

11   Bill Williams, *The Making of Manchester Jewry 1740–1875* (Manchester: Manchester University Press, 1976), vii.

12   Williams, *Making of Manchester Jewry*, vii.

tolerant regard for Jewry on the part of the gentile middle class, notably illustrated in the pages of the *Manchester Guardian*. By the 1880s, however, this situation of pervasive consensus had started to fragment as a result of the rapid growth through increased immigration of a Jewish working class. Some of the Jewish immigrants from Iberia settled in the south of the city in Withington, and there was a pocket also in Salford, but many found employment in the garment trade, which in Manchester was based in small workshops rather than the larger factories to be found across the Pennines in Leeds. By the early 1890s there were over 250 such workshops, employing close on 2,000 Jewish workers mainly in the Strangeways, Red Bank and Lower Broughton districts, the core area of the Jewish working class. Their arrival prompted the removal of better-off Jews further up Cheetham Hill Road towards Prestwich, Whitefield and Bury. By 1910 a total Jewish population of around 30,000 was displaying signs of internal tensions that had not been evident earlier.[13]

Some elements of this new Jewish working class were not only less disposed to accept middle-class leadership, but were treated with more hostility by indigenous residents than was the established Jewish middle class.[14] Anti-semitic propaganda was in circulation by the 1880s in newspapers such as the *Manchester City News*. Williams notes that the social tension between established Anglo-Jewish families and the east Europeans proletarians had its roots in religious and political differences – particularly

---

13   Lloyd P. Gartner, *The Jewish Immigrants in England* (London: Allen and Unwin: 1960), 40, 43, 90–1, 145, 160; V.D. Lipman, *Social History of the Jews in England, 1850–1950* (London: Watts and Co., 1954), 67; Bill Williams, 'Heritage and Community: the Rescue of Manchester's Jewish Past', in Tony Kushner ed., *The Jewish Heritage in British History: Englishness and Jewishness* (London: Frank Cass: 1992), 128–46; Rickie Burman, 'Jewish Women and the Household Economy in Manchester, c. 1890–1920' in David Cesarani ed., *The Making of Modern Anglo-Jewry* (Oxford: Basil Blackwell, 1990), 55–75; Laski, 'The Manchester and Salford Jewish Community'.

14   Bill Williams, 'The Anti-Semitism of Tolerance: Middle-Class Manchester and the Jews 1870–1900', in A.J. Kidd and K.W. Roberts, *City, Class and Culture: Studies of Social Policy and Cultural Production in Victorian Manchester* (Manchester: Manchester University Press, 1985), 74–102.

socialism and Zionism – brought by the newer immigrants. These features caused elite Jews to attempt to 'anglicise' the immigrants through measures of social control, a strategy designed to ensure continuing tolerance for their own social position.[15] By the twentieth century, then, the Jewish community was far from homogeneous, divided by ethnic, religious, political, and class differences, and manifesting a complex set of attitudes towards the question of assimilation.[16]

II

Howard Jacobson's novel *The Mighty Walzer* (1999) is a celebration of the east European Manchester Jewish community. It offers a particular fictional representation of ethnic life and culture. The community is remembered from an end-of-century perspective by the middle-aged narrator (the novel's hero, Oliver Walzer) as it was in the 1950s. It is a memory that merges with the author's own reminiscences of his life as a teenager at the same time and in the same place. The novel therefore has a distinct historical and autobiographical perspective focused on the gradual coming of age of the character Oliver and the writer Howard. It is a story of changes – changes in a life, in a family, and of a sport. It has been described, not surprisingly, as a 'rite of passage' novel.[17] Its story time spans a period starting with the fictional Walzer family's life before Oliver's birth, when his parents were growing up in Cheetham Hill; it proceeds through Oliver's own middle age, when he has left Manchester behind for a rootless single existence as a lecturer in vaguely artistic matters in Venice; and it ends, appropriately,

15   Williams, *Making of Manchester Jewry*, 331–3. See also Alan Kidd, *Manchester* (Keele: Keele University Press, 1993), 124.

16   Bill Williams, '"East and West": Class and Community in Manchester Jewry, 1859–1915' in Cesarani ed., *Making of Modern Anglo-Jewry*, 15–33.

17   See Jonathan Bate, 'Ping Pong Boy', *Times Literary Supplement*, 20 August 1999, 19.

with Oliver's return to Manchester for his father's funeral. As in almost all Jacobson's work he interrogates his own experiences of Manchester life in the 1950s to reflect on the questions of Jewishness and Jewish identity which have been the chief subjects both of his novels and of his non-fictional work in the past decade or more.[18]

Jacobson approaches Oliver Walzer's history in a warmly nostalgic and affectionate mood, as well he might for it is his own history to a large extent. The past is recreated with fondness, and the memories are good ones. Jacobson's perception of the Jewish place in Manchester life is of a community finely poised in a social spectrum. He positions it as semi-respectable, not fully assimilated and accepted, and creates an immigrant assimilation of an in-between, apologetic kind: not too little integrated, but neither too much, just enough, treading a delicate line between Anglicisation and Jewish orthodoxy. Walzer's family and the many other families in Cheetham Hill had in a very Jacobsonian sense *got by*. They were not part of the established Jewish middle class whose achievements in the world of commerce had allowed them to be absorbed into the society of the English middle class and celebrated in the annals of Manchester's economic and artistic achievements.[19] The branch of immigration from which Walzer's family came had achieved nothing of great import – in the arts, business, the learned professions or even sport – to receive acclaim and acceptance by the host society. They had, to a degree, raised themselves up by the self-help means that the city's nineteenth-century philosophy had so lauded. Walzer's father Joel, a market trader, is a wonderfully humorous example of this process. Equally, though, there are indications of a resistance to elite *mores* which resulted in Jewish support for socialism; Walzer's mother, for example, as a young woman in the 1930s had associations with free-thinking left-ish elements: 'She knew communists [...] she corresponded with men who were fighting with the International Brigade in Spain' (39–40) – reminding us that east European immigrants

18   See Howard Jacobson, *Roots Schmoots* (London: Penguin Books, 1993); 'Being Jewish ...', *Guardian (G2)*, 11 June 2004, 2–3.
19   See Williams, *Making of Manchester Jewry*, 336.

did not always accept the lead of the conservative Anglo-Jewish middle class in politics. But neither, in Jacobson's eyes, were the Walzers and their neighbours the victims of any vigorous discrimination. Of the Mosleyite presence in the 1930s (Manchester was something of a stamping ground for fascists) there is little indication, and none relating to the serious anti-Jewish rioting that occurred in Manchester and other major cities in the 1940s when Jewish resistance movements were campaigning to end the British Mandate in Palestine.[20] The Walzers' neutrality in itself is regarded as something of an achievement, an ambivalence they strove hard to preserve, and it accounts for the contradictory attitude towards Jewishness expressed by both Jacobson and his fictional characters. It allowed them just enough space to be English and at the same time afforded them a mark of Jewishness. They were Jewish English, rather than English Jews, careful not to invite attention from non-Jews. 'Stay shtoom. Don't draw attention, that was what we grew up with' Jacobson has said. 'If we saw a Jew driving a big car around Manchester, it was, "Don't do that, there'll be a pogrom."'[21] It is the main concern of Oliver Walzer's father: accommodate, live and let live, don't rock the boat. *'You don't upset the shaygets'* is his persistent refrain (104). The one outstanding signifier of Jewishness – religion – is rejected. Jacobson's family was not outwardly religious. They did not observe the Sabbath, though at the same time retained a slight feeling of guilt about it.[22] For Jacobson himself, when visiting orthodox relatives in Llandudno, the observance of religious rituals is regarded

20   Geoffrey Alderman, *Modern British Jewry* (Oxford: Clarendon Press, 1992), 319; Tony Kushner, *The Persistence of Prejudice: Antisemitism in British Society During the Second World War* (Manchester: Manchester University Press, 1989), 200–01. The contrast with Morris Beckman's account of anti-fascist campaigns in the Ridley Road area of Dalston, east London, in the late 1940s is very marked. Beckman's group was involved in some violent clashes with resurgent Mosleyites who sought to whip up opinion over the Palestine issue against local Jews. Morris Beckman, *The 43 Group* (London: Centerprise, 1992).

21   Allison Pearson, 'Howard Jacobson' 27 April 2004, <http://www.telegraph.co.uk/arts>

22   See Todd M. Endelman, *Radical Assimilation in English Jewish History 1656–1945* (Bloomington: Indiana University Press, 1990), ch. 6.

with some scepticism, if not incredulity.[23] Towards the end of the novel
the middle-aged Oliver explodes at the thought of his daughter marrying
an orthodox Jew in a ceremony from which his sisters, for having married
gentiles, are excluded:

> Yes, you are right, your father is a Godless bastard. But answer me this: if the Creator
> whom you and that wet-mouth Shmuelly worship holds it as a matter of urgency that
> the feelings of Aunty Hetty and Aunty Sandra are to be considered of no account
> because their husbands are defiled by the prepuces which were His fucking inven-
> tion in the first place, what the Christ are you doing giving credence to a word He
> says? Honouring God isn't compulsory, you know, even if He exists. You may choose
> not to. (348)

Equally, they were not ashamed of their origins, but at the same time
wanted to 'move on'.[24] Before the Walzers' male child was born, in the
early 1940s (the same time as Jacobson's own birth) the family had moved
from Cheetham Hill to Heaton Park, a small step on the petty-bourgeois
ladder. Oliver's father Joel never made much money, certainly not enough
to take the family to Southport, the epitome of Lancastrian Jewish respectability. He was, and remained, a market trader, a dealer in tsatske – 'a toy
or plaything, a shmondrie, a bauble, a whifflery, a nothing' (14). He works
the markets in the Manchester area selling his nothings, a life dedicated to
communicating trivialities – cheap trays, plastic poppet necklaces, travel-
lers' refreshment packs, lamps, bags of chocolate truffles (misshapen). With
these the Walzer house is stocked and decorated; tsatske, for Joel Walzer, is
both merchandise and an aesthetic. Looking back Oliver wonders whether
this accounts for his own failure to be serious and dignified. He ends up
himself being a dealer in academic tsatske.[25]

---

23   Jacobson, *Roots Schmoots*, pp. 12–17.
24   Howard Jacobson, interview with Joan Bakewell for 'Belief', BBC Radio December
     2004.
25   See Howard Jacobson, *Roots Schmoots: Journeys Among Jews* (London: Penguin
     Books, 1993), 4. This autobiographical passage is almost identical to Jacobson's
     description of the Walzer household's production of goods for market sale (*Mighty
     Walzer*, 105–6).

Like his mother and father Oliver, though Mancunian to the marrow, is simultaneously only too aware of distant origins, of a life before Manchester. This sense of heritage, however, is more ethnic than religious. Eastern Europe exercises a mysterious hold on his psyche. 'Bug country, that was where we came from, the fields and marshes of the rock-choked River Bug, Letichev, Vinnitsa, Kamenets Podolski – around there. All we'd been doing since the Middle Ages was growing beetroot and running away from Cossacks' (5). Carrying this influence with them, Oliver's and his father's generation of Mancunians adapt it into a distinctive local vernacular, separate but not too separate from that of non-Jewish people. They have a patois. None of them speaks Yiddish, yet they incorporate into their speech a lexicon of Yiddish terms just as non-Jewish Mancunians perfect their own colloquialisms as a means of bonding together with whatever group they feel they belong to. It can lead to ambiguities, as when, after a table tennis match against Allied Jam and Marmalade, Selwyn Marks claims to have detected anti-semitism on the part of their opponents:

> 'Are you telling me that's why you lost now', Twink said, 'because they were anti-Semites? I suppose the net was anti-Semitic.'
> 'I'm not saying it's why I lost. I'm just saying it's what they are.'
> 'You're messhugge', Aishky said. 'They were nice people'.
> 'Then why did they call Oliver Mordechai?'
> 'Mordechai? Who called him Mordechai'
> 'The one with the shmatte bat.'
> Aishky and Twink wanted to hear it from the horse's mouth. 'Oliver, did he call you Mordechai?'
> 'Not that I remember. Why would he have called me Mordechai, anyway?'
> 'Because he's an anti-Semite. Mordechai the Jew.' [...]
> 'No', I said. 'He said, "Better luck next time, me duck." Me duck, not Mordechai.' (74)

Sport occupies a central place in Oliver's early life (just as the memory of it figures prominently in his middle age); to a large extent it also holds the novel together by exposing the fundamental dilemmas of the poor immigrant position. In this *The Mighty Walzer* is groundbreaking. For one thing, the place of sport in immigrant culture – Jewish culture in particular

– has been generally ignored by scholars of immigration and minorities.[26] Ironically, since virtually all historians of immigration are themselves immigrants, Jewish historians appear almost to have imbibed the old myth that Jewish men were not physical; that they exhibited certain 'effeminate' characteristics.[27] Few historians, immigrant or otherwise, have turned their attention to this area, and those who have seem unable to decide whether the relative absence of Jews from organised sports in Britain is a reflection of lack of interest or of social exclusion. There is some evidence of the latter in golf, for example, with the black-balling from exclusive golf clubs of applicants from Jewish families. The apparent lack of a Jewish presence in cricket, on the other hand, may simply be explained by a lack of interest in the sport.[28] Considering the importance of sport to immigrant communities, as a means both of gaining acceptance from majority cultures and also of seeking to retain an element of ethnic distinctiveness, it seems a topic that is worthy of fuller investigation. Oliver Walzer's chosen sport is not connected to any such establishment activities as golf or cricket. His story is about table tennis, a sport of recent origins and humble neighbourhood proportions. It is a sport that has received scant attention in the growing

26 In the now well-developed historical literature of immigration, especially Jewish, there is much attention to economic, religious and political matters but scarcely any reference to the place of sport in Jewish life. See Alderman, Kushner, Cesarani, Endelman – among the more recent generation of scholars.

27 See Bryan Cheyette, *Constructions of 'the Jew' in English Literature and Society: Racial Representations, 1875–1945* (Cambridge: Cambridge University Press, 1993) ch. 1; *Between 'Race' and Culture: Representations of 'the Jew' in English and American Literature* (Stanford CA: Stanford University Press, 1996), ch. 1. The idea of the 'effeminate Jew' acquired some support in the early twentieth century from the writing of the young German Otto Weininger, whose *Sex and Character* (London: William Heinemann, 1906) advanced some massive generalisations about women and Jews (and the British) and seemed to confirm existing conservative views on women and anti-semitism.

28 See Richard Holt, *Sport and the British* (Oxford: Oxford University Press, 1990), 133, 351; on golf see John Lowerson, *Sport and the English Middle Classes 1870–1914* (Manchester: Manchester University Press, 1993), 22–3; on cricket see Jack Williams, *Cricket and Race* (Oxford: Berg, 2001), 41–3.

literature of sport history in this country over the past twenty-five years.[29] It should not surprise us to learn that Jacobson was himself a fine player in his youth, and like David Storey in *This Sporting Life* he brings deep personal knowledge and understanding to his descriptions of the game. The novel not only alludes to sport in metaphorical terms, as a way of illuminating aspects of social behaviour; it also contains detailed *real* information about the game and its origins, development, and international context. Jacobson has also claimed (perhaps with an intentional irony) a certain Jewishness about the game as he knew it. 'Table-tennis was a very Jewish activity [...] It was an intellectual game; you almost played it in a suit [...] it was like athletic chess.'[30] And Oliver Walzer comes to see in the Jewish table tennis clubs of Manchester a unique style of play which contrasts with that of other ping-pong traditions: the southern style, exemplified in Oliver's partner and adversary Lorna Peachley – an 'all-round game of exaggerated loops and non-stop jigging' (153); or the game he encounters as played by boys from north-east Lancashire at the Ribble and District Table Tennis Academy in Burnley, who are 'greedier in their play, more pinched and avid, colourless, without flourish or bravura' (151). In later years, as a student in Cambridge, Oliver partners a man from Sri Lanka, 'a class act' as he describes him, whose style of play reminds him of the Jewish game in Manchester: 'the only non-Bug and Dniester ping-pong player I'd ever come across who had *wit* in his game' (319) [my italics]. For Oliver, table tennis embodied fun and sociability. It was not, in the last analysis, a game to be taken too seriously.

This mentality had its place in table tennis history. The game contrasted markedly with the 'betting sports' – football, boxing, horse-racing, greyhounds – for the virtual absence of any serious commercialism, media exposure, or stars. In the 1950s, to be sure, the names of Victor Barna, Johnny Leach and the Rowe twins gave the sport some national recognition, but it was essentially a game played by local people in local clubs. It

29 See Richard William Cox, *British Sport: A Bibliography to 2000* (London: Frank Cass, 2003).

30 Francis Gilbert, 'Family Influence: Howard Jacobson', *e magazine*, 11 February 2001, 30.

had originated in a country-house context as a domestic, social game for both sexes, played for pleasure. In the interwar years it began to develop an organisational structure of leagues which brought together players from a variety of occupations and associations – churches, pubs, businesses, public services, leisure centres, schools, families. In the absence of attention from academic historians one has to talk to former participants or dig down to locally produced commemorative volumes of clubs in an attempt to re-create the game's story.[31]

Table tennis is the making of Oliver. He comes upon it by accident, finding a ball in Heaton Park lake (it is, he later learns, a ball of some distinction – a Halex***), and discovers that he is a 'natural'. Before ever setting foot inside a ping-pong hall he is an expert, honing his skills at home by playing, Bradman-style,[32] against the plaster whorls on the living-room wall. The Halex*** comes back at unpredictable angles, sharpening the boy's reflexes. His bat is pure improvisation – a copy of Stevenson's *Dr Jekyll and Mr Hyde* 'in the soft green pitted-leatherette Collins Classic series' (15). With such home-based resources Oliver nurtures his talent. This introverted, domestic introduction to sport is typical of the boy, who is shy and withdrawn, pampered by the many women members of the family and given to secret pleasures in the lavatory. He also dreams of becoming a great table tennis player who will beat the new far-eastern champion Ogimura. Oliver the quiet daydreamer is, according to his father, a 'kuni-lemele': 'a rustic simpleton. Not quite the village idiot, more the shtetl schlemiel' (26). It is an aim of the male members of his family to bring him out of his shell, and table tennis provides the means of doing so. Specifically, it happens

31   See John Bromhead, 'Win or Lose: A Sample of Table Tennis History', paper presented to the British Society of Sport History, Leicester, April 2004. Bromhead argues that the competitive side of the game developed eventually to a point where the purely social aspects declined, to the particular detriment of women's participation.

32   The Australian batsman Don Bradman, who dominated world cricket in the 1930s, claimed to have developed his technique and co-ordination by throwing a golf ball against a corrugated iron water tank and playing the rebound with a cricket stump. See Charles Williams, *Bradman: An Australian Hero* (London: Abacus, 1997), 17.

when his father takes him to the Akiva Social Club, and the world of the table tennis leagues of Manchester and district opens to him.[33]

Akiva is a club for Jewish players but, in keeping with the Walzers' equivocal philosophy, it competes in a mixed league. It is a world in which, for the first time, he relates on equal terms with adults, or at least 'sort of' grown men as (with their curiosities and foibles) Oliver regards them. ('They've all got something wrong with them' he exclaims to his family on arriving home after the first night at the club). The members take the twelve-year old in with much warmth and good spirit, and he acknowledges that he might, at other clubs and among other people, have been given a much tougher initiation into the sporting life. Compared with the eccentric domestic life of his family and the curious onanistic culture of his grammar school, the Akiva is a rational and orderly real world of competition rules (extracts from which introduce many of the chapters) drawn up to ensure fair, orderly play. Jewish clubs, the implication runs, are no strangers to the English concept of 'fair play'. Clubs have secretaries, matches are organised events, there are travel schedules, and there is a kind of dress code to which most members adhere. Oliver has a tracksuit with 'a wildly rhetorical "A" for Akiva' (65) embroidered by his aunt, modelled on the perfect outfit favoured by his mentor Twink Starr.[34] It is life with a purpose, and gives Oliver the chance to achieve something, to live up to the expectations his father has of him.

It is, moreover, another way of reinforcing his Jewishness while simultaneously integrating into English society. The Akiva team players are all Jewish working-class men and lads with a rich Mancunian-Jewish outlook, but Oliver's introduction to the league is in the most un-Jewish

---

33   Jacobson has presumably taken the name 'Akiva' from Rabbi Akiva, a great scholar of Judaism who was involved in the rebellion against Rome (132–5 CE) and subsequently executed. Akiva is associated with an optimistic world view – 'he could look at utter devastation and see future glory.' (See <http://www.ou.org>). The twin themes of rebelliousness and optimism chime well with the narrative.

34   Though his other mentor, Aishky Mitofsky, 'played in the clothes he came home from work in' (61) confirming Jacobson's assertion that ping-pong could almost be played 'in a suit'.

surroundings of the Allied Jam and Marmalade factory club. Here, with a
new bat to replace *Dr Jekyll and Mr Hyde*, he is beaten by stolid gentiles;
not good players, but 'canny' ones. Oliver is taught his first lesson in table
craft. He is also made aware of the austerity and imperfections of playing
the game in this local, make-do milieu, where resources are limited and the
conditions far from perfect. The rooms always seem cold, there is furniture
to lose balls behind and trip over, and floors are often unnecessarily polished
and slippy. But the caretaker, a shayget, takes pride in polished floors, so
nobody complains. You don't upset the shaygets. 'This was my first lesson
in the ergonomics of ping-pong: every feature and dimension of the playing
area must contribute to your discomfort [...] Tribulation, that should have
been ping-pong's *nom de jeu*. No wonder the game came naturally to sun-
starved Slavs and Magyars' (70). Oliver begins to believe that the game is
in the blood, an ethnic characteristic. Why have east Europeans dominated
it for so long? But equally, perhaps, it suits an indigenous Lancashire tradition in which the art of cotton spinning and weaving over two hundred
years linked with the craze for Yo-Yo that had taken his father as a youth
to the World Yo-Yo Championships in the Higher Broughton Assembly
Rooms in August 1933, and from there to his son's passion for ping-pong.
'Wristiness', he imagines, 'was in their blood' (4). And so all players, Jews
or gentiles, perform their natural art in the quintessentially British form
of voluntary association, through which so much of the country's amateur
sport has been fostered. Manchester table tennis, moreover, was open; for
although Oliver plays for a Jewish club there is no separate Jewish *league*.[35]
The races are thus conjoined in association, and for Oliver table tennis is
his route into manhood.

35   See Laski, 'Manchester and Salford Jewish Community', *Manchester Review*, 1964.
     The attempt to extend the Manchester Maccabi tennis club into a 'base of culture and
     sport for all the youth activities of Manchester' was not successful, chiefly because of
     the separate interests of the small Jewish clubs (presumably those like Akiva). (107).
     A Jewish Table Tennis League was formed in Manchester in the 1970s, mainly from
     north Manchester synagogues. It waned in the 1990s, when a rump of players joined
     with the Manchester Maccabi and formed a team in the Manchester District Table
     Tennis League (see <http://www.manchestermaccabi.org.uk>).

Oliver, Twink, Aishky, Sheeny, Selwyn and their team-mates at the Akiva bring an eccentric style to their playing of the game. They play a very Jewish game. All, in their different ways, are tragic ping-pong players. The despicable Gershom Finkel, who breaks the heart of one of Oliver's aunties by running away with another one, has played for England; he has been that good. But he is banned forever from international competition for betting against himself in a match against Sweden. 'He lost every match. Not by much, but by enough' (166). Aishky, who loves to win matches with dramatic smashes (and therefore often loses them by striving for that final flourish) loses fingers on his right hand in an accident; he then amazingly learns to play just as brilliantly left-handed (the Manchester League struck a special medal for him), only to lose left fingers in another accident. He devotes the rest of his life to studying the Holocaust. When Twink is called up for national service the Akiva 'as a fighting ping-pong force' (180) comes to an end. It has been a phase in Oliver's life, and he has learnt from sport something about both life and himself. Table tennis has brought him into contact with questions of winning and losing, and of the values to be cultivated, and the values to be despised, in a life. For all that sport has done for his personal rite of passage Oliver comes to see it with a deep scepticism.

In contrast to views that developed in the nineteenth century about immigrant Jews being provident, goal orientated, and individualistic, rising from the ghetto through a need to achieve,[36] Jacobson provides us with a different narrative. The Mighty Walzer dreams, to be sure; he lacks nothing in imaginary 'grandiosity'. But in practice he cares little for the thrill of winning, and nothing for any conventional material enrichment ('swag') that victory might bring. This mentality is not confined to the world of sport. He is like his father in this respect. Joel's financial management is so chaotically careless that he eventually goes bankrupt. It is the 'buzz' of the 'gaffs', the excitement of market life that entrances him. Oliver is the same with table tennis. Winning in itself, especially against clearly

36　See David Feldman, 'There was an Englishman, an Irishman and a Jew … Immigrants and Minorities in Britain', *Historical Journal*, 26, 1 (1983), 185–99.

inferior opponents, offers neither pleasure nor sense of achievement. He
is good enough to win the Manchester Closed Junior championship but
nearly 'blows it' because he knows he can beat his opponent easily, and so
shrinks from securing what he sees as a hollow victory. What is winning
all about, why is it so important? There is a kind of pleasure in losing, and
Oliver takes a self-pitying delight in it. Above all he despises the strutting
postures of the winners.

> Grandiose in my ambitions I may have been, but in the final analysis I was never
> comfortable winning. I didn't like the way it made me feel. And I never liked the
> way it made other people look. I remain a devoted student of the subject to this
> day – the illness of winning. I watch it day in and day out on television [...] Nastase,
> McEnroe, Navratilova, Coe, Christie, Lewis, Budd, Klinsmann, Cantona, every
> member of every Australian cricket team, Tyson, Eubank, Ballesteros, Norman,
> Hill, Schumacher, Curry, Cousins, Torvill, Dean. A roll call of the psychotic [...]
> The ultimate B-movie. *The Horror of the Human Will*. Forget the Creature from
> the Black Lagoon. Forget the Fly. This one's really sticky. This one's come out of
> soup too disgusting to describe. And the telly commentators call it character. (256)

With the end of Akiva Oliver graduates to the much tougher competition of
Hagganah, where the players look like 'veterans of the Israeli independence
wars' (209); they refuse on principle to play for England, even though they
do not keep Shabbes, because the international team plays on Saturdays:
'If they want to pick Jewish players they have to respect how Jews live. Let
them play on a Sunday' (209–10). These are hard men, who are not afraid
to upset the shaygets. Oliver is not happy in this unambivalent environment, from which he withdraws after a life-changing match against the
egregious aspiring winner Stanley 'Royboy' Rylance of Railways. Royboy
is so anxious – over-anxious – to win that Oliver decides to give him the
game: 'If he wanted it that badly he could have it [...] I gave it to him as a
gift. I had neither the character to win nor the character to consent gra-
ciously to his winning. So I gave it to him' (264–5). Oliver never played
table tennis in Manchester after that.

He does play, however, when he reaches Cambridge as a student and
makes the transition from semi-isolation in Manchester to the heart of
the gentile Establishment. Indeed, it is Oliver's prowess at the table that
secures him a place at the notable sporting institution, Golem College.

Here again, playing for the most part against ludicrously poor opposition, he encounters his old distaste for winning. But he also comes to reflect on what, in his eyes, are seen as the true values of sport. In believing that winning is less important than the existential pleasure of playing a game Jacobson articulates through Oliver a sentiment that comes very close to that of the ethos of the Victorian amateur: the 'lover' of the game.[37] What else explains Oliver's concerns about the changing 'technology' of ping-pong that so affected the game in the 1950s? It was all to do with the bat, and sponge rubber. It is another rite of passage for Oliver – 'to sponge or not to sponge' (208) – which coincides with his joining Hagganah. 'Every match was hard these days. Harder to win and harder in the sense of less sociable and easeful' (209). It marks the passing of the game of the vellum bat, even the sound of which brought its own pleasure: 'plock plock, plock plock' was sweeter than sponge's anonymous 'oof plock, oof plock'.[38] 'The game', says Gershom Finkel, 'isn't worth a candle any more. The new rubbers have killed it. I wouldn't go to the bottom of the street to watch a match' (197). But watching was not what it was about. The table tennis that Oliver remembers was a game that held his community together, and helped him fashion a sense of identity. When the Akiva comes to an end, with Aisky minus several fingers on both hands, Twink conscripted into the army,

---

37 See Lincoln Allison, *Amateurism in Sport: an Analysis and a Defence* (London: Frank Cass, 2001).

38 Oliver's reaction is connected with the changing 'technology' of the game. His heroes – Bergmann, Barna, Leach – would have used a bat with a plywood middle covered on each side with dimpled synthetic rubber. It encouraged the artistry of spin, with the chop as the standard defensive stroke. Long rallies were a characteristic feature of this form of table tennis. In the early 1950s this style began to change as a result of new technology (sponge bats) and tactics introduced in Japan. The bat became standardised in the form of the 'sandwich' bat, i.e. the traditional layer of wood in the middle, covered with a thin layer of sponge, and an outer covered of dimpled rubber. Oliver's game had been essentially a defensive one; the new technology made it a speedier, more attacking game analogous to the 'serve and volley' approach introduced into lawn tennis around this time. See Chester Barnes, *Advanced Table Tennis Techniques: How the World's Top Players Win* (London: Angus and Robertson), 10–12.

Sheeny Waxman gone over to Hagganah and Oliver thinking of following him, Selwyn Marks taking up swimming, and his brother Louis emigrating to Israel, Oliver asks Aishky what he will do now 'for sport'. 'Sport? Who's been doing sport?' asks Aishky. 'We both laughed. Of course ping-pong wasn't sport. Football was sport. Cricket was sport. Ping-pong was – But we both knew, without saying, what ping-pong was' (181).

III

David Nathan, reviewing *The Mighty Walzer* in the *Jewish Chronicle*, found that it recreated and celebrated a world of northern Jewish communities of the 1950s.[39] But is that fictionialised world also not a very fanciful one, an ultimately misleading, perhaps stereotypicalised, representation of times past and present? Do people *deliberately* lose? Was being a Jew in Heaton Park quite so untroubled an existence as Jacobson makes it appear? Perhaps the paranoia of the unfortunate Selwyn Marks, who believed that the gentiles were always out to get him, is a truer expression of the community's persona. Throughout the novel Jacobson gives us a sense of the tenuous nature of Jewish relationships with Manchester gentiles: 'you don't upset the shaygets'. It is a defensive approach to social relations. Jewishness is not *celebrated* so much as preserved in attenuated form *within* the community. Jacobson actually says little about the shaygets. They are opponents at ping-pong, often people, as with 'Royboy' and the players of Allied Jam and Marmalade, not to be admired. The novel's world is an introverted one, equipped with a number of self-sealing devices that prevent its engaging with the world outside. There is nothing that Oliver does before going to Cambridge that takes him away from his tightly circumscribed community. This is not assimilation of the kind sought and experienced by middle-class Jews in the nineteenth century. It is self-imposed semi-exclusion, as is his

39   David Nathan, 'North-West Passages', *Jewish Passages*, 20 August 1999, 24.

eventual exile as a lecturer for tourists in Venice. Could it be that Oliver's seeing winning as a more troubling state than losing is part of this defensive psychology? In the novel's splendid finale, Oliver re-visits a Manchester which (predictably) fails to live up to his memories of the city; it has been 'Torn apart to make room for tsatske precincts for the post-industrial poor' (332). In the artlessly named G-Mex (formerly Central Station) he finds taking place the Ninth World Veterans Ping-Pong Championships where, in the international company of veterans of all ages and various states of renown, he loses some of his grandiosity, acknowledging that he had never been exceptional as a player, only 'so-so' (357). He is made aware, however, of people's enduring fascination for sport:

> Why, there were men here, playing in the over-eighties' competition, wearing knee-supports and elastic hose and bandages round every joint, so arthritic that they required the assistance of a third party to retrieve any ball for them that didn't finish up in the net. They had to hold on to the table between strokes, some of them, so that their own momentum wouldn't knock them over. Could *their* imaginations still be rioting in futurity, looking forward to the day when they'd be world beaters? (361)

When his old adversary and girlfriend Lorna Peachley, whom he has not seen for 35 years, gives a brief show of affectionate recognition he surmises what it might mean: love, forgiveness? Neither. 'Just that she remembered who I was. Which is all any of us Walzers has ever asked' (387). It is an appropriately self-deprecating note on which to end. Life, like politics, is the art of the possible, especially for expatriots of the Bug and Dniester. In the last analysis 'grandiosity' is not their style.

'[...] We both knew, without saying, what ping-pong was.' Oliver's remark about his beloved game represents a Jacobsonian paradox. Of course ping-pong is in one sense a classic example of Britishness. The nation that Marx noted for its capacity to 'join' – to form clubs – which had a continuous tradition of voluntary associational life stretching well back into the eighteenth century,[40] also produced the Akiva. By taking the kuni-lemele

---

40 See Peter Clark, *British Clubs and Societies, 1580–1800: the Origins of an Associational World* (Oxford: Oxford University Press, 2000).

Oliver there and leaving him inside until he was accepted Joel was *forcing* his son into assimilation. What he imbibes there, however, is a peculiarly bastardised, Walzerian sporting ethos. It contains some of the principles nurtured in the British amateur tradition – in which playing for the *love* of the game is crucial – while rejecting other aspects: in particular, the desire to win. If sport is, as we are frequently told these days, a zero-sum game 'about winning', it is clearly not so for Oliver. It can also be about losing. It depends on mood, but mood depends to a large extent on the opponent. When the opponent is so clearly fixated with winning, when as with 'Royboy' sport has become a culture in which the need to achieve surpasses all other considerations, making it a ridiculous obsession, then Oliver is happy to lose; happy to reject a conventional masculinity, and to revert in some sense to being the 'feminised' Jew; to lose, indeed, to his girlfriend. Sport is not 'about winning' – at least it is not *all* about winning. It is also about being yourself, growing up, and enjoying the company of eccentric friends. Somehow it is not an activity for fully grown men.

In *The Mighty Walzer* Jacobson gives us subversion on a grand scale on a number of fronts. In his view of Jewish life, which is not competitive and not obsessed with success; in his view of assimilation, in a neighbourhood that was Jewish, but not embattled; and in a family whose memories are mercifully happy ones, with no horrific experiences to recount. It was a family that was also stable, or at least as stable as a household could be where financial management was conducted according Joel's surreal accountancy. And in his view of sport Jacobson questions much of the received wisdom about its potency in society. Would those arch framers of public-school games in the nineteenth century, on which the entire edifice of sport has been constructed, have recognised their vision of moral manliness in the world of the Akiva?

Index

BRITISH IDENTITIES SINCE 1707

The historiography of British identities has flourished since the mid-1970s, spurred on by increasing national consciousness in England, Scotland, Wales and Northern Ireland, and since 1997 by devolution. Historians and other academics have become increasingly aware that identities in the British Isles have been fluid and that interactions between the different parts of the British Isles have been central to historical developments since, and indeed before, the Act of Union between England and Scotland in 1707.

This series seeks to encourage exploration of identities of place in the British Isles since the early eighteenth century, including intersections between competing and complementary identities such as region and nation. The series also advances discussion of other identities such as class, gender, religion, politics, ethnicity and culture when these are geographically located and positioned. While the series is historical, it welcomes cross- and interdisciplinary approaches to the study of British identities.

'British Identities since 1707' examines the unity and diversity of the British Isles, developing consideration of the multiplicity of negotiations that have taken place in such a multinational and multi-ethnic group of islands. It will include discussions of nationalism(s), of Britishness, Englishness, Scottishness, Welshness and Irishness, as well as 'regional' identities including, for example, those associated with Cornwall, the Gàidhealtachd region in Scotland and Gaeltacht areas in Ireland. The series will encompass discussions of relations with continental Europe and the United States, with ethnic and immigrant identities and with other forms of identity associated with the British Isles as place. The editors are interested in publishing books relating to the wider British world, including current and former parts of the British Empire and the Commonwealth, and places such as Gibraltar and the Falkland Islands and the smaller islands of the British archipelago. 'British Identities since 1707' reinforces the consideration of history, culture and politics as richly diverse across and within the borders of the British Isles.

Proposals are invited for monographs and edited collections, including those that arise from relevant conferences.

Vol. 1   Ben Wellings: English Nationalism and Euroscepticism: Losing
          the Peace
          293 pages. 2012. ISBN 978-3-0343-0204-3

Vol. 2   Catherine McGlynn, Andrew Mycock and James W. McAuley (eds):
          Britishness, Identity and Citizenship: The View From Abroad
          362 pages. 2011. ISBN 978-3-0343-0226-5

Vol. 3   M. H. Beals: Coin, Kirk, Class and Kin: Emigration, Social
          Change and Identity in Southern Scotland
          289 pages. 2011. ISBN 978-3-0343-0252-4

Vol. 4   Andrew Francis: 'To Be Truly British We Must Be Anti-German':
          New Zealand, Enemy Aliens and the Great War Experience,
          1914–1919
          317 pages. 2012. ISBN 978-3-0343-0759-8

Vol. 5   Shanti Sumartojo: Trafalgar Square and the Narration of
          Britishness, 1900–2012: Imagining the Nation
          236 pages. 2013. ISBN 978-3-0343-0814-4

Vol. 6   Jeffrey Hill: Popular Politics and Popular Culture in the Age of
          the Masses: Studies in Lancashire and the North West of England,
          1880s to 1930s
          277 pages. 2014. ISBN 978-3-0343-0936-3